'An affecting tale that reminds us o
too much about appearances and not enough about the natural
affections of the heart. The sense of loss is palpable.'

Louis de Bernières

'A memoir not of misery but of love deflected and deferred...
From his reflections come two simple conclusions: that love is
not spontaneous but grows from long-term commitment, and
that blood is not thicker than water.'

James Robertson

Praise for Brian Johnstone's previous books

'A Poetic master...[a] skilled builder, who knows how to
weight his words and fit them together with care.'

Susan Mansfield, *Scotland on Sunday*

'Nothing in here is humdrum, nothing is over-personal. It's a
kaleidoscope of language as well as of the world.'

Sally Evans, *Northwords Now*

'Writing grounded in reality...illustrating how we cope and do
not cope with change and time.'

John Idris Jones, *Inpress*

'Great power and sharpness of focus...the fruit of distilled
meditation.'

Edmund Prestwich, *The Manchester Review*

'Johnstone's poetry is often vigorous and muscular in its language,
... which, in its gravity and resonance, recalls early Heaney.'

Oli Hazzard, *The Poetry Archive*

'Full of stilled moments and nicely shaped incidents.'

Robyn Marsack, *Scotland on Sunday*

Also by **Brian Johnstone**

Poetry

Dry Stone Work
Arc Publications, 2014

The Book of Belongings
Arc Publications, 2009

Homing
The Lobby Press, 2004

Robinson, A Journey
Akros Publications, 2000

The Lizard Silence
Scottish Cultural Press, 1996

Poetry in translation

Terra Incognita
L'Officina (Vincenza), 2009

Double
Exposure

A MEMOIR

Brian Johnstone

Published by Saraband,
Suite 202, 98 Woodlands Road,
Glasgow, G3 6HB,
Scotland

www.saraband.net

10 9 8 7 6   5 4 3 2 1

ISBN: 9781910192672
ISBNe: 9781910192689

Typeset by Iolaire Typography Ltd.
Printed and bound in Great Britain by Clays Ltd, St Ives plc.

Contents

Poems

For JNJ & SJB

Introduction

THIS BOOK IS a conversation with the past. A conversation with the inhabitants of my own particular past, and a dialogue with previous selves.

Like many memoirs, it concerns a search. But it is a search not for any 'long-lost' relative or shadowy individual. Rather, it is a search for what lay behind the decisions, actions and outlooks that shaped the past, that formed the people whom I once believed I knew, but now realise I didn't. As such, it is a search for my own past as much as for the past of others.

This though, is *not* a misery memoir – nowhere, and at no point, can I claim anything approaching misery to have been my lot. If the nature of this book is to be qualified at all, it is a baffled memoir, a perplexed memoir, a disconcerted memoir. All the stories I recount here are told as I saw them unfold. Necessarily there will be deviations from the way in which they were experienced by others. But this is my story. I can only tell it as it happened to me.

As a writer, poetry is my default literary response. Many of the elements explored in this memoir first surfaced in my poems. I have come to realise that these poems are the storyboard around which the book has grown. They have been my route back to the past, and are integral to the narrative. They are the links that bind the story together, the markers that punctuate the conversation with the past.

In exploring the secrets and evasions that run through the narrative – the absence of trust, or the wholesale disregard for its necessity, which lay behind the experiences I write about – I have come to see the individuals concerned and the pattern of their lives in a new and more sympathetic light. I have tried to show that I attach no blame to anyone; that I hold no grudges. We are all creatures of our time and we all act accordingly.

To extend the photographic metaphor of the title *Double Exposure*, if this memoir is anything it is an attempt to 'fix' and then 'stop' this story – and the people involved – in time.

Brian Johnstone
12th May 2016

Author's Note

IN ORDER TO guard the privacy of surviving family members and of the individuals concerned, the names and nicknames of all persons, both living and dead, who appear in this narrative, have been altered. The letters quoted in various chapters are all verbatim as received, although some have been edited for the sake of brevity.

About the Author

BORN IN EDINBURGH in 1950 and educated at the University of St Andrews, Brian Johnstone is a poet, writer and performer. He has published six poetry collections to date and is featured on the Poetry Archive website, curated by Andrew Motion. His work has been translated into more than a dozen European languages.

Brian Johnstone has been active on the Scottish literary scene for more than 25 years, organising poetry events in Edinburgh and Fife. A founder of StAnza: Scotland's International Poetry Festival, he was Festival Director from 2000–10. In 1991 he co-founded Edinburgh's Shore Poets, and he ran Cave Readings for the Pittenweem Arts Festival for five years during the 1990s. He lives in the Fife countryside with his wife, the artist Jean Johnstone.

For more information see brianjohnstonepoet.co.uk

Time is not a single train, moving in one direction at a constant speed. Every so often it meets another train coming in the opposite direction, from the past, and for a short while that past is with us, by our side, in our present.

Claudio Magris
from *Danube*

... we also have appointments to keep in the past, in what has gone before and is for the most part extinguished, and [we] must go there in search of places and people who have some connection with us on the far side of time...

W G Sebald
from *Austerlitz*

Prologue

I T WAS 1957, sometime towards the end of summer. In the city of Edinburgh, our family was going up in the world. We were moving from the tenement flat we had lived in since the midpoint of the century to a terraced house in a suburban street with no little conceit of itself.

Ours was a young family – at least we children were – but neither of our parents was in the first flush of youth. They had married late, in the aftermath of the war. They had much time to make up.

Taken as a whole, we would have been the very model of a '50s nuclear family, but for the fact that both offspring were male. Six and four respectively, we boys had been looking forward to this move for months, in particular to the garden we had never had before and to the prospect of new friends.

One day, a few weeks before the removal van arrived, I wheeled my red tricycle across the main road outside the door to the family flat. As the elder of the two boys, I had an inspection to make. Climbing into the saddle, I pedalled the mile or so to our new home.

Men were busy there, laying carpets, hanging curtains, painting the outside woodwork. They made a huge fuss of me, giving me a tumbler of milk and letting me explore the garden while they got on with their work. I picked some flowers and put them in the boot of my trike to take home for my mum. I knew she'd be pleased to get something from the new house.

Cycling home, I had been gone for nearly three hours, but no-one would think anything of that. It was the 1950s. Children were left to their own devices and my mother had been busy with the packing, happy to get me away from the flat and out from under her feet.

Back home, I parked the trike at the foot of the tenement stairs and took the bunch of flowers up the two flights to our flat. I was right – Mum was delighted with them. She was also delighted that I seemed to appreciate the move to the new house as much as she did, that I valued all the sacrifices my parents were making to go up in the world.

As for me, I liked the garden – and the garden shed.

1

After the Tone

IT WAS CLOSE to midnight when I got home one cold October night in the penultimate year of the twentieth century. The phone was bleeping when I came in, its light flashing to indicate a new message. On other nights that late, I would have left it to deal with in the morning. But the final event of our brand new festival had finished that evening, so, hoping that it might be a message of congratulations, I pressed play and waited for the anticipated, 'Well done!' or 'Great start!'

Nothing could have prepared me for what I heard. The now obsolete mini-cassette tape has long since been wiped and the aged phone disposed of, but it went something like this:

I'm ringing as I think you are the son of the late Mrs Beatrice Johnstone of Morningside in Edinburgh. If not, please disregard this message. But if you are, you might be interested to know that her daughter, your half-sister Maria, is in Scotland just now. And she's trying to contact you. This is her husband speaking – she feels too emotional to call you herself. So, please do ring me back on this number if you would like to get in touch?

That was followed by a landline number whose area code I didn't recognise. Then came the long bleak tone of a phone hung up. And silence.

I have no memory at all of what I did next. But I vividly recall those moments – returning home after the success of our new-founded festival, the answerphone bleeping, and my utter astonishment at the message. The half-sister to whom the message referred was someone I had never heard of, had no inkling even existed. But what made the message even more shocking was the memories it brought back, the past perplexities it evoked.

What I *do* remember is what I did subsequently – although due to the late hour, not until the following day. It was then that I called my brother to discuss the situation. Relaying the phone message had a similar effect on him. The two of us were amazed. The content of the message – the revelation of this half-sister – was extraordinary, uncanny even. But its means of delivery was astonishing too.

'What a weird way to get in touch with news like that,' my brother said. 'It's earth-shattering.'

'Don't you think,' I suggested, 'it would've been a bit more sensitive just to say some information about an unknown family member had turned up?'

'Sure – then the guy could've waited until we'd made contact before revealing what his news was all about.'

How many people, we wondered, would choose to leave such a highly charged piece of information as a phone message?

'Actually, wouldn't a letter have been more appropriate?' I said. 'My address *is* in the phone book, after all.'

What I could not know then was the assumption behind the chosen means of communication. In fact, as I discovered later, the phone message had been left in the belief that I would already know about this half-sister. This was not the case. I had no idea whatsoever that such a person existed. Neither did my brother. But she and her husband had no means of knowing that.

★ ★ ★

After the Tone

My mother – the Beatrice Johnstone referred to in the phone message – had died aged eighty-five, the previous March. A woman of very definite opinions, she would not have reacted well to her full Christian name being used. Christened Beatrice for one of her grandmothers, who had died tragically young, my mother always loathed the name and had never used it. She had also dropped the diminutive Beattie decades back. It had been the name of her childhood and youth, which she had long since shortened further to Bea – the name by which all of her adult friends had always known her. And the name that my father – who had also instigated a change, from the 'Tom' of his youth, to the 'Gilbert' of his mature years – clearly preferred for his wife.

But, just over six months earlier, I had registered her death. This had required the use of her full name.

At the time, both my brother and I were still rather raw from mourning our loss. As well as that, the last year or two of my mother's life had been something of an emotional rough ride. Her health had been breaking down – difficult for anyone – but more so for a sport-obsessed woman who had been fit all her life. She was also exhausted by her recent removal from the suburban Edinburgh family home where she had lived alone since our father's death twenty-two years before.

Fiercely independent for as long as we could remember, Bea had resisted all suggestions that the house was too much for her. As she entered her eighties, my brother and I were becoming increasingly concerned that the two-storey end terrace Edwardian villa, to which we had moved in 1957 and where we had spent most of our childhood, was becoming more and more of a burden.

This is a situation familiar to most people with elderly parents: a desire to see the parent maintain independence, but offset by a concern that they should still be able to cope, still enjoy the same independence without any excessive additional risk. That dilemma can weigh heavily on the next generation of family members and can so easily give rise to resentment – even distrust – on the part of the aged parent.

At family gatherings – Christmas, Mum's birthday, visits from relatives and the like – my brother and I would choose the moment to head for another room and have anxious discussions about her future.

'How can we persuade her it really is time for a move?' we would wonder. 'And how can we get her to see this won't be the end of her independence?'

Leaving Bea in the sitting room chatting with our wives or playing with my brother's children, we used to think we would never be disturbed. But no matter how many cups of tea or glasses of sherry we plied her with, it never worked.

We would pretend we had only been trying to wash the dishes or make a fresh pot of tea; that we were admiring my brother's new car or taking a look at something in the garden. We would say all we needed was to get some air. But it was no good. Our mother would seek us out with cries of, 'I *just* know you're talking about me! I won't have you discussing me behind my back. Stop it at once!'

We never did get far with these sessions. Perhaps Bea's wartime work with the Air Ministry had made her extra alert. Maybe she was suspicious by nature. Perhaps older parents develop a sixth sense as to when they are the subject of discussion. Or maybe this had derived from similar experiences earlier in her life – there would have been many of those.

In vain, we tried to reassure our mother that we were only thinking of her, only looking after her interests. Yet she was fully aware it was *her* life we were attempting to redirect. And she was determined to resist it. The conflict was clear. We could plan all we wanted, but getting Bea to agree to anything – that was always going to be the biggest step.

Various plans were mooted. But nothing as drastic as a care home. We imagined our mother in a small flat of her own, maintaining her independence. We had our own ideas as to how this could be accomplished. But she was insistent she would never countenance one suggestion we made – splitting the family home into two apartments, the lower of which she would retain. So the best option seemed to be sheltered housing – somewhere with a manager on site in case of emergencies. And she was ideally placed for it. Just around the corner from her house was a new block of such flats, recently built in 'the field' – a patch of wasteground we had played in as boys. Bea would not even have to move to another part of town. And, by way of a bonus, this block was even closer to her beloved golf course.

But, was she to be persuaded? She was not. Getting her to accept advice from her own children was well-nigh impossible. The family home meant too much to her. As did making her own decisions.

'It's the house I bought with Gilbert, which we shared for years,' she said. 'I owe it to your Dad to keep it – and to keep up the garden'. So much of her past – her identity even – was tied up with the family home.

But a resolution came more quickly than we expected. Behind all her resistance, my mother *was* becoming aware of how many difficulties her deteriorating health was causing to her household routine.

The family home was absurdly large for her needs. The sole occupant of a kitchen and scullery, two public rooms and five bedrooms, she now lived in just three of those. Although the large lounge was brought into use for a week each Christmas, it and the other surplus spaces were chilly and uninviting for most of the year. Much of the furniture was immediately post-war in style – several pieces still boasted the *Utility* mark – and all were heavy and cumbersome. But each item had to be moved for cleaning and, she insisted, replaced on the exact same spot. To do otherwise would reveal the wear marks on the equally aging carpets. There was room after room to hoover – or 'vac', as she'd have said. Acres of woodwork to dust – doors and skirting boards, mantelshelves, windowsills and her much admired pitch-pine staircase. Countless surfaces to polish – the dining table and sideboard, the cocktail cabinet, the spare bedroom furniture – all unused for most of the year, but requiring her special touch, her personal attention. Appearances *had* to be kept up.

The look of the old place was also breaking down. It was beginning to be an embarrassment. Rhones were springing leaks and downpipes were rusting. The garden was rapidly getting beyond her. As someone with such exacting standards, she would, if she could, pick up every fallen leaf that strayed into the flower beds and religiously remove every weed that dared to show face.

Indoors, it was the same. Curtains were fraying to such an extent that to draw them any way other than gingerly was to risk the fabric coming away in your hand. Her favourite royal blue stair carpet was wearing out – I found her one day inking in the bald patches with matching biro. The bathroom cistern was such a problem that visitors had to be shown the precise way to pull the chain. Failure to get this right – and there were many – caused a continuous stream to debouch into the lavatory bowl.

But she was reluctant to spend money on any replacements, knowing how much the sheer scale of the undertaking would cost. Having already coped with dry rot – the blame for which she always laid at the door of her slovenly neighbour – she was unable to face any further disruption. The plaster dust from the dry rot repairs was too awful a memory. It haunted her. Still present in the fine film she could not help noticing on all her polished surfaces, its residue was apparent even years after the event – or so she claimed.

On one occasion, towards the end of her time in the old house, I suggested getting some new flooring for the kitchen. But it was no use – she was adamant that the lino would 'see her out'.

'It's not that old! It was only laid in '57 – when we moved in,' she reminded me, 'It'll do for ages yet.'

It was a relief, therefore – but really no surprise – when she announced to us that she was going to move into the very block of flats my brother and I had spotted some time before. And it was a decision, she was adamant, she had made entirely by herself.

'I was chatting to a friend from church the other day,' Mum let slip, almost casually, 'and she told me one of the flats round the corner was on the market. It's very nice in there, she said – so I've been to have a look. Anyway, I've had a good think about it and I've decided to put in an offer.'

A neat way of avoiding having to accept our advice – or at least of having to admit to it. But it *was* her decision – that was important. We had no grounds for complaint. The move was on.

Her offer accepted, our mother was happy for my brother and me to organise the work on the new flat – as long as she had final say on the colour scheme. But it was impossible to persuade her to relinquish any of the tasks involved in the sale of the family home. As a former legal secretary, she had more experience than either of us. Before long she impressed us both by advertising the old house in the Edinburgh property supplements, conducting a series of viewings and making her decision as to who the new owners would be.

To her credit, she decided to accept a lower offer on the place so that a family with young children could be the new occupants.

'This was always a family home,' she explained, 'and I'd like it to be one once again.'

* * *

My brother had been closely caught up in dealing with the break-down of our mother's health. He was still living in Edinburgh, only ten minutes up the road from Bea, while I was based in Fife, an hour or so away to the north. However, I was more directly involved in her removal from the family home. I had taken a year off from my teaching post to write. My first collection of poems having been recently published, a follow-up was uppermost in my mind. However, I was rapidly dragooned into organising the house clearance and the preparation of the new flat. Since to her way of thinking I was 'not working', my mother deemed me available to help her sort through the detritus of forty years under the same roof. Down-to-earth as ever, she was unable to consider my writing as work.

We talked a lot during the long hours of sorting and sifting, but then, we always had. While I was keen to avoid the hole-by-hole, shot-by-shot accounts of her almost daily games of golf, I was happy to chat with Bea about all sorts of other topics. We would talk regularly on the phone – often having hour-long calls when she would give me full accounts of her life day-to-day – but she was always ready to listen to what I'd been getting up to. She much preferred, though, to hear about the goings-on at the various schools I worked in and my life in the teaching profession than about any of my activities in the literary world. I think she worried she might not understand these. The neces-sity of grasping a topic straight away was something she was emphatic about. She would shy away from talk of poetry or books, art or music fearing always that she would be out of her depth in those areas.

One of her many received opinions was that to talk knowledgeably with 'the male of the species' – something she always prided herself on being able to do well – a woman had to have a good understanding of 'what is going on in the world', a workaday grasp of current affairs. This she undoubtedly had. But she tended, latterly, to be about three weeks to a month out of date. In her desire to get her money's worth out of every newspaper, she would read them cover to cover and, in her later years, would get somewhat behind in keeping up. Still, she was always happy to discuss the state of the country – largely terrible, she thought – while we went for long walks in the summer, or runs in my car in the winter. Very much typical of her class and generation, her opinions were never the most progressive and I frequently found myself challenging them. Even so, she was always ready to argue a point and even, on occasion, to concede one.

Most of our chats during the house clearance, though, were about the past – her past – prompted, on occasion, by the contents of unidentified boxes or discoveries at the back of cupboards. Having kept an almost obsessively tidy house – a trait I do not share – I was discovering my mother's aptitude as a hoarder – a trait that I do share.

Battling over bits of string that 'might come in handy' was trying. Getting shot of the contents of a long obsolete coal bunker was a struggle. And persuading her to part with her collection of carefully saved and scrupulously ironed wrapping paper was well-nigh impossible.

However, finding in her old sewing trunk the remnants of my grandmother's wedding dress, dating from the first decade of the twentieth century, was a poignant moment. I could scarcely believe what Bea was telling me as she unfolded the aged tissue paper to reveal a meticulously preserved silk bodice, complete with applique satin roses. I had been very fond of Grandma, who had survived until I was fifteen, the only grandparent living in my lifetime, and this discovery brought her vividly to mind, conjuring her in all the vigour of her youth.

On the other hand, finding the inflatable rubber cushion Bea's father had used to make sitting in his armchair more comfortable during recurring bouts of haemorrhoids, was less emotionally engaging. I never knew my grandfather, who died several years before I was born. Naturally, I had heard stories of him – as a dedicated collector of antiques, as a dignified and successful businessman, but also as a strict disciplinarian and sometimes overbearing *pater familias*. This particular discovery did at least underline a certain vulnerability in him, which I had never considered before.

But in time the work was done. The house was cleared and all that was to be preserved had been transferred to the flat that my mother was to call home, though – while we never knew it at the time – for much less than even a full year. All that remained now was to make a final inspection of the house, lock it up and hand the keys over to my mother's lawyer.

I was concerned that checking over the now-empty family home would be too distressing for Bea, but I had underestimated her. She was keen to take a final look and together we walked through the empty rooms and hallways – a process I would have to repeat only a matter of months later in the more constricted environment of her sheltered flat.

AN ACCUMULATION OF DUST

The house had outgrown circumstance, but
you held on. Pressed between the pages of your past,
you stuck to them, reluctant to move out, to recognise
the brittleness of age. And when it came, the move
stirred up the sediment of forty years and more.

Not long in your new shell, and now the haste
to prise you from the last, seems ill advised. I run
a finger through the dust you would have mopped up
in a trice and wonder if an old shell, empty, cold,
was not a better home to play out fading days.

Double Exposure

We broke apart the old one in a week. You walked
with me through vacant rooms accompanied by ghosts
we hadn't laid. And now, the hoover picks up dust
from carpets that outlived you, as I pick up misgivings,
doubts, from small, undusted corners I forgot.

Now the family home, and the flat we had hoped she would enjoy for
a long time yet, had both been forsaken. But what our mother had left
behind was more – far more – than dust.

* * *

Bea died suddenly in March 1998, only four months after her move to the
sheltered flat. It was unable to shelter her from deteriorating health and the
condition that had dogged her for the previous few years.

Six months later I was phoning my brother in a state of disbelief.
It was the next morning, the one after I had received that late-night
answerphone message, the morning after what proved to be a night of
much sleepless tossing and turning. Passing the content of the message
on to him had as shocking an effect as the original had had on me.
And what added to our confusion, deepened its effect, was the fact
that this was not the first time such a bombshell had been delivered to
us. We had experienced a similar shock close on a quarter of a century
beforehand.

That extraordinary coincidence apart, what my brother raised was
a consideration much more practical and level-headed than anything
I had thought of. Given our mother's recent death, his concern
was that this call might be from someone seeking to make a claim
against our mother's will. Was someone trying to lay hands on our
albeit meagre inheritance? As Bea's estate was going through the legal
processes involved in its winding up, this was a plausible suggestion. A
family man with three young children, my brother was understandably
concerned that their futures might be affected.

Impractical being my default setting, I had never considered this. I was shocked – true; puzzled – undoubtedly; but concerned – I cannot really say I was. Still, my brother had a point. How could we be sure that this person *was* our half-sister? In the worrying contemporary world of identity theft, personality scams and the like – nascent but developing in the late '90s – how could we be certain this was not some sort of attempt to perpetrate a fraud?

As I was due to leave on holiday the very next day, it was important not to leave this question hanging in the air. We needed to know more before doing anything – and certainly before responding to the phone message. That decision made, any attempt to get in touch with this just-revealed half-sister should, we agreed, be put aside for now.

What we needed first were some facts.

2

Adults & Betters

WHO WERE MY parents? A question I never asked myself as a child. They were just Mum and Dad – it was always that way round. *My* mum and dad – same as they had ever been. Each with their own characteristics, their own little foibles. Each a vital part of our family unit.

At an early age I could never conceive of anything different. Gilbert and Bea as children – impossible to imagine. Having any sort of life before they were married – equally beyond conception. This sense of disbelief can only have been enhanced by the fact that neither of my paternal grandparents was alive, so there were never any visits to my father's old family home; in fact, in my early childhood, I didn't even have an inkling of where it had been located. On top of that, my one surviving grandparent, my grandmother, no longer lived in Bea's childhood home, so that connection had also been broken. Grandma, bent double with rheumatoid arthritis and walking always with a stick, was visibly a much older person. So the generations appeared to be immutable to my infant eye, set in stone since the dawn of time.

Equally impossible to my child's mind was conceiving of any part of the family unit as having an existence independent of it. But differences within it became apparent early on. Hierarchies were recognised and pecking orders established. Seniority was acknowledged.

With my father being away on week-long business trips every month or so, and my mother being the traditional stay-at-home housewife of the period, she was the one who mattered. Mum was always there to greet my brother and me on our return from school; always ready with the tea on the table each evening; always there to get us up in the morning. Everything in the house was my mother's realm – the house being the *Woman's Realm,* as the magazine of the period proclaimed.

There were rarely any 'wait till your father gets home' deferrals. But when Gilbert was at home, Bea would occasionally be forced to call on my father if the jockeying for position between us boys got out of hand.

'They're fighting again, Gilbert! Stop them, quick!' she would cry, and Dad would rush in to prise us apart.

But most of the time as pre-teens we were biddable to our mother's will, even protective of her, especially when Dad was away on business. The family home ran on smoothly, with any potential disruption to standards or routine largely under control. And never, in my experience, was there any disagreement between my parents as to a course of action. No, that was for later – much later.

* * *

To Bea, politeness was the ultimate virtue. Rudeness, or simply the neglect of courtesy, was another thing she couldn't – and wouldn't – tolerate. Irksome though they were to us as boys, we were trained in the accepted norms of politeness – always to use Mr and Mrs when addressing our 'adults and betters'; to use Uncle or Auntie for those so-called 'borrowed' relatives my parent's friends were held to be – it being unacceptable for children to refer to adults by their Christian names; at all times to say 'please' and 'thanks' – and to say them in a sincere manner; always to write thank-you letters after receiving Christmas or birthday presents; and, when all others were taken, to offer our own seat to a grown-up on the bus or the tramcar.

Holding the door open for an adult, especially for a lady or an elderly person, was another of these norms. So insistent on this was my mother that on occasion I would see her take revenge on those who didn't come up to her rigorous standards. Leaving a shop, she would defer to those coming in, particularly older or more obviously harassed shoppers. Seeing such a person approach, she would step back from the door and politely hold it open for the other customer, anticipating a courteous, 'Thank you.'

More often than not, this was forthcoming. But when it was not, Bea would say loudly to the customer entering, 'I beg your pardon!'

'Sorry... but I didn't say anything,' was the usual response.

In a flash Bea would come back with, 'Oh, I thought you said "Thank you" – I must've misheard.' And she would sweep out of the shop having taught another ingrate a sharp lesson.

The antithesis of politeness for her was vulgarity – being 'common' as Bea would have it. My mother abhorred vulgarity of any sort. This extended all the way from dubious jokes to slovenly speech. She would cringe at any incidence of blue humour, looking pained when my father guffawed at the frequent *double entendres* of *Round the Horne* and *The Navy Lark* escaping from the wireless.

She had a particular dislike of the Scottish comedian Lex McLean and would rail against his popularity. She would insist on us only watching BBC television in case we stumbled upon his regular show and were corrupted by his 'filthy mind'. This was easy for her to do when we were together in a house with a television – on holiday or visiting relations. But, not having a set at home, we would visit neighbours to watch there. Bea even asked the aging spinsters, who were happy to give us access to their TV almost anytime, to ensure that we only saw BBC programmes. It was a constant worry to her that we would be exposed to the degraded standards of STV and thus the twin evils of dirty jokes and 'bad English' – her received opinion of Scots vernacular.

Although she wouldn't have called it that, Bea was an early exponent of recycling. Either that or she was an avid upholder of the 'make do and mend' approach of the wartime years – take your pick. Jam jars were scrupulously washed out and reused, plastic tubs the same; string and wrapping paper were hoarded; vegetable scraps were saved up for the pig swill lorry – still calling regularly in my childhood. Elbow patches were sewn onto jerseys and jackets; socks were darned; and old pullovers were ripped down and reknitted.

As she got older, familiar items around the house would be dropped or knocked off surfaces. None that could be repaired, however ineptly, were ever discarded. Others suffered from age and wear. Dickey window catches would be secured with clothes pegs, broken handles with bits of old flex. But her favourite kitchen cabinet refused to conform.

Never taking to fitted kitchens, Bea had stuck with her own take on a *Utility* brand style, particularly evident in her 1950s metal storage cabinet. She was wedded to its fold-down shelf for mixing baking ingredients, to its ventilated doors to keep foodstuffs fresh and its twin drawers overflowing with cutlery. The move from the flat in '57 had prompted a repaint by my dad to bring the cabinet up to date with 'modern colours'. Since then, resplendent in pillar-box red and butter-milk magnolia, it had stood its ground in the centre of the kitchen wall. The room itself, always referred to by Bea – but Bea alone – as the 'breakfast room' adjoined the former scullery, recast in the same spirit as the 'kitchenette'. The latter – a working space with cooker and sink – was more traditionally decorated in green and cream, while the former featured Wedgewood blue walls and a lemon yellow ceiling to offset the red faux-leather chair covers, the red Formica table-top and the red Fablon-covered windowsill. The cabinet was essential to the overall effect. But now its drawers were collapsing and the complicated system for opening and supporting the fold-down shelf was giving out. Mum tried various things as wedges and packing to keep it in service but eventually the whole cabinet gave way to creeping metal fatigue.

She was distraught. Nobody made anything comparable in the 1980s. She wanted her kitchen to stay the way it had always been. It was sheer good fortune then, that an almost identical cabinet turned up in what we would now call a retro shop. I was able to source the same shades of red and cream and paint it up to match the old one. Mum was delighted. And again ahead of her time – retro, before the term was current.

* * *

My father was a man of less definite opinions. But a man of regular habits and preferences nonetheless. In common with so many who had seen wartime service in the forces, a sense of normality and an almost staid daily existence were what he valued most. He had lost many friends and comrades in action. His way of life and family relationships had been hugely disrupted. On top of which he had lost his closest RAF comrade in a car crash – and that shortly after this friend had acted as his best man. It is easy to see that a tranquil and unruffled life was what he needed. Easy also to see that having two boisterous young boys roaring about the place would have tried his patience at times. At many times.

Normally placid, my father would 'put his foot down' when he felt things were getting out of hand. Prone to sudden explosions of temper, he could react with fury if his authority was challenged by either of his sons. This could be over trivial things like not wanting to eat something we'd been served at table, or more serious infractions such as fighting over toys, or arguing about whose turn it was to sit in the front seat of the car.

But the unpredictability of his explosions meant it was difficult to be sure of anything. This, it seems, was common in men returning from the pressures of war. Quoted in Turner & Rennell's *When Daddy Came Home* are wartime children who remember that family relationships 'could not withstand even trivial anxieties' and that 'upheaval and disruption' tended to cause 'arguments and anger'. While I don't wish to overplay this aspect, it is true that we were never disciplined in a calm, serious manner, but always in the heat of temper, on the spur of the moment.

One of the worst instances of this was understandable. And Gilbert's anger must have been building as he drove up the quarter mile of main road, the full view of our end-terrace house getting closer with each yard travelled. As he approached the turn into his parking space at the front door, the cause of his irritation would have become increasingly visible. Its location proved beyond doubt that I had disobeyed his strict instructions. For my part, I had convinced myself that I was merely interpreting his injunction – even if I was not quite obeying it to the letter.

Adults & Betters

My brother and I had recently learned to climb drainpipes. For some time, I had been obsessed with running along the high walls of our garden and climbing onto the shed roof, so the drainpipes were an obvious next step. Once again, it would have been me leading my brother astray that was blamed for his tackling this too. But how much more interesting was a house roof than a shed roof. Even more so as, behind the sloping slates of the façade, our roof was flat. Flat all the way to the top of the terraced street. Once up there we could run up and down the street at our leisure, waving and shouting greetings to our earth-bound chums, peering into everyone's back gardens and 'spying on' the inhabitants of the next street over.

This practice had already been put a stop to. The aged sisters who lived next door had complained to our father of being alarmed by the thump of our footsteps overhead. So we knew we weren't supposed to run up and down the terrace roofs any more. But Dad had only instructed us to cease that activity, not thinking to specifically ban us from the rooftop.

'So, why not just stay on our own roof?' I suggested to my brother. 'That wouldn't annoy anyone.'

'Sure thing,' he responded, ever keen on another wheeze. Setting a 'bad example' was so easy.

As our house, being an end terrace, had a pitched section of roof on two sides, my idea was to treat the central enclosed area as a sort of courtyard. A roof garden, even. I'd seen these in magazines. They looked alluring. All the range, too. Shinning up a back drainpipe carrying a rope, I lowered this down to my brother and hauled up two or three pot plants and a couple of saplings in containers to our new garden. A pair of deckchairs next, and a bottle of fizzy lemonade. Settling down for the afternoon with some comics in the sun, we thought we were set up. Our own roof garden – the height of fashion.

It was the potted saplings that gave us away.

Driving up towards the house, Gilbert had immediately spotted that, where before there had been a clean line of grey slate, the profile was now broken by a bunch of spindly branches swaying in the wind above the apex of the roof. He was through the front door, into a rage and out the back to the garden in seconds. Nothing would persuade him that our wonderful roof garden was a good idea. Nothing would have persuaded him of anything in that mood. We were peremptorily ordered to climb back up – under supervision – and remove all items from the roof right away, ourselves included.

'You are *never* to go onto the roof again!' Dad commanded, 'and you are *never* to climb drainpipes again! *Do you understand!?*'

We did – of course. Stupid idea anyway…

'And don't you *ever* indulge in *any* such tomfoolery *ever* again,' he fumed. The matter was closed.

But this was a side of our father that we saw rarely in our young days. It would grow more pronounced as we grew into the fractiousness of teenagers. As we challenged his authority, took advantage of our adolescent cockiness. As we 'argued the toss' – his stock phrase for any disagreement. But as younger boys, we generally did as we were told, and felt we had a friend in Dad.

We knew not to disturb him when he was ensconced in the dining room using the table as his work desk. He would be in there for an hour or more each evening 'doing his writing', as our mother called it. I imagined this as some sort of homework for grown-ups – which, of course, it was.

As a commercial traveller working from home, my father had accounts to complete, orders to process and so on. In all his own papers, he was always represented as a very formal A.T.G. Johnstone Esq. His neat handwriting or business-like printed script would be in evidence on all sorts of documents – file covers, envelopes, letterheads, invoices, accounts. So neat that I would also ask him to put my name on my school jotters and covered textbooks just for the look of it.

Car-bound for a living, my father was a natural driver. At least that's what people always said.

Does such a thing exist? If it does, my brother is one too. But it is true that Gilbert drove with skill and tenacity all his life. I can never recall him having an accident of any sort. He was always a tolerant driver although apt to complain when he was being held up by anyone of less skill or a lesser sense of urgency.

'Blooming pintle,' he would mutter, not quite under his breath, as a car in front of him crawled along.

Where that term came from I never knew.

He was always in the car – for his work, to drive my mother to the shops, to fetch and carry for my grandmother, to drive my brother and me to Cubs or Scouts, and to take us all for runs at the weekend. Attractions were legion in the vicinity of Edinburgh: Queensferry to view the Forth Bridge; Carlops to visit our great-uncle's farm; North Berwick for the open air pool; even Dunfermline for a visit to the abbey, once the new Forth Road Bridge had been opened.

Although he must have had his fill of being behind the wheel on his weekly business rounds, he never seemed to mind the Sunday runs that my mother – house-bound for her working week – loved and looked forward to.

Until, that is, the invention that transplanted the wireless – the ever-so-portable transistor radio.

WILD THING

Slap it hard with every beat, play
percussion on the back seat of the car
until the driver gets the notion
that it's time the radio was off, time

he drew the line, his fatherly concern
for welfare more towards the leather
of the vehicle's upholstery
than distraction from the road

he's steered down many times before
taking the '60s family for runs
he'd sooner have declined, since
he's driving every working day for pay

21

to keep the wolf he'd spotted lurking
at the corner of the street as far
from his own door as effort can, only
to find the wild thing howling in his ears

from pirate stations sons insist upon,
his two boys loudly baying for the chase.

While he would frequently insist that the radio be turned off, our father would only ever complain when my brother or I were 'playing up' in the back seat. But, more often than not we were urging him to speed up over hump back bridges so we could 'feel the bounce' or to 'race the train' where the road to the seaside ran parallel to the main east coast line.

When we got too fractious or started to fight over some toy or comic, Dad would pronounce, 'If you don't stop that you can just get out and walk.' This regardless of where we might be.

It was a threat never carried out, of course. We would generally manage to calm ourselves but, on occasion, it was a case of the car being drawn into a layby or a road end and the two of us being given a general dressing down – even more mortifying if we were ordered out of the car first and had to endure the humiliation of a row on the roadside.

★ ★ ★

The 'new house', as my mother would still often refer to the suburban end-terrace villa we had moved into in 1957, had appealed to me at the age I was then mainly for its garden, and for the many parks and open spaces in the neighbourhood. By the time I was 'into long trousers' – a coming of age ritual at fourteen – the place had begun to feel stultifying and vapid. As the pretentions of the teenager grew, so the alienation of this house bore down on me.

The 'best room' was a case in point. Rarely used, that was perhaps just as well since it was dim and oppressive at the best of times. East-facing on the ground floor, its view was interrupted by a dense, light-excluding privet hedge which, at night, was bathed in the eerie glow of an amber street lamp right outside the window. The presence of the hedge gave rise to another consequence of wartime exigencies. Previously bounded by railings, since wartime had found the front garden also hedged in, the railings were summarily removed. Like others in a similar situation, they were fated to be melted down for the war effort.

When the house was built in Edwardian times, this room had been conceived of as the dining room, with the much brighter drawing room above it on the first floor. My parents, however, used it as their lounge, having the upstairs room as their bedroom. This used to depress and frustrate me as the first floor room, with its generous oriel window, commanded a panoramic view taking in several of the local streets and, in the distance, Edinburgh Castle, Blackford Hill and a broad swathe of cityscape. How much better it would have been as the 'best room'.

But Mum couldn't countenance that. 'No-one else has an upstairs lounge, so *we* can't,' was her take on the matter.

The boredom of the house was best exemplified for me by another view, that from the actual dining room, which perversely my parents used as a family room. Here was where Gilbert and Bea sat of an evening, where they listened to the wireless, read the newspaper and chatted. It was where the television, bought only when I left home for university, was placed. And it was where I would listen to jazz concerts, poetry readings and drama productions on the BBC's Third Programme. My problem, though, was what faced me from the chair next to the wireless. With my eyes unoccupied, I couldn't help staring out of the window as I listened intently. This window framed the opposing halves of two identical beige coloured semi-detached villas; the gap between them filled by the bland face of a tenement, and a tiny strip of sky visible above its rooftop. Not a single tree or any natural feature was visible. The sheer sterility of the view came to symbolise what I saw, in the smug certainty of my youth, as the vacuous conventionality of life in that house, a sterile environment I was increasingly determined to flee.

Double Exposure

My teenage years had seen me move out of the bedroom I had shared with my brother since we had moved from our tenement flat in 1957. As we tried on our different adolescent personas, getting along with each other was becoming more and more vexing. I begged my parents for a room of my own.

There were two possibilities. One room, fancifully called the study on the sole basis that I had swotted for my exams in there; or another, the playroom, which still held a cupboard full of our childhood toys. My preference was for the latter. It was away from all the other bedrooms. It was close to the back door. It was an interesting irregular shape, unique in our house. It had its own internal staircase leading up from the kitchen. This and the coomb ceiling gave it a rather 'groovy' attic look. I would be able to decorate it in a 'cool' contemporary style. After much pleading, it was agreed. The toys would have to go. The tin soldiers, the toy farm, the plastic cowboys and 'injuns', the clockwork railway and its station were all out to the bin in an instant. The old playroom would be my new bedroom. Away from my brother who, now that I saw myself as a sophisticated teenager, was driving me crazy with his immaturity. As doubtless I was driving him crazy with my pretensions.

The new room was the only major project I ever undertook with my father. Together, we sanded and painted the staircase, then emulsioned the walls – one feature wall a bold terracotta, the others a stark contemporary white. We laid new carpet and hung the curtains. But something was missing. Already an avid reader and an embryonic jazz fan, I had to have shelves for books and records, with space for a radio and a record player.

Dad and I headed into town to Lawson's Timber Yard to secure the material. Lawson's of Lady Lawson Street (was that a coincidence?) was a warren of interconnected spaces stacked with battens, planks, beams and sheets of hardboard and ply in any dimension imaginable. Huge saws would cut the timber to whatever shape and size was required. The whole place reeked of sawdust and wood shavings, resin and glue. Slotting the planks for the new bookcase into the boot of Dad's Cortina and tying the regulation red duster onto the protruding ends as a hazard warning, we turned for home. Over the next weekend, we worked together in the garden to stain the wood with a solution of potassium permanganate – a neat trick Gilbert had learned in the RAF – and to varnish and assemble the shelves ready to set them up. Within a month, I was in my new room – my *own* room, for the first time ever. Grown up at last, I thought.

What I hadn't foreseen was the hilarity – at my expense – this room would cause. It was the former maid's room of the Edwardian house, hence its back stair and proximity to the kitchen. When later I stared bringing girlfriends home to spend hours listening to records in my room – with luck, punctuated by the angled-for snogging sessions – Dad would never miss a chance for a joke. Cracks about the maid's room 'not being short of maids', about 'old maids not being what I was after' and so on would reduce me to silent fury and cringing embarrassment.

Another hitch I hadn't anticipated was the stair up to the room opening off the kitchen. While this was handy for the back door, and was close to giving me my own private entrance, it also put me just upstairs from the most frequently used room in the house.

When the snogging progressed to stronger stuff, my mother, knowing full well what was going on I now realise, took her turn at embarrassment. She would claim to be anxious about strange noises coming from up the stairs and pose leading questions.

'Are you all right, dear?' she once asked a girlfriend, 'I thought I heard you crying or something.' Cue more cringing on my part.

But luckily, pumping up the volume on the stereo system I had upgraded to by then would usually muffle anything too audible from those down below.

★ ★ ★

In my mind, I was out of there already. Our 'four of a family' was what I had known all my life, but moving on, moving out, 'moving on down the line' was what I wanted now. My parents were part of my past. I gave them no further thought. By eighteen I was off to university. By twenty I had moved out. By twenty-one I was married. We could make as much noise as we wanted now.

3

Four of a Family

M Y PARENTS HAD been married in 1950, at the fulcrum of the twentieth century – and at the start of a fresh new decade to boot. But, more tellingly for them – and for those of my generation – it was five years after the end of hostilities in the Second World War.

But nobody ever called it that when we were growing up. It was never 'the Second World War', or even 'World War II', but always simply and starkly *the* War. As in 'before the War', 'during the War', but much more rarely 'after the War' – the War itself being an omnipresent point of reference. To my brother and me, the War was no more nor less than a fact of life, one we experienced through my father's collection of relics – his Air Force uniform cap, his old military groundsheet, his tin of medals and his Desert Campaign sunglasses, complete with their leather sand protectors.

To many of my contemporaries, and to me no less, it felt almost as if the War was still going on, continuing right through our childhoods. In comics, on the radio, at the pictures, it certainly was. And in the combative games boys of all sorts played, it was acted out with gusto – in playgrounds, in the streets, in swing parks and back gardens, and on the numerous patches of wasteground occupied by gang huts, dens and hidey-holes.

★ ★ ★

In contrast to the omnipresence of the War, and its existence evoked through our father's memorabilia, I can recall no evidence of my parents' marriage anywhere in the family home. There may have been in the flat we lived in until I was six, whose ornaments I have no memory of at all, but I doubt it.

True, my mother had always worn wedding and engagement rings. My abiding recollection is of them gracing her long, slender ring finger. A more vivid image though, is of her engagement ring lying on the kitchen mantelpiece. There it was placed safe and dry any time she did the washing up, and there I would notice its presence as I passed while helping with the chores or heading out to play. But as for my father, he would wear no rings – the War again. Asked why, he told the story of a soldier he'd seen catch his ring in a hook on the back of a troop vehicle as he jumped off. The lorry, accelerating away, had torn the man's finger off at the knuckle.

But, we would discover later, there may have been another reason behind his lack of a wedding band.

To my child's eye, the most vivid memento of my parents' marriage was their wedding photograph. But there wasn't a single print of this in the family home. The house was strangely devoid of pictures. A shop-bought print broke up one wall each in the dining room and the lounge, and a print of Iona Abbey hung above the spare bedroom fireplace. A small photo of my late grandfather stood in its frame on the sideboard and a few faded postcards and age-curled snaps were lined up along the kitchen mantelpiece. But that was it. There was a large half-moon mirror in the hall, vital for my mother to check her appearance before going out, and a curious contrivance featuring an old rear-view mirror hung for the same purpose close to the back door. Otherwise, the walls were bare, relieved only by the restrained patterns of the wallpaper and the play of light on their empty surfaces.

My parents' wedding photograph *was* in evidence though. Just not there, in the family home. But in my grandmother's house, it had pride of place above her dining room fireplace. It was a posed black and white group portrait, signed with a flourish in the name of some city studio but displayed in a rather ordinary, undecorated frame. Gilbert and Bea stood centre stage, flanked on one side by their best man – the late RAF chum of my father's – and on the other by the bridesmaid – my mother's best friend Joan, a 'borrowed aunt', being a family friend rather than a relative.

But the picture was decidedly unglamorous in terms of today's glitzy industry devoted to preserving 'wedding memories' in all conceivable media. It never struck me as at all odd that my mother wasn't dressed in white, in a 'proper' wedding dress. But then, growing up in a house with only one female occupant, there was no talk of weddings and their particular fashions. My view might also have been influenced by my uncle's wedding photo, taken at his wartime marriage, which hung in the same room. While he was dashing in his army major's uniform, his bride, like my mother, was dressed in a smart suit rather than a gown and veil.

At that age, I knew nothing of hasty, on-leave wartime weddings, with little or no time to plan anything or make any special purchases. Nor was I aware of the restrictions placed on dressmaking and couture by rationing. So I must have accepted these get-ups as normal. I did notice though, that while my aunt and uncle's photo showed them framed in a church doorway, my parents' was shot indoors in a studio of some sort.

Asking about that difference in locations, all my grandmother ever said was, 'Your mum and dad got married in a registry office – that's why.'

And I suppose I just left it at that. Only much later would I put those facts and others together to come to what seems now like an obvious conclusion.

★ ★ ★

My brother and I were born in the first three years of our parents' marriage, I being the elder, my brother two-and-a-half years younger. I remember being told later how much I seemed to resent his arrival, a state of mind I understand is common amongst first-borns. My mother used to relate with mock horror – and to my endless embarrassment

– how I would poke my brother with nappy pins to make him cry; and how once, when left alone with him for a few minutes, I had almost drowned him in the baby bath while pretending to wash his face; or worse, the time when, playing at barbers, I had half scalped him in my infant attempt to give him a haircut.

But I need to be wary of how accurate these memories are, particularly as they come from the first years of my childhood. 'We fit our facts to our feelings,' Jenny Diski writes in one of her *London Review of Books* Diary columns, 'and our memories obediently adjust to reflect those feelings back at us as recollection.' I am as prone to that as anyone. I can never entirely trust what I remember – or think I remember – from the earliest part of my life. Knowing that my mother was inclined to assure me that I *must* remember some incident or other, I am sure many of what I think are *my* memories will have been planted there through years of her story telling. In truth, it is impossible to be fully confident of the veracity of any memory. Transference and incorporation are rife. The novelist Tatiana de Rosnay touches on this when she writes that 'one day...this story that lives with me will live with you as well'. Once related, she says, any account can transform into 'the memory of who we were...of what we can become.'

It is striking how often other writers dealing with their early years express the same reserve, the same wariness. All our initial memories are necessarily patchy. Most of them are of faces and scenes whose significance is long gone. They are more like dismembered and jumbled pages, fallen from a book with a broken spine, than akin to a well-ordered and indexed volume. Is it ever possible to distinguish what you can really remember from what someone told you later? Even if it were, would we not find that many of what we believed to be genuine memories would prove false – or at least embellished – on closer scrutiny?

My infant feelings towards my brother must have been more ambivalent than my rough handling of him would seem to indicate. There were also many stories of my looking after him in a caring elder-brother sort of way. I can see now that my motive might well have been to 'pull rank', but I was always glad to have my brotherly care flagged up by my never-too-doting mum. She would happily recount how I had run alongside one of the donkeys on Elie sands to make sure my brother didn't slip from the saddle; how I would take him by the hand and, looking left, right and left again at the kerb, as I had been taught, help him cross the road safely; and even how I'd tried to keep my uncle's Cairn Terriers from licking his face, only to find myself being bitten by one of the critters for all my efforts.

One particularly vivid, even hauntingly traumatic memory makes me sure that brotherly empathy really was there. It is of an incident early in my brother's childhood and the graphic recall I have of it convinces me of its truth. The family was out on one of our frequent runs in the car, this time into the Pentland Hills just to the south of the Edinburgh suburbs. Our father had parked off a side road next to a bridge over a burn, and we were all absorbed in gazing down into the water, looking for fish and playing Pooh sticks. Suddenly, for no reason anyone could remember, my brother made a dash for the other side of the bridge, perhaps to be the first to catch sight of a particular stick as it floated its way under the arch.

What happened next is something I have always been able to see in my mind's eye. All of a sudden a car seemed to appear out of nowhere, speeding down the narrow country road. It caught my brother in mid carriageway, bowling him over and running right over the top of him. My strongest visual image is of his small body rolling across the tarmac, as the car skidded to a halt after the accident. I don't remember much else other than being back in our own car, my mother distraught and cradling my brother in her arms, while Dad sped into town to the 'Sick Kids' hospital – me, baffled and open-mouthed, sobbing all the while on the bench seat in the back.

My brother, who was only three at the time, must have been saved by his small size. The car, it transpired, had gone right over him, his sole injury being a deep gash across his cheek. This looked awful as it bled copiously. Only five myself, I was convinced that it would be the end of my wee brother. But happily, it was not. Flanked by my parents, I sat in the corridor of the hospital, gulping the Dettol and carbolic air, while the doctors ministered to him behind closed doors. Amid much screaming, his cheek was stitched back together. Apart from rather a livid scar, he made a fine recovery.

THE MARK OF TRACKS

Because I had already crossed the bridge,
was watching for the sticks you dropped below
to float on through, I hadn't heard it. But
our father had, and turned too late to stop

you run, in time to see you roll about
the road, like thistledown, beyond the sole
car in a day just skidding to a halt.
Our mother staunched the blood, her picnic set

abandoned in the grass. Back in my seat,
I gawped, too baffled by the strangeness as,
foot down and crashing through the gears,
Dad got you back to town and to a doctor's touch,

to stitches fixing in the mark of tracks, the cut
the road had made, would take down all the years.

For someone who went on to spend the majority of his working life behind the wheel, and eventually to run his own taxi firm, the road had early demanded a heavy price.

★ ★ ★

As boys, we would always look forward to going 'down town with Dad' on a Saturday morning. It was long before seat belts or any real sense of in-car safety. Lined up along the bench seat in the front, my brother in the middle, me on the nearside, we three males of our family would head down Morningside Road, past Bruntsfield, through Tollcross and into the centre of the city.

One of the main reasons for this, and for Gilbert himself taking us into town, was to have our regular haircuts. It was always a short back and sides for us – no arguments. This operation was enacted at the salubrious premises of Davison Ltd, Gentlemen's Clothiers and Hatters, on Frederick Street. The store operated an extensive barbers' salon in the basement. Ushered downstairs by our father, who seemed to know all the white-coated barbers personally, we would be taken to one of the long row of leather-upholstered chairs and greeted by Mr Purvis, our regular. His fellows all the while would be snipping at someone's pate, shaving a stubbly chin or stropping a cut-throat razor on the leather strap that hung by the side of each chair. A board would be placed across the arms of Mr Purvis's chair and either my brother or I – we used to argue over who should go first – would be hoisted onto the board, enveloped in a white sheet, and the operation would begin.

Our hair was never allowed to grow long so the hair cut would be over in a few minutes. To smooth down sticky-up locks, the barber would apply a small amount of hair oil – despite our repeated pleas for Brylcreem –and we'd be done. But the moment I remember most was after we had been shorn. Coming back up into the street, it would always feel so horribly cold around the neck and the back of the head. Small wonder. We had virtually no hair left there at all.

Other trips down town with Gilbert would take us into the hushed domains of the bank or the building society. There we'd be expected to sit quietly at the back while our father enacted his financial transactions. A bank I could understand, especially as Gilbert's branch had the word 'savings' in its title – I even had a small savings account of my own at the local post office, and, before that, a red pillar-box 'bankie' to post my pennies into.

But what was a building society? Was Dad involved in construction? Did he have a hand in some of the new blocks of flats that were springing up locally? If I ever did ask, I cannot recall an answer, only being rather puzzled by the name. Curious to think that both of these premises are now restaurants, much like many of Edinburgh's other purpose-built finance houses. They seemed so stable and immutable at the time.

As did my father's regular garage. This was Jones Motor House, just off the busy thoroughfare of Morningside Road. A vast-seeming concourse of petrol pumps, workshops, ramps, inspection pits, air pumps and oil drums, full of interesting mechanical smells, it was peopled by an army of brown-coated or boiler-suited attendants who would see to our car's every need. No self-service here. Gilbert would draw into the forecourt in his latest company car and, without seeming to issue any orders, would have his window chamois leathered to a sparkling sheen, his oil checked and topped up from a huge metal jug, and his petrol tank filled with speed and efficiency from one of the lit-up pumps that lined the space. This garage – no-one ever called them petrol stations then – occupied the whole area below the Plaza Ballroom. The closed-up and unused aspect of the old dance hall should have been a portent. I have no memory of when the whole site was cleared, but it cannot have lasted much beyond the '60s. In the spirit of the new Morningside, it is now a branch of Waitrose.

My father appeared to know every short cut there was to get him to wherever he needed to be in town. He would weave through side streets, up back alleys, down narrow wynds and emerge in a familiar part of the city centre like a magician. This was a skill he passed on to both his sons – though most particularly to my brother who employs it to this day in his work as a taxi driver. Like the banks and building societies of the past, though, so many of these routes have changed. Were he here today, Gilbert would be unable to use the majority of his famous short cuts, most having been bollarded off, converted to one-way streets or demolished. There are countless areas of the city my father would scarcely recognise, even if he could locate them, and countless others where he would be convinced he was in an different city altogether.

* * *

We were an almost clichéd 1950s nuclear family, albeit with a bias to the masculine. Two respectably married parents; a father who went out to work; a mother who was a stay-at-home housewife and child carer; the standard two children; and a nearby grandparent who visited regularly and was very much part of the family.

It is all too reminiscent of the classic mid-century *Janet and John* school reading books. These depicted the precisely two-point-zero children featured as part of an average British family, living a typically middle-class life. Except for my brother being a 'John' rather than a 'Janet', we were a classic. 'Four of a family', as my father always said.

Life seemed almost the same in our household as it did in the books. Father set off to work in the morning, smartly be-suited, briefcase in his hand, his trilby hat angled slightly on his head the only concession to individuality. We would watch his Ford Consul head off down the main road and out of sight, knowing he would be back at the antic-ipated hour each evening, in time for tea. Mother did the cooking, her meals planned and budgeted to the extent that we knew what we would be having for 'high tea' on each particular day of the week. It was always boiled eggs on Monday, fish on Tuesday, spaghetti on Wednesday – tinned, of course – and so on, right through to Sunday, which was invariably mashed banana and milk, since we'd had the larger traditional Sunday lunch earlier on. Life was secure and predictable – as predictable as the school uniforms we put on each weekday, as the home knitted sweaters we were given for Christmas, as the Chilprufe underwear we were enveloped in each winter and the Start-rite sandals we were released into all summer long.

This predictability, however boring it might have been, was part of my mother's careful household management scheme. Having spent nearly twenty years before her marriage as a secretary in various city offices, she had applied her undoubted business skills to organising the household down to the last iota. This was vital to her in order that money could be conserved – saved to put towards her sons' privileged but aspirational schooling, towards her desire to live in a respectable house in a decent part of town, and towards having a proper family holiday each summer. She would often tell us how much she and our father were sacrificing to ensure all of that.

What *we* felt we were sacrificing though, as a surrogate Janet and

John, was a 'Spot' or a 'Tiddles'. It was an absence we were frequently accused of 'harping on about'. But my mother, being fanatically house-proud, would allow no domestic pets, despite her sons' pleas. Both my brother and I loved animals at that young age. But it was no use. At least my mother's proscription allowed me to become a keen and regular dog walker for the many neighbouring old folk. I would call for their pets almost daily, as I would call for my friends to see if they were coming out to play.

The pet owners' houses held a strange fascination for me. Smelling so different from our antiseptic family home, their upholstery would be coated with dog hair, and richly aromatic baskets would sit by the fireside. The aging dog lovers seemed to have no care for appearances and never worried about chairs being shoved out of place or muddy prints being left on the linoleum. Their pets were loved and at ease, spoiled with treats and bouts of stroking. They seemed to be part of the household, imbuing their slightly shambolic homes with a warm, vaguely tweedy atmosphere. I was always welcomed, given a treat of my own, and encouraged to make a fuss of whichever dog was being taken out that day.

Our mother did relent a bit later, allowing garden pets – a guinea pig, some rabbits and a tortoise – but they were never a huge success and didn't last long. The only animals she ever permitted inside the house were my uncle's dogs, majestic Alsatians – which the War prohibited us from calling German Shepherds – and a bowl of desolate goldfish that sat on the kitchen windowsill for a few years. But there was always a sense of relief when we tired of these pets and Bea was shot of them at last.

★ ★ ★

So, what a nice respectable family, the neighbours must have thought. Such nice tidy boys, so smartly turned out. See them setting off to walk to school in their bright new blazers, leather satchels slung on their backs. See them well scrubbed in their Cub uniforms, 'bob-a-jobbing' assiduously round the neighbouring houses. See them sitting quietly in church as their father, a kirk elder, takes up the collection. See them kitted out in junior kilts for a cousin's Highland wedding, smiling sweetly in the photographs.

See them carrying the messages for their mother on shopping trips to Morningside Road or running errands to the corner shop to get her regular twenty-pack of Kensitas. See them in their Ladybird T-shirts, long socks and khaki shorts; see them playing on the swings in the local park or climbing trees in the wasteground up the road; or riding their second-hand pushbikes up and down the hilly suburban streets. See them opening doors for ladies; offering seats to their elders; always saying 'please' and 'thank you'. And only ever having one home-made cake – on earlier strict instructions – when guests were in for tea. So polite; so thoughtful; so well brought up.

And their father doing well in business, promoted to management, every two or three years a new company car, always raising his hat to a lady, shaking a friend by the hand; their mother keeping the house so neat, never a speck of dust; and her baking – you never tasted anything so good.

All perfect – in the perfect world that was settled, post-war, suburban, middle-class Scotland.

4

The Way She
Told Them

G ROWING UP IN 1950s Scotland was anything but 'touchy-feely'.
We were secure, yes – our parents were there, but rarely if ever,
as we'd say in the current idiom, 'there for us.' The stoicism of the
period required that we just got on with things. But, despite this almost
stand-offish lack of emotional engagement, there was plenty of time
for talk – for family anecdotes, stories of 'before the War', tales of that
era it is almost impossible for a child to conceive of – the time of his
parents' youth.

The fact that my parents' youth lay well before the enormous historical watershed of World War II served to add both to my inability to
conceive of what they must have been like at that time and my deep
fascination with the period. The obstacle that the War created in time –
when seen from the 1950s – was one barrier that needed to be crossed.
Another was the way in which history appeared to have stopped at the
same time as the War came to an end. Everything that had happened
to any adults in our family circle – with the sole exception of Gilbert
and Bea's marriage – seemed to have taken place prior to the return of
peace in 1945.

Perhaps the peculiarity of this state of affairs is one of the reasons I was captivated by history from a very early age. The first books I was drawn to were about the past – historical adventures for boys as well as the more prosaic history texts on the school reading list. So keen was my desire to absorb the past that I even managed to get punished for it. The first time I ever received 'a dose of the belt' was in my primary three class, at the age of seven. The particular offence that invoked the use of the tawse was no more than my eager reading of the class history textbook – the legend of Bruce and the spider, if I remember rightly. But the mistake I made was to do so on the sly during a mental arithmetic lesson. At least the teacher responsible for my punishment – one Miss Dalhousie – had a historical sounding name. And at least her response didn't create in me an aversion to history – or to reading. But it may well be responsible for my lifelong aversion to maths. However, I had the inheritance of that post-war stoicism to help me put up with it. Teeth gritted, injustice had to be accepted, had to be borne.

Along with that stoicism there was also an inculcated sense of shame that prevented me telling my parents about this punishment – indeed, any punishment – prevented me from even thinking of doing so. Of the many times I was disciplined for a misdemeanour at school – whether belted, given lines, a punishment exercise or detention – I never once confessed my sins to my parents. Never once – despite feeling that many of these instances were unjust – would I have sought their help in seeking redress. All were kept quiet, too shameful or embarrassing to admit. As were all the other secrets of schooldays – the bullying by older, more physical boys; the continual gropings endemic in a single-sex school; the victimisation by one particularly malicious teacher; the smoking behind the bike sheds; the punch-ups behind the old air raid shelters; and a legion of other scrapes both caused and experienced.

To her dying day my sports-loving mother believed that I had been, if not an enthusiastic, at least a participatory rugby player during school games periods. Far from it. My technique during those miserable, bone-freezing lessons was to stay as close as possible to the rear of the games master, in the belief that no-one would pass the ball directly at him and hence I wouldn't have to submit to being tackled by any of the beefy toughs that pounded around the pitch. This ploy was largely successful, but it did mean that I emerged from the changing rooms after the game with a suspiciously clean kit. This was easily remedied. A quick stop off at a patch of mud or a dirty puddle on the way home and my shorts and jersey could acquire enough evidence of wholehearted participation in the game to convince anyone. True, it gave Mum more washing to do than had I gone home with a clean kit, but at least it spared her from the disgrace of owning up to a sports-averse son.

In terms of secrets, children are privileged in a way. If they can keep their council, they need never 'fess up.' If there *are* family mysteries rattling their bones in the cupboard, the younger generation will have a good chance of finding them out at some point in their mature years. As this narrative shows, such secrets have a habit of revealing themselves despite never having been so much as hinted at by their keepers or suspected by those that might have discovered them. Parents, on the other hand, rarely get to share in any confidences their children have opted to keep from them. Far from the secrets of younger generations being things that will die with their keepers, they are things which their potential discoverers – that particular generation's parents – will die without being able to access.

A common view of the 1950s – and one to which my mother would refer nostalgically in her later years – is that the era was much safer and less threatening than more recent times. There may be an element of truth in this, but my suspicion is rather that standards of safety and perceptions of risk were simply more lax then. There were many situations of potential risk that I kept secret from my parents. This was not out of any particular inclination to childhood secrecy. It was much more a result of the inherent shame that ignorance and lack of openness promoted. No-one would ever 'open up' to us kids so, in return, there was no inclination on our part to share any worries or concerns with an adult.

Our family home, situated in the midst of its Edwardian suburban streets, was also close to one of the city's lunatic asylums, dating from the late Victorian period. This was the 'loony bin', as we casually referred to it in those days before political correctness. Its proximity had its advantages. We would encounter the less at-risk patients strolling in the neighbouring streets, buying their daily paper at the corner shop, or wandering in the hospital grounds in which we children had free rein. This gave us an inherently unprejudiced view of mental patients coupled with a vast area of parkland and woods where we could play unmolested. Unmolested – as far as our parents knew, that is.

I don't know about any of my playmates from that time, but my own benign view of 'loonies' changed dramatically after an incident that left me with a nasty bleeding gash across my cheek. Encountering a patient I knew by sight at one of the gates from the hospital grounds onto the adjacent hillside, I mistook his gesture for a wave. In fact he was – for some unfathomable reason – lashing out at me, his ragged fingernails causing the wound. Confused and upset, though not particularly hurt, I ran home. But rather than tell my mother what had happened, my instinct told me to concoct a story to explain the cut. The deeper message from my instinct – the one that prompted my keeping what had happened a secret – was that I would end up in trouble myself as a result of the incident. I was just too fearful to tell my mother the truth.

Thereafter I was much more wary of anyone who appeared to be odd or out of the ordinary. The local 'loonies' released for the day were now to be shunned, as were any other 'weirdos' I encountered: the drunks who were ubiquitous in certain parts of Edinburgh's Old Town back then, the 'neds' from the housing scheme beyond the hospital grounds, the aging tramp who would wander around the city centre bizarrely dressed in army cast-offs. But none of this I *ever* discussed with my parents. My feelings were always kept secret.

As were so many other incidents and accidents: the 'rough boys' who tried to steal my bike in the park; the stone I threw at a friend, nearly blinding him; the dodgy looking swimming pool attendant, who hung about the changing rooms leering at naked boys; the gang who had tried to 'torture' me and my pals with embers from a bonfire; the little girl who caught her leg in the spokes of a wheel while getting a 'backie' on my bike. And the creepy station porter who would regularly 'inter-fere' with me while bribing the friend I was out train spotting with to keep quiet with bags of sweets. Even this one, captured in an early

poem – a foolhardy but almost scientific attempt to prove or disprove
what I'd been so frequently told.

RITE OF PASSAGE

Down sloping path and greasy steps
we gain the cutting. The forbidden,
we thrill at its touch, alone.

On to the line. A set of points
resists our strength. A can to kick
and ballast stones to rattle round inside.

The wheels will suck you in,
my mother said. A lie, no doubt. Still,
comes the train, headed for the future.

Backs against the wall, we wait
for our proof. Friends, daring each other.
Boys, being boys, being men.

A roar, that cloud of steam train smell,
it shudders by. My stare bobs
in the red light, sucked in alright.

Perhaps I was in a double bind. The freedom had by children in the
'50s was liberating. Perhaps the urge to keep it 'under your hat' was a
means to maintain that freedom. But I doubt I was capable of thinking
that through then. Much more likely is that the 'buttoned up' attitudes of adult life had transferred to children's experience, inducing a
constricting blend of shame and fear, which ensured that everything
was kept under wraps in case it was considered either wicked or blameworthy. A juvenile version of the older generation's wartime stoicism
prevailed.

Double Exposure

Like the poet Richard Gwyn, I had been brought up 'with the received knowledge that any display of feelings was somehow shameful.' The common injunction 'don't make a fuss' was one we all took to heart, especially as males. After all, 'big boys don't cry' had been a repeated mantra throughout our early years. Any instances of tears had always been met with this response, even when couched in soothing terms. Why would we then even think of raising concerns that showed us in a less than perfect light as real boys – as 'boys, being boys, being men' as I say in the poem. No, our junior secrets were kept amongst ourselves and, for the most part, carried lightly.

⋆ ⋆ ⋆

It is infancy – and early childhood – when the parent–child relationship is at its most guileless. What was most real to me then was the street on which we lived until I was six. Morningside Road – our 'high street' until 1957 – seemed to me a cornucopia. Rationing, of course, was still in place, but what did I know of that. The shops at the foot of our close – or 'common stair' as my mother called it – appeared to sell everything you could want. And Mum, *my* mum, seemed to know everyone.

Shopping, or getting 'the messages' was life enhancing. I would flit from shop to shop, as a 'wee chap' holding onto my mother's hand, then later, in my primary one class at school, as a 'big boy' striding in ahead of her to greet each shopkeeper cordially. I was always made a fuss of, given a 'sweetie to myself', or a biscuit to munch. Everyone seemed to warm to me, and to my brother too when he came along. Never a cross word was said. Until the scene in the fishmonger's, that is.

I must have been overeager to inspect the fish on display. I liked to watch the drip, drip of the ice they rested on, and to ogle their weird faces staring balefully up at prospective customers. One minute I was peering through the glass of the display cabinet, the next I was climbing up onto the ledge at its foot to get a better view. What the fishmonger actually uttered, I have no idea, but his shout was enough to make me drop to the floor and burst into tears. My mother was furious. The shopkeeper protested that he was only worried I might fall into the cabinet, but it was no use. No-one had the right to shout at her son. Mum stormed out of the shop and never went back. In the busy high street that was Morningside Road there were other choices, but only one other fishmonger. Despite my mother complaining all her days that the fish there were 'too wet' – a strange complaint about seafood – she never returned to her original shop and was quietly satisfied when it shut down decades later.

Almost everything could be bought in the vicinity of our flat. The block in which we lived held a greengrocer, our regular butcher, and the licensed grocer Bea patronised almost daily. I loved to watch the wheel of the huge bacon slicer rotate and the thin slices of meat slide off to land with a faint thwack on the greaseproof paper laid in place by the shop assistant. The scales too fascinated me, as sugar was weighed out, lentils were rattled into the pan and flour was measured and bagged, balanced by one or more of a set of gleaming brass imperial weights.

A particular item of attraction sat on the counter in the chemist's shop, just at eye level to me as a five-year-old. This was a cast iron contraption collecting money for charity, known as – to use the derogatory terminology of the day – the 'jolly nigger penny bank'. I would have donated our life savings to him, if I'd been allowed to. But all I was ever permitted was a single penny per visit. I would slot this into the 'minstrel's' hand, press the contraption's lever, and watch entranced as his hand rose up to his mouth. The eyes would roll enticingly, his tongue would flip the coin backwards and it would vanish with a clunk into what I imagined was the 'minstrel's' copious copper-filled belly.

The shop immediately next to our stair door was captivating for a different reason. The sweetie shop, as the confectioner's was always known, was a cave of delights – visual, olfactory, mouth-watering and, if I was a 'good boy', flavoursome. Every time I went in there I must have gone through all the facial contortions of the *Fry's Five Boys* chocolate wrapper – desperation, pacification, expectation and, with luck, acclamation, followed by realisation. As I got a bit older I was allowed to go down the stair on my own to spend my pocket money

– at least the proportion I wasn't encouraged to save up for 'something special'. And it was there I bought my mother the first present I gave her – a box of chocolate teddy bears purchased, Bea told me years later, with my own money. I was touched to find the empty box preserved amongst my mother's mementos after her death.

Within the next few blocks were all the other shops needed for 'the messages' or for the settling of bills for items we had delivered to our door – the daily papers, the coal, the milk and so on. Milk arrived in its pint bottles in the early hours of each morning from the shop everyone referred to as E & D's – the Edinburgh and Dumfriesshire Dairy. Until I was seven or eight this was delivered from a horse-drawn milk float which would linger at the bottom of each stair while the milkman rattled up and down with his crate of bottles, responding to the orders put out the night before on a slip of paper stuck in the top of one of the empties. I used to gaze transfixed at the huge carthorse idling in the street, munching on the oats in its nosebag or huffing clouds of steam from its whiskery nostrils come the cold weather. I was also fascinated by the float which, although it had no sides to it, never seemed to lose any of the stacked crates of milk as it clattered along the cobbled streets.

A bit further along from E & D's was a baker's with delicious smells wafting out of the adjoining bake house morning and night. Another of Bea's class prejudices was on display in there. Despite my father's stated preference, she would never buy a plain loaf, declaring that it also was an item of 'common' taste. But Gilbert quietly accepted this and tucked into pan loaf instead. Nearby was Rossi's Ice Cream Parlour – another cause of childish appeals. A hugely attractive lure to us as boys, but one that fell foul of Mum's 'no eating in the streets' diktat. We were allowed to slurp at a cone when we were out for the day at the seaside – but in Morningside Road, in public, never.

★ ★ ★

While I was part of a large and widespread family, all of its members were sufficiently dispersed, and of such different ages, that we saw little of them. They were much less real than the characters that peopled

Morningside Road. As one tends to do with the deceased, many of our relatives were only evoked through tales and anecdotes. With the single exception of a snap shot of my maternal grandfather, these relatives – dead or alive – were not even represented in photographs around the family house when I was a boy. This further added to their almost non-corporeal nature.

Although I was not conscious of it at the time, this may well have discouraged me from making any enquiries about my father's family. As well as his reticence about the War, Gilbert told us nothing whatsoever about his parents and remarkably little about his siblings in their youth. The only thing I remember him saying about his childhood was to explain why he was unable to swim. All his brother and he had experienced by way of open water was summer paddling in a beck close to their Cumbrian childhood home. In truth, Gilbert did not talk about his past and made only a few scant remarks about anyone in his family, and then only if pushed.

I was aware that both of my paternal grandparents had died well before I was born but, extraordinarily, I don't think I had seen a picture of either of them until after my father's death. To this day, although I still retain a vague image of a stocky man in a large homburg hat, I couldn't be certain of recognising my paternal grandfather, or my grandmother, were I to find more shots of either of them now. I did know of one figure from my father's past, his best man who appeared in the wedding photo on display in my grandmother's house, but he had been killed in a car crash when I was an infant. I also remember a few of Gilbert's Edinburgh friends – various 'borrowed' uncles – playing with us boys in our younger days, but they too fade from the scene early on. We did have an aunt and an uncle on the paternal side but, as was echoed in my mother's family, they lived far from Edinburgh, both south of the border and we saw little of them.

I can only remember a single instance of a visit to each of these relatives during all of my childhood, although I'm sure there must have been more casual solo visits by my father when travelling on business. As kids, we only made the one long trip down to Gloucestershire, where my aunt lived in a curious 'born again' household with a female companion and that lady's 'backward' sister, as the terminology of the time would have it. I can remember being toured around the sites of the area – castles, cathedrals, ruined abbeys, half-timbered villages – which I loved, being a history-obsessed child. And it was there that I remember meeting my first American. This was a visiting evangelical preacher from the Midwest. Sporting a plaid lumberjack shirt and casual slacks, he was so unlike the black-clad ministers of the Kirk that I could hardly believe he was a reverend. As a family we attended one of his strange-to-us services in the local mission hall. This featured lots of congregational interjections which made my father literally start out of his seat with a 'Good God! What was that?' It was not the way things were ever done in the dour Church of Scotland.

In the case of my uncle though, my childhood memories are even fainter. The one visit I remember was when the two families – ours, and his with his four boys – met up during their summer holiday on the Solway Coast of Cumberland. All I really remember was being disappointed by the muddy beaches – so unlike the golden sands I was used to in Scotland. There was though, a period in my early teens when one of those four cousins was a student in Edinburgh. At that time he used to come round regularly for tea at the family home but, again due to the age difference, he spent more time with my parents than with us young lads. Only recently have I realised, through information from another cousin, that I had another aunt on my father's side. But, while I vaguely recognised the name, I had no idea she was an aunt and have no recollection of ever visiting her.

This tenuous grasp on my father's family led to a sense of disconnection that was equal, if not greater, than the similar feeling my mother's family engendered. There were occasional suggestions of a dispute my father and my uncle may have had with their sister. Although it's scarcely believable, it was suggested that this was over whether to spell their surname with an 'e' at the end or without one. That story, I now believe, was merely a front. Although completely unaware of such things during my childhood, it is clear to me now that my aunt and her 'companion' were living in what was effectively a lesbian relationship. Whether this was actively so is another matter. But it seems much more likely that this was the basis of the dispute than any spelling disagreements. But, of course, no-one would discuss such matters openly in the '50s, let alone be inclined to take a tolerant approach to them. That my father and uncle were reconciled with their sister says more about their mutual love than the received attitudes of the day.

There were also dark hints that my father and uncle had once had an older brother who may have been killed in the First World War, or may have committed suicide – something no-one on my father's side of the family seems at all sure about. If this latter speculation is true, it may provide one of the reasons for my paternal grandparents upping sticks and moving south of the border in the early part of last century. This could be yet another reason for my father's silence about his past; for his never talking about his parents the way my mother did. But, as I discovered after his death, there were many more reasons behind this reticence.

So guarded was my father, that as a kid I was even unsure as to exactly where he had been born. He had spent his youth, I knew, in the Cumbrian town of Penrith. He had even taken us, on the way back from our aunt's in Gloucestershire, to see the house his family had lived in before the War. But had he been born there, or in the Dumfriesshire town of Annan, where his family had originated? I didn't know then, and I never managed to find out until after he died – when I found out a great deal more.

* * *

My mother had also come from a larger family than our own mid-century unit, although it was not particularly large for its period, the decade before the First World War. Born in Aberdeen, she grew up in a tidily symmetrical combination of two boys and two girls, my mother being the third born and the second of the girls. In contrast to my father's reticence, Bea was chattily garrulous about her family and her regiment of relations.

What came out of the stories she told when I was both a child and an adult were the distinct natures of her siblings. The oldest, her elder brother was sporty, musical, full of fun, tall and handsome – there was always a bit of hero worship there. Although he lived to a great age, dying only a few years before my mother, I actually saw very little of him. Most of his life was lived in London and retirement took him down to Cornwall, rather than back to his native Scotland. Nonetheless, I have vivid memories of the excitement his visits engendered, somewhat coloured by the vaguely frightening presence of one of his series of Alsatians. A talented, amateur jazz-age musician, with a keen enough ear to pick up tunes on one or two hearings, he featured in Bea's stories of parties in their youth, playing stride piano or strumming the ukulele and singing. What I remember most from his visits during my childhood is his pounding the keys of the second-hand upright we had in an upstairs room, vamping out the popular show tunes of the '30s. To this day, somewhere in the attic, I still have a 78rpm on 10-inch shellac that he recorded in a booth in Binns, one of Edinburgh's city centre stores – four tunes jazzed up on the music department's piano.

My mother's younger brother we saw even less. Always quite frail and delicate, he too had moved south of the border and visited rarely. My only real recollection of him is on a fishing trip with my dad and my brother out along the east coast. Or perhaps it's only the snap shot I have of him on a riverbank showing my brother how to cast that has planted the image in my memory. My mother's sister, on the other hand, we would visit as a family from time to time. Although I suspect we'd have done so more often had she not lived in Glasgow, a city my mother regarded with disdain, convinced of the infinite superiority of Edinburgh. Indeed, any time we wrote to this aunt – thank-you letters mostly – we were always told to put 'Renfrewshire' as the address, rather than 'Glasgow', despite the fact that she lived well within the Greater Glasgow boundary. Although the address was technically correct, I always ascribed it to an act of postal snobbery. Whether it originated with my aunt or my mother, I can't say, but I always suspected the latter.

While it is easy to poke fun at my mother's received opinions and innate snobbery, I in no way attach any blame to her for this. She was a product of her time and her class. No-one can choose their background. Such snobberies, though more hidden, are still very much with us, particularly in class-bound Britain. Propped up by the country's divisive private education system, by attitudes to regional and class accents, by the London-centric media, and by the persistence of class-based politics they are often as entrenched as they were in my parents' youth. They are, as Polly Coles says in *The Politics of Washing*, 'imprinted on our collective consciousness' like photographs on paper, part of the 'DNA of our culture.'

Despite my mother's relations being married and settled down, and all but my mother's elder brother having several children, we never really mixed with our cousins. All of them were a good deal older than my brother and me. While we did visit the few relations who lived in and around Edinburgh, most of them were of the generation above my parents – great aunts and uncles. But, as one of those peculiar children who enjoyed the company of elderly people, I was always happy to listen to them talk. Or I would wander off on my own to explore their houses, opening doors and peering into cupboards as I went. Being of a more interesting vintage than the 'up-to-the-minute' style my mother aspired to when I was a young boy, their homes seemed eccentric and were intriguing to my nascent imagination.

No, any engagement with my parents' generation of family members was almost exclusively through the stories that Mum told about the inter-war period when they'd all been young, and gay – in the sense that's been overridden by the meaning attached to that word nowadays. Stories about how she, a tomboy, had followed her older brother everywhere, climbing trees, shinning up drainpipes, cycling, swimming, skating, riding and playing endless games of badminton and tennis. One particular story that I can't help wanting to visualise featured this very brother taking part in a school gymnastics display, where every member of the team was dressed as the cartoon character Felix the Cat – jumping, skipping, vaulting, climbing ropes and balancing on beams. I would give anything to have witnessed that. Another tale had the four siblings climbing a peak in the Highlands in thick mist, guided to the summit by the sound of hymn singing from a party already at the top, and presumably seeking divine aid in finding their way down again. Yet another involved my mother getting thrown out of Edinburgh's Caledonian Railway terminus, the Caley Station, by the Transport Police. She and a group of her friends had been frolicking about on the luggage trollies in a state of elation after an all-night party. What larks!

While my mother seemed to me to get on well enough with her sister, the stories she told of that sibling tended to stress her different character. More bookish, she was reputed to have read all of Scott's Waverley novels by an early age, a feat I might have attempted were the self-same novels – a handsome leather-bound edition inherited from my grandfather – not regarded as mere ornaments. Taking a prominent place in my mother's display cabinet that stood proudly in the lounge, they were not to be moved in case doing so spoiled the look of the room. At least the Stevensons and the D K Brosters were alright to take out and read, being lower down on a less prominent shelf.

My younger uncle featured to an even lesser extent in Bea's stories. He would appear more as a bit player in accounts of tennis matches, swimming galas and holidays at Gullane, their family's preferred summer resort on the East Lothian coast. But always alongside other characters from her wide circle of relations and friends.

Inhabited by the myriad members of an expanded and extended family, my mother's stories ranged through cousins, aunts and uncles, second cousins, cousins once removed, all interconnected in a company whose cast only she could portray. In the wings were various family friends – those ubiquitous 'borrowed' aunties and uncles – the family's long-term maid, Hannah, and various grooms at my great-uncle's livery business. But few of these players on my mother's stage were known to me. There was, though, one exception. At the head of this whole conglomeration, during most of my childhood, was the benign presence of my grandmother.

Living in Edinburgh, just up the road from my school gates and only a mile or two from the family home, Grandma, as she always liked to be called, was someone I saw a great deal. I still remember my surprise when, after her death, I found some photos of her in her younger days. A tall and elegant woman in her Edwardian youth, the only Grandma I had known was a little old lady. Almost crippled by arthritis, she would walk with a stick all the days I knew her.

Whether this ill health made me, her eldest grandson, more protective of her, or whether it was her kindness and warmth that attracted me, I don't know. But every week or so I would drop in to see her, making a detour on the way home from school. There I would be regaled with tumblers of Creamola Foam and a Perkin biscuit or, if I was lucky, a couple of sugary-sweet 'French Fancies' from the baker's at the end of the road. All of which would be accompanied by still more tales of the family, but this time a generation or more further back.

An accomplished piano player in her youth, and married to a passable amateur violinist, Grandma would tell stories of how the whole family used to gather round the piano, each one singing or playing their favoured instrument; of one great-uncle who'd had a career as an opera singer and another relative who'd been a concert pianist; of my great-uncle's stables where my mother learned to ride; of another great-uncle – a dire warning, this one – killed by a burst appendix, too frightened of the surgeon's scalpel to face the operation that would have saved his life. And of the grandfather I never knew, of his time in the whisky business, and his interest in antiques, many of which were still in evidence around Grandma's flat.

Even farther back took her to my great-grandfather and his business as a coal merchant. Photographs of this still exist, one in particular showing my infant grandfather perched on top of a decorated cart horse outside the coal office, with a bowler-hatted great-grandfather proudly holding the bridle. His coal depot was at Port Hamilton, the old Union Canal basin between Edinburgh's Fountainbridge and Lothian Road, long since filled in. He would walk there from his home at the foot of Viewforth every morning.

And, what's more, despite the passage of time, Grandma could even remember his favourite joke. Inviting friends, relations, business contacts – anyone within earshot, I suspect – to visit him at his office if they were ever in the vicinity of Port Hamilton, he would come out with it, doubtless pausing for effect before the last phrase.

'If you're ever passing the canal, *do* drop in.'

I find it extraordinary to think that I can tell the same joke my great-grandfather told generations back, its groan-invoking one-liner making its first appearance over a century ago. Since it's by no means really that funny, my great-grandfather doubtless wearied those who heard it told just once too often.

While all of this historical extended family seemed to exist only in these stories, it would still come alive in my own imagination. But the relatives themselves were almost nebulous in their lack of firm reality. To such an extent that I can remember, as a very small boy answering my grandmother's door, being baffled when I was told that the tall and distinguished elderly gentleman who stood there was none other than Great-Uncle Frank, the very opera singer, now retired, of whom I had been told so much. Until then he had only existed for me as a figment of Grandma's tales. Here, it seemed to me, was a character from fiction – or even ancient history – pulling at the doorbell.

★ ★ ★

However reliable or fallible they might be, such tales played a role in creating the image of a family I had vivid impressions of, but really barely knew. Through the stories my mother told and retold, I built her experiences up like Meccano, creating a viable if shaky structure through which to assemble her past. That structure, though, is necessarily unreliable, unsafe. I can no longer say whether this particular emotion belongs to that particular memory or whether I have taken it, like a stray piece out of a different set of Meccano, from another recounted incident altogether. Or worse, from that store of feelings we all build up throughout our lives – not just from direct experience but also from the constant bombardment we are all subject to from a media never shy of emotional incursion.

It is this aspect of recollection that the writer Jenny Diski describes as 'excitingly corrupt', going on to charge the very facility of memory with an 'inclination to make a proper story' of what fragments we retain of the past. As she says in *Skating to Antarctica*, 'Who can say that this image is correct and not an image from a film or picture, or another part of one's life which, seeming to fit with the general story, is pressed into service.' Psychology shows human beings essentially to be creators and retrievers, framers and reconstructors of their own narratives. Given what a keen storyteller my mother in particular was, it must have been a considerable challenge to her to completely expunge from her stories the secrets revealed to us after her death. And those others we subsequently discovered. The constantly reiterated tales of her younger days must have forced her to be ever on her guard against even the tiniest slip.

But secrecy is a habit that, once ingrained, cannot be removed. Once that habit has been acquired, memories 'begin to distort'. In her own memoir *Giving Up the Ghost*, Hilary Mantel talks of how family members 'confabulate to cover the gaps' and in doing so 'cobble together a narrative' to the best of their abilities. But as a narrative is expanded, teased out over the years, she says, 'distortions breed distortions'. Was Bea's internal self-censorship something that inclined her to embellishment – even invention – in what she *did* relate? As psychologist and writer Charles Fernyhough explains in *Pieces of Light*, 'memory is an artist as much as it is a scientist.' Was the very act of reiteration my mother's means of training herself to instinctively 'edit out' the elements of the narrative she considered shameful or unworthy – those she was determined at almost any cost to keep secret? Could this mean that her own particular narrative is even more suspect than usual? Might it, in fact – to use a phrase which she was prone to overuse herself – be 'most unusual'.

5

Crossing a Line

M Y FATHER – Arthur Thomas Gilbert Johnstone – had, like my mother, died in March, but that was back in 1976. His age at the time – only sixty-eight – seems very young to me now. After a minor 'warning', as they were often described then, and a second more major heart attack from which he was still convalescing, he succumbed to a third while resting in the dining room of the family home. He had just carried my mother's vacuum cleaner – a heavy, ancient model – upstairs for her, trying to spare her the effort. We think he must have felt ill again and, not wanting to worry Bea, had sat down to catch his breath. He died alone in his favourite chair.

My wife and I had no telephone in the spartan farm cottage we lived in at the time. By chance, that very evening I had gone down to the call box at the edge of the village to ring my brother. I was given the news then.

Walking back up the farm track to our cottage, my mind was full of competing memories and regrets. I was just a few hundred yards from the front door where I had waved my father off after a family visit only a couple of months before, not knowing then that the next time I would see him would be in an intensive care ward – and that this would be the last time I would see him alive.

The previous Christmas, my parents, with a couple of aunts in tow, had come up to Fife for a day out. After lunch, Gilbert and I repaired to the kitchen to do the washing up while my wife played the lady of the house and chatted with the other visitors. Maybe it was the domesticity of the moment; maybe it was because we were the only males in the company that day; but in our bit of craic over the soapsuds and dishtowel, I felt we had crossed a line. A line that was largely of my own creation, but one that I was at last beginning to see as both unnecessary and artificial. The line between our parental and our adult relationships was beginning to give.

'This is the start of something new,' I'd thought to myself. It was. But I could never have imagined the form it would take.

★ ★ ★

In the autumn of that year, around six months after my father's death, both of us brothers, together with our wives, were summoned to the family home. My mother had something important she wanted to talk to us about. She had been dropping hints – some more veiled than others – that there was some vital family business we had to discuss. This had been going on almost from the day my father had died.

Of course, my brother and I had put our heads together, puzzling over Bea's behaviour. We had never been a family for holding such meetings and this summons was unprecedented. As the hints firmed up into a specific date when we were all to gather, our speculation had similarly firmed up.

'What the hell could this be about?' we asked each other. 'Do you think it could be something good or some more bad news?'

'Should we expect it to affect us – or is it just going to be something about Mum?' my brother wondered.

'God knows!' was my only response.

Try as we might, we failed to come up with any suggestion of what could be behind this summons.

As a family we had never been prone to soul bearing discussions or any sort of group conferring. Putting things out of our minds was always *our* way of it. As with many other families of the period, we were distinctly 'hodden doon'. In this, my parents' behaviour was typical of their generation. There was always a certain emotional aloofness, an unwillingness to dig any deeper than the surface in our interactions. Like the family Richard Gwyn writes about in his memoir *The Vagabond's Breakfast* we 'endured a collective adherence to a code of non-disclosure.' This sense of propriety was both a throwback to an earlier part of the century and, I believe, a consequence of shared endurance in wartime. It seemed we all had to subscribe to an unwritten agreement to keep hidden anything that might provoke or disturb. Show us a carpet and we would sweep our worries under it.

But our worries began to surface when Bea launched into what felt almost like a prepared speech. Saying how difficult the whole thing was for her, she went on to explain that she had promised Gilbert she would do this. Whatever 'this' was.

'That doesn't make it any easier to do,' she said, addressing my brother and me, 'but there's something you both need to know.' Agog, we perched on the edge of our Parker Knolls.

Perhaps it would've been clearer if Bea had started with the more easy to grasp aspects of her revelation, easing us into the surprising, unforeseen and downright astonishing information about our father's life that was about to follow. But no, instead she opted to open with the bombshell.

'I have to tell you that you have a half-sister,' she informed us. 'She's your father's daughter, living in London. And I want you boys to get in touch with her right away.' The information failed to sink in at first, but Bea continued.

'What we never mentioned to you before,' she went on, almost casually, 'is that your dad was married before he and I met. He was divorced just after the War. Your half-sister – Catherine Mary Johnstone – is the daughter of that marriage.'

Eager to get her task over, our mother went on to fill us in on the background to this first marriage – about which we also knew nothing – and the birth of our half-sister, Gilbert's daughter, whose existence we had never so much as suspected.

And then came the remark Bea was most emphatic about, 'You owe it to your dad to meet her. You *must* meet her – for *his* sake.'

And thus, in a heartbeat, our father's family had increased by one. Our 'four of a family' – one of Dad's stock phrases – had evaporated like early morning mist. My mother had changed status – she was now a second wife. And so had I – I was no longer my father's first-born. My brother was now his third child. Another sibling had been parachuted into our lives. Gilbert had three children. Not the two we had always accepted, always believed in.

Like some strange generational game of musical chairs, the funeral march had barely ceased and we had all risen from our seats to move round the family circle and sit down again, but in a different place from the one we'd been in before. The shape of the ring had altered, elongated. An unknown and unguessed at figure was seated on the margin, long abandoned and ignored. And in amongst the familiar chairs we all knew, there was another – strange and unfamiliar – placed almost at the centre of the group. Its occupant was holding out a hand to us. An eager hand, we were told. But were we ready to grasp it?

I have little recollection of the details of that gathering. Just of feeling stunned – even a bit annoyed. Dad's early death had been a hard blow to us all and here was our nuclear family turned on its head. Here was a secret he had kept from us for no reason apparent at the time. And it was all too late to ask for any explanation. The man it most concerned was gone. And to me it almost felt as if my trust in him had gone too.

★ ★ ★

Much has been written, filmed and broadcast about the expected joy of finding so-called 'long-lost' family members. My own initial feeling at this sudden revelation was largely one of resentment. While today I get on well with my father's daughter, whom I very much regard as my sister, it has been a troubled relationship for all sorts of reasons. But none of these, I must be clear, were connected with Catherine herself. And none to the subsequent discovery of a second half-sister.

Despite the numerous ups and downs of adolescence in the '60s, and of three strong-minded and argumentative males in the one family, there had never been any breakdown in our relationships. Despite our father's job, which could take him away on business for the best part of a week at a time, effectively rendering my mother a single parent on a regular basis, we had always been a tight-knit family. The paucity of relatives close by and the lack of close family friends had made us so. And now, at one fell swoop, that unity was disrupted, challenged, denied. And denied at the most sensitive of times – right after the death of a parent.

There had been no discernible hint of any sort that such a disclosure might be made one day, that such a secret even existed. Not that anything can prepare you to receive such a piece of news. Far from being delighted to discover that I had a half-sister, I was stunned. We all were. Shocked, even. But emphatically not – as the popular media would have one assume – dying to rush off and meet her. We needed time to take it all in. Time to adjust.

It was at this point that the moral blackmail kicked in. Our mother was insistent that we *had* to meet Catherine, that we must do it 'for Dad's sake'. It had been his dying wish that all of his children get together.

'*All* of his children!' my brother and I thought. 'And we'd always believed it was just the two of us!'

Despite this, however, we did agree to meet Catherine. If only once. We would see how it went.

'But,' we told Bea, 'we need time to come to terms with this.' Above all, we realised, she mustn't rush us.

And so the back story came out. My father – despite his total silence on the matter – had indeed been married before. Long before. Before he moved to Scotland. Before the War even.

'He never got on well with his first wife,' my mother said, 'and she deserted him. Ran off with someone else while he was serving his country in the Air Force. Can you believe it?' Her tone suggesting that this was something *she* would never have done.

* * *

Crossing a Line

It sometimes feels as if I never knew my father. This revelation only served to heighten that nagging sensation. Obviously I knew him when I was a child and a youth, though his work related absences made him less of a presence than my mother. But the crucial point is that I never knew him man to man in that maturing of the father–son relationship I envy in many of my friends. Throughout our life together, he was always 'my father', I was always 'his son'. Despite instances when he was very much supportive of me, going many an extra mile on my behalf, we never got beyond the parent–child demographic. His often authoritarian manner and his insistence on being obeyed without question made it almost impossible to discuss anything with him. Indeed, he would characterise any attempts at discussion, however reasoned, as dissent, batting them down with his stock response of, 'I'll not have any arguments.'

My father and I were much further apart in ages than many of my peers were with either of their parents, and Gilbert's work meant he was away from home on a regular, if infrequent, basis. But I have little doubt that this lack of adult interaction was more down to me than to him. I was all of twenty-five when my father died, and I had been married for almost four years. But it is easy in retrospect to see just how immature I was. The beginning for me of more adult attitudes only began with Gilbert's death. What saddens me most about this is that I feel we were on the verge of a more equal relationship when he suffered the heart attack that killed him.

A short time before that, when I had just started my first teaching job, Gilbert had taken me out for a pint to celebrate. In his own way he was trying to kick-start grown-up interaction. But that gesture was his sole attempt at moving us to adult getting-on. All I remember is the sensation of being uncomfortable with the whole situation. Only just grown out of the hippie identity of my student days, I was still thirled to the 'hip versus straight' view of lifestyle. And I was very much a self-appointed member of the former category. Inclined to see myself as some sort of challenger of societal norms, I had even carried this attitude over into my nascent career. After all, my main driving force during teacher training had been the recently published *Teaching as a*

Subversive Activity, and I had looked more to A S Neill and R D Laing than to my course tutors for guidance.

We had gone, on my father's suggestion, to a local suburban lounge bar on the edge of the Braid Hills, rather than to any of the more 'alternative' hostelries in the back streets of the city centre which I favoured. It was a doubly unfamiliar set-up. We had never done this in the past. And Gilbert had never been a pub type anyway.

'What am I doing in a 'straight' pub with an old man in his sixties?' I wondered, sipping uneasily at my tankard of gassy Export.

Perhaps if there hadn't been such a difference in our ages this feeling would never have arisen; or perhaps if the War hadn't separated our experiences so much we would have found more in common, and found it more readily. But who can say?

We had got on well with each other most of the time when I was a boy. During the school holidays, I would often 'chum' my father on his business rounds. A commercial traveller all his life, he had worked for various pharmaceutical companies since settling in Edinburgh before I was born. By the time I was old enough to accompany him, he had built up an impressive range of contacts and his rounds would take us to numerous parts of Edinburgh that I had never visited on family occasions.

The Royal Infirmary, the 'Sick Kids' – as the children's hospital is still known – the Western General or the Princess Margaret Rose Hospital were all regular calls, as were the numerous pharmacists, druggists, manufacturing chemists and capsule makers dotted around the city. But however intriguing the area or impressive the building, however fascinating the comings and goings of the building's personnel, I would rapidly get bored and be eager to move on to the next stop. As soon as Dad reappeared, shaking hands with a customer and striding across the car park – sample case in one hand, briefcase in the other – I would wonder what fascinating establishment we were headed for next.

Getting older, these trips had taken on a different complexion. I became my father's driver. Always eager to learn, I had begun pestering him for driving lessons before I even reached the legal age of seventeen. But as soon as I did, Gilbert took on the task of my tuition.

Crossing a Line

The first lesson was a disaster narrowly averted. But averted only by my father's steady nerves and quick reactions. Having selected a quiet, wide and empty side street in an area not too close to home, Gilbert moved me over to the driver's seat and ran me through the rudiments of the controls. Being an opinionated and cock-sure teenager, of course I thought I already knew these backwards. I was nonetheless made to practice clutch control, gear changing, checking the rear-view mirror, indicating and easing off the handbrake all in a methodical manner – and, more importantly, all stationary.

Then came the moment for the first move. Gilbert ran me through it, going over the points above, expecting me to edge the car forward, perhaps hesitantly, perhaps haltingly. Instead – forgetting in an instant all he had talked me through – I jerked my foot off the clutch, and the car shot forward, slewed across to the other side of the street, narrowly missing a pedestrian on the pavement, and came to a halt just short of a lamppost as my father pulled furiously on the handbrake and the engine stalled. I don't recall whether I was given a dressing down on the spot or whether this was kept until we got home, but Gilbert must have been determined to teach me as he continued with the lessons until I was proficient enough to give him a few days off behind the wheel and drive him to his more distant business calls.

I got my first car a couple of years after passing my test. Bought for £50, it was a beat-up old mini-van with the registration number 127 JOG – which doubled as a group chant my friends would use when they had to bump start the jalopy for me – an all too frequent occurrence. Gilbert was very helpful to me in buying this vehicle – and its replacement. I had ignored his advice and, within weeks of acquiring the van, had driven down south to the rather ponderously named Bath Festival of Blues and Progressive Music. Held in a Somerset valley near Shepton Mallet, the approach roads featured steep inclines and long halts in the sun while the traffic inched towards the site. Those, and the combined payload of three friends and a girlfriend, meant that almost inevitably the radiator overheated and blew. My friends and I parked the mini-van on a verge and footed it the remaining mile or so to the festival. A weekend of musical and other highs ensued. But, the show over, I got the blues for real when I discovered the car had been stolen while I was grooving to the progressive sounds on stage. My girlfriend and I had to return ignominiously by train, me fuming to myself that my father had been proved right.

Gilbert also helped me find a back street garage for cheap repairs to the successor mini-van. Although he must have sighed inwardly at my many juvenile prangs, he seemed not at all abashed when the van's stoved-in bonnet was replaced with a glaringly bright red fibreglass replica. Nor was he put out when I later bought a retired Morris postie van, its number plate mounted on the roof of the cab. Not so my mother. She insisted I parked round the corner from the family home in case the neighbours disapproved – or worse, thought the position of the number plate marked the van out as a commercial vehicle.

It was down to me to reciprocate my father's kindnesses with consideration. But I confess I didn't. Dad was there to help me,, was the attitude I took – every bit as juvenile as those prangs. I even once dumped a clapped-out Dormobile on him and left him to arrange for it to be repaired and auctioned. This on the dubious grounds that he was the one who had checked it over for me before I bought it and so must, *a priori*, be responsible for it now it had failed. The fact that I was about to start work as a teacher was my justification for not having time to see to this – and Dad *was* retired, I pointed out. Having reached my quarter century, and being about to start my first professional job, did not seem to have added to my maturity.

There was little sign of my father and me nudging towards a more adult relationship. The vast difference in our experiences of life must have contributed to this. I doubt whether the generation gap has ever been wider than between those generations on either side of the Second World War.

While I hesitate to use such a term, there is one that I feel is at least relevant to this dichotomy. 'Survivor's guilt' is a commonly recognised phenomenon associated with the outcome of a disaster, the aftermath of a conflict or, in its worst-case scenario, with surviving massacre or genocide. It appears it is well-nigh impossible, having come unscathed out of some terrible experience, ever to escape the sensation that the survivor does not deserve still to be living. That such a one has no right to survive when others – and others often perceived as betters – have not made it through. What I would liken to this, though plainly not of the same order, is that sense of guilt at having been born into a generation lucky enough never to have had the challenges to which the previous two generations were subject. Never were those of my generation – at least in the UK – called up to war. Never were they subject to the relentless losses of war. Never were they forced to confront their own fears and inadequacies the way my parents' and grandparents' generations were. We missed it – through luck, or better judgement, or just simple chance. This was something about which it was easy to be smug, even superior, in my hippie youth. We were all going to create this new world where these conflicts of past times would not arise. That was the old way. We were the new.

I have long abandoned such naïve notions. But, as I grow older, I am almost surprised to find myself subject to an increasing sense of discomfiture – something at least akin to survivor's guilt – about my generation's avoidance of the War. I have grown into an increased understanding of its cost, both personal and communal. I am better able to appreciate the terror and fear to which my parents' generation were subject. Not in a 'shock, horror' way or even a 'pity for lost youth' manner, but through the growth of a deeper and stronger sense of empathy which I can say was absent or, at best, dormant in my younger years. I will never be able fully to appreciate what previous generations went through and yet I now find myself more able to grasp the actuality of it and to empathise with their wartime experiences.

This is something that has crept up on me unexpectedly. The writing of this memoir has added to it. As has the reading and research, the exploration of family photographs and the examination of documents that preceded it. But it is more than that. It is a sensation tied up with the regret I feel at not knowing my father better – at not working at knowing him. The regret that the secrets he – and my mother – kept from me, prevented me from knowing him as I would like to have done. The regret – common to many, I am sure – that I was not then who I am now.

Someone else who has identified this phenomenon is Richard Gwyn. In talking about the War as the 'essential divide', he sees it as a specific marker of the 1950s, a kind of blemish on a generation, one which is extended by the increased father/son age gap consequent on time spent in the forces. Like Gwyn, I experienced this same wide age gap. My father was all of forty-three when I was born, putting him in his sixties during my fractious late teenage phase. Although the War would have been a barrier between us come what may, had we been separated by fewer years it is conceivable that we'd have felt less alien to each other, less antipathetic to each other's lifestyles.

Twenty-five – my age at my father's death – is young, very young, and an age at which one has far too many notions about oneself. Gilbert was always an affable and garrulous man – a 'hail-fellow-well-met' sort of chap, as he'd have been described then – who got on well with everyone. Despite not finding it in himself to be tolerant of my youthful notions and conceits, he would almost certainly have got on with me, given time. No, I was the one who struggled to see this side of him, only to get an all too brief hint of it before it was taken away.

★ ★ ★

My father, we discovered later, had married his first wife in 1939. The couple had moved to a remote village in the west of the Lake District not long before the start of the War. Their daughter had been born there in 1940. The family had stayed on in their village home after hostilities broke out, but eventually Gilbert had left to join the RAF. In his absence, his first wife had taken over his job of selling veterinary supplies to farmers. This meant she had a car and a petrol allowance – a rare and fortunate privilege in wartime. But it was one that may well have led to the encounter which precipitated the break-up. However it happened, their relationship proved just one of so many ill-founded marriages that did not survive the separations and temptations of wartime.

Gilbert's young wife was stuck in an out-of-the-way village, missing the social life she had enjoyed before her marriage. On a visit to relatives in Manchester she had met an American officer and, like so many other wives left at home, must have seen him as providing an opportunity for some relief to her boredom, of bringing some fun back into her secluded life. We will never know exactly what happened, but the background is there in numerous accounts by those in similar circumstances.

None other than Barbara Cartland has described these situations. Soon to become famous as a romantic novelist, she served as a wartime marriage guidance counsellor. Things would have started harmlessly, she suggests, with women looking for 'a little change from the monotony' of daily life and missing a man 'to appreciate them.' My father's first wife was a former research chemist from Manchester, so being isolated in a remote Lake District village must have made her feel even more cut-off and solitary. As Cartland goes on to say of women in these circumstances, 'she is lonely, he smiles at her, she smiles back and it's an introduction.' It would just have been 'rotten luck' that she was already married. They meant no harm – but, before long, things would have changed, developed. And that's how it must have happened with Gilbert's first wife. From these beginnings, she had gone on, almost inevitably, to fall in love with this man.

By the time the War was nearing an end, she had come to the conclusion that her marriage had been a mistake. Still serving in the forces, but by this time back in England, my father had received a lawyer's letter out of the blue. His wife wanted a divorce. He was devastated. Quickly arranging for compassionate leave, he had made a hurried visit to try to persuade her to change her mind. But she was adamant. Their marriage was at an end.

Having fallen for her American serviceman, Gilbert's now estranged wife planned to follow this man across the Atlantic when the War ended. It was only later that she discovered he had lied to her – he was already married. Her hopes were shattered. But she was still emphatic that her marriage was over. The romance had shown her a way out of her isolated life, reminded her of what she had given up in leaving the city. There was to be no turning back. She wanted to make a fresh start.

She had a brother in Canada. Using a recent small legacy, she decided to start a new life there. Taking her daughter with her, they moved first to Ottawa, but after spending some time in Canada, the two of them settled in Texas. At some point my father and his first wife had got divorced – or, as they said in the idiom of the time, Gilbert had 'given her a divorce.'

* * *

But my half-sister Catherine had grown up curious about her father and harbouring happy memories of him from her infancy. She had visited Britain several times on holiday and had eventually come back to the country for a job in London. This was in the late '60s, almost a decade before Gilbert's demise.

At this point in the story our mother came out with another revelation, one that seemed even more incomprehensible than the original surprise announcement. Catherine had – Bea went on to say – been in touch with our father for nigh on ten years, almost since her arrival on these shores. A further bombshell. A further secret kept from us.

'Why on earth,' I demanded of Bea, 'didn't Dad tell us about this himself? Or at least, why didn't he tell us when we got a bit older? He could've expected us to have had a bit more understanding by then.'

'For God's sake! We're both in our twenties now,' my brother pointed out. 'We could... we *should* have been told!'

Never mind how resentful we were feeling, both of us felt we would have been much less so had we been taken into our parents' confidence, if not from the start, at least once Gilbert's renewed relationship with his daughter had settled down and become permanent.

But there was so much more to this than was apparent from the bare facts. It was – our mother confessed – on *her* strict insistence that our father had never revealed to us either his first marriage or his daughter's existence.

'You see,' Bea said, 'when we got engaged, almost no-one knew that I was marrying a divorced man. I only told your grandma, my sister and my best friend – your Auntie Joan – that Gilbert had been married before.'

It seemed that, to her, the shame of our father being seen as a 'second-hand man' – a term she claimed was current at the time – had been something she could never bring herself to face. One of my mother's many received opinions, here being cited as justification. It was not so much a lie that had been told at the time, as an omission of the facts. Yes, our old friend of recent coinage – being 'economical with the truth.'

Of course, the original decision on this secrecy may not have been my mother's. It is plausible that it might have been foisted on her by her family. Even if she did acquiesce herself, the concealment might have been instigated by my grandmother, or even by Bea's siblings, perhaps even referring back to their ever-upright father's stance of abhorrence at divorce in doing so. An element of moral blackmail is even conceivable, an insistence that a dead father's opinions be honoured – and my grandfather had only died a few years before my parents became engaged. There would have been no reason to acknowledge my father's divorced status for their wedding to take place in church as they planned. The Church of Scotland has no restrictions on divorcees remarrying.

It is true that divorce was much rarer in '50s Britain and was viewed as something, if not to be ashamed of, at least as something to keep quiet about. The period was characterised by an almost feverish desire to 'get back to normal', one which included a rejection of 'wartime morality'. Establishment figures from Parliament to the judiciary were vocal in this campaign, none more so than Geoffrey Fisher, Archbishop of Canterbury at the time, who insisted that every single divorce made for 'an area of poison and a centre of infection' in the life of the nation. Despite his having no authority in the Church of Scotland, he was a respected voice of the establishment nonetheless. In such an atmosphere, it is at least easy to understand the power of the stigma and to sense the origin of the secret, even if not to understand its maintenance over the years.

But it seemed to me at the time – in my self-professed 'liberated' mind-set – that it was this accumulation of secrets that made the situation even more objectionable. That the insistence on the part of my mother on secrecy being maintained *ad infinitum* was going too far. She further revealed that Gilbert had pleaded with her to agree to his bringing all three of his offspring together. That she had flatly refused to countenance this, from fear of the concealment of his divorce getting out, I found too just much to bear.

'How could she have done this to Dad?' I asked myself. 'How could she have thwarted his dearest wishes, and all to save face?'

'The deception might just have been understandable in the early '50s,' I told Bea later, 'but it doesn't bear consideration in this day and age.'

* * *

In the short period between my father's leaving hospital to convalesce from his major heart attack and his death a week or so later, I had phoned home numerous times to see how he was doing. I also attempted to fix up a day when I could get down from Fife to visit him. Each time I phoned, my mother always told me that, despite what he might say himself, he was still very weak and was not yet up to seeing visitors.

'Just give it another few days,' she had said, 'Maybe after the weekend Dad'll be up to a visit.'

And, of course, we all thought we had plenty of time.

But I cannot get rid of the nagging doubt that perhaps – just perhaps – my mother had another motive in keeping me from visiting then.

Was she selflessly protecting Gilbert from the stress of having to tell us about his daughter, to reveal what they had both so long concealed? He may well have planned to do that, since he'd have had me there together with my brother, who was still living in the family home at the time. He may even have told my mother that he was going to do so and she may have been trying to postpone this until he was stronger. Or was it perhaps stress to herself that Bea was worried about? Was she frightened that, should Gilbert speak up about his past, the secrets she had insisted were kept from us would come out? Was she scared that this would rapidly put them beyond her control? That they would show her up in a poor light, sow the seeds of resentment at such a worrying time? Or, to take a more charitable view, did she just need time to think through how she would respond?

A combination of both, I think.

In the end I put off – or was put off, I can't say which – for too long. Gilbert died before I got down to see him back home one last time.

Arriving at the house some hours after his death, I found my father wrapped in a sheet and laid out on the lounge carpet where he had been placed by a kindly neighbour, a friend from my parents' church. Turning back a corner of the sheet, I bent to kiss his forehead. It was as cold as the atmosphere in the unheated room, never used except on special occasions. It is an image I can never forget, and one that was startlingly brought back to me through a visual misapprehension in our own home many years later.

TRACE

It was a recognition of shape. The long body bag
of our duvet rolled loosely on the floor and lying to me,
as your chrysalis of sheet had done in a different room,
late in the day you ceased being my father.

Deceitful, it caught my breath and threw it back
two deaths ago, to eyes that would not cry, as fingers
shaking, folded back the neat hemmed edge of cotton
to your chin, unshaven, your face, sunk cheeked and empty

as I felt looking at the husk of you, the mirror misted over
and obscure. But now I want to find you there again, unroll
this quilt, spool back to what we should have shared
with time and patience, pick the stitching out.

My father, you were rolled into that sheet before
my hand had eased its grip. I cannot feel
your fingers in my palm but only absence, the impress
of a word in pencil someone accidentally erased.

Double Exposure

I had visited my father many times while he was in hospital following his second heart attack. I had said all those loving things that my upbringing and the mores of the time impeded my saying, except in extremis. So, while I have many regrets about my relationship with my father, I have no regrets that I didn't bid farewell to him in the way I'd have liked to, in the way he deserved.

6

Once Bitten

CUFFLINKS ARE THINGS I have rarely worn. And they would definitely not have been part of the image I sought to cultivate in the '70s fag end of the hippie era. But, for some reason back then, I needed to borrow a pair from my father to complete the get up I had planned for some party or other. Fancy dress, I shouldn't wonder. I expected him to lend me an old pair, some that wouldn't be missed were anything to happen to them – my father had few illusions as to my responsibility at that age. I was surprised, then, to be offered the discreet gold cufflinks I had seen Gilbert wear many times when dressed formally for church or going out to a function.

Handing the cufflinks over to me, my father said, in an almost offhand manner, 'Now, you *will* take good care of these, won't you?'

'Don't worry, Dad,' I said, 'they'll be fine.'

'You know, these links were a gift from someone who once meant a lot to me,' he added, 'so look after them.'

Wrapped up in myself, and in the prospects of whatever occasion I was headed for, I missed the opportunity to ask him who this might be. The matter went the way of all casual remarks. It was only after he died that I discovered – or perhaps realised (I can't now say which) – that the person in question was his first wife. As my father never wore a wedding ring all the years I knew him, I think it's safe to assume that he did not do so during his first marriage. Could these cufflinks – gold, after all – have even been his first wife's wedding gift to her new husband?

This small episode took place several years past the date of my half-sister Catherine's first arrival in Britain. She and Gilbert would have had many opportunities to meet up by then. He would have had plenty of time to contemplate bringing his sons and his daughter together. Was my father trying to create an opportunity for me to ask him more? Was he trying to open up to me about this person he said had meant so much to him? True, I *had* noticed the initials, paired with his own on each of the opposing faces of the cufflinks but, stupidly, negligently even, had never given them so much as a passing thought.

At the time, my not-long-married wife and I were staying the night in the spare bedroom of the family home. This privilege was accorded to us only after our marriage. In that era single rooms were *de rigueur* for the unwed, at least they were under my parents' roof. It would never have occurred to me to suggest otherwise. But now that I was married and respectable, rather than solo in my teenage bedroom up the back stair, we were accommodated together on the upper floor of the house.

That evening, while my wife soaked in the bath, I was in the spare room getting ready to go out. Gilbert must have been pottering about in my parents' adjacent bedroom when I asked him to find me the cufflinks. Had he seen this as a fortuitous opportunity to let me know that he too had been married relatively young? Did he maybe want to wish us better luck than he'd had? Or was there more to it?

By then my parents would have had many discussions about my father's desire to bring the offspring of his two marriages together. This desire, I now know, was consistently thwarted by my mother. Might this remark of his have been an attempt to spark my curiosity? After all, I'm certain he *did* have other, less valuable pairs of cufflinks, so it seems likely that he made a specific decision to lend me the special pair. We were alone together on the upstairs landing where he could have answered any question I might have posed without my mother, downstairs in the kitchen, hearing what was being discussed or supposing he had set the whole thing up. Was this his grab at an opportunity to open up, a desperate effort to break the impasse in which he had been trapped? Poor man. If it was, I feel for him. He must have been hugely disappointed that I didn't take the bait.

If bait it was. I may be reading far too much into this. Would my father have risked going against my mother's express wishes like that? I don't want to suggest that he was in any way under my mother's thumb – although how can I be sure of the dynamics of their relationship, especially at this distance? But it's unlikely he would have wanted to challenge her directly. I can imagine how torn he would have felt between love for his wife, our mother – the one woman who had stuck by him – and love for his daughter – the one who had sought him out when he had considered her lost forever. Would he have risked hurting my mother – perhaps damaging their relationship – to realise unilaterally what he and his daughter wished for? Impossible to say. But I can't help wondering if that transient moment on the upstairs landing was an attempt to engineer a resolution, to make it seem as if he'd just stumbled into it by chance.

After my father's death, but before becoming aware of his first marriage, I suggested to my mother that I would like to have these very same cufflinks as a memento. I was puzzled when she prevaricated. But as Bea said to Catherine in one of their letter exchanges:

> I still have the gold cuff links your mum gave to your dad and I would be happy to give them to you. Actually, Brian borrowed them one Christmas and he asked me after his dad died if he could have them. He hasn't got them yet and I feel they are really yours by rights as they were given to Gilbert by your mother. If he asks again, Brian I mean, I will stall till I get him told about you.

What I did not know then – and so could never have realised – was that she felt duty bound to offer them to the daughter of Gilbert's first marriage before she could answer my request.

Ages later, once the air had cleared in the aftermath of the revelations, I mentioned to my mother the remark Gilbert made about his first wife – and why he had insisted I look after the cufflinks. I didn't, of course, mention how I'd subsequently interpreted its import. I was surprised at her reaction. She was hurt. Gilbert, she said, had always told her that his first wife had meant nothing at all to him. Yet it seems beyond credibility that he would have married someone who did not mean *anything* to him, at least at the time. Surely what my father had intended was that his first wife had long since ceased to mean anything to him by the time he met my mother?

Was this an instance of that same hint of jealousy Bea's reaction to Gilbert's daughter seemed to evoke? Resentment at having settled for a man on whom someone else had previously had a claim? Or was it another case of making realities out of selective memory? That compulsion she always had, to keep up appearances at all costs?

★ ★ ★

It has become clear to me over the years that my father was a charming and genial man. He liked women and enjoyed their company as equally as he did that of his male friends. Perhaps he was not the most decisive of characters himself but he made up for any lack of resolution through his choice of partners. From what I have been told about his first wife's character, I can appreciate that both his marriages were to strong-minded women; to women who were strangely alike in some ways. Both, it appears, believed they had married beneath them. So Gilbert must have been persuasive as well as charming.

His first marriage had been destroyed, it seems, through no fault of his own, though there is no way of ever knowing its hidden under-currents. But like many marriages of the time, the separation brought about by the War had caused it to wither and die, before it had even had time to fully flower. The freedom of opportunity to which wartime conditions had given rise had severed it at the root. He had lost his first wife irretrievably. So he must have been very afraid he might lose his second wife. And doubly anxious not to risk any action that might precipitate this.

Gilbert must have been prepared to go to almost any lengths in order to preserve his new relationship and the family life he and my mother had built together. Even if this meant concealing his first marriage. Even if it meant later keeping his daughter a secret from his sons. The notion of being 'once bitten' is very much applicable to my father. Even if it doesn't exactly apply to the bad luck of his falling in love with his first wife, he had undoubtedly been 'bitten' in her unforeseen decision that their marriage was over. And doubly so through her removal of his daughter from his life.

'Twice shy' is equally characteristic of the state of mind he must have been in with his daughter's reappearance and Bea's resistance to her being acknowledged publicly. Gilbert was caught in the dilemma of whose love to prioritise, how to balance his affections. For decades, even despite his second marriage, a corner of his heart must have held a hidden remembrance of his first wife and his only daughter, a yearning to know what had happened to his little girl, even if he had long ceased to have any feelings for her mother. But that was the past, over and done with, is all he can have been able to think.

When his daughter asked him, years later, why he hadn't kept in touch with her, he described his feelings of helplessness and bewilderment when the marriage ended. His sense had been that as a girl she belonged with her mother. The distance between England and their initial landfall in Canada had meant that he believed he would never see her again. It broke his heart. But he couldn't stop her leaving when his first wife emigrated. His daughter, he must have believed, was lost to him forever.

It is clear that more than just a single relationship is lost with the end of a marriage. Even if there are no children, many friends, relatives and acquaintances can be lost when a couple spit up. Countless individuals simply 'lack the words and the social skill to deal with divorce', as Jenni Calder says in her collection of life study essays *Not Nebuchadnezzar*. Was Gilbert one of those? Was he in a state of shock and rendered if not literally, at least emotionally speechless by the situation he found himself in? An emotional trauma that would have been all the more devastating coming at the very point when, the War being over, he'd have been contemplating a happy return to his wife and daughter, a resumption of his old life. He had lost not only his family, but the home he would have been looking forward to getting back to, the rural lifestyle he had only just begun to enjoy when the War had intervened. Was this what was behind his reluctance – his inability – to make any attempt to maintain contact with his daughter. Was he in denial of the whole situation? As Calder concludes, 'like death, divorce is a territory we pretend is not ours.'

When Catherine returned to England she was in her late twenties. Her reappearance brought back to Gilbert intense memories of the life he had shared with her and her mother in the early years of the War, before he was called up. The sudden emotional impact must have been overwhelming. It was bound to raise fear and jealousy with Bea. As Laurie Lee has suggested, 'memory can be more real than events' – the actual past may not quite fit recollections, but 'the shape, the feeling remains.' My mother would undoubtedly have sensed that. Meeting his daughter again, Gilbert would have carried back to the family home a sudden ardour for at least one element of his past life. A past life my mother had believed was buried and gone.

★ ★ ★

It has always puzzled me – and puzzled my sister even more – that my mother regarded divorce as so very scandalous. Obviously, her background and the received opinions of her family and her class had played their part. While her opinions may well have been her own, I can never be sure what notions had been put into Bea's head by others. She was very prone to quote received opinion, often bizarrely unfounded, as fact.

There were many occurrences of this. Whatever the weather, she always insisted on sleeping with her bedroom window open by at least a crack. She would often refer, almost with a sense of pride, to finding snow that had drifted in to her childhood bedroom overnight. Asked why she insisted on an open window, she would explain it was to combat the dangers of oxygen deprivation.

'It's well known that lack of oxygen can cause illness – even death,' she hinted darkly.

Once, when staying the night with us in later years, this spartan attitude was again revealed. This time her ploy was to reject out of hand an extra pillow.

'Everyone knows that a second pillow gives you a double chin,' she announced. I never offered her one again.

When ecological concerns became more prominent in the '80s, she had her response ready. My suggestion that the CFCs in the hair spray she used would be damaging to the ozone layer did no more than give her an opportunity to explain that she had considered this and had a remedy at the ready.

'I know all about that, but I make sure it's not a problem,' she said. 'I always check the bathroom door is shut tight before I use the spray.'

My mother's extended family seemed stable, staid almost. I am not aware of any instances of divorce amongst her relatives which could have influenced her attitude. But she may well have been advised by her elders not to broadcast the fact of my father's divorce.

'Nobody needs to know about it, Beattie. Better to pretend that it never happened,' I can imagine them saying.

I feel she would have thought that, while other people might get divorced, it wasn't an acceptable course of action in her family, even as a last resort. Given her innate sense of propriety, I can easily see her taking that position.

Of course, divorce was much less common in the 1950s than it is in the first part of the twenty-first century. On the other hand, it had increased in frequency greatly in the period immediately after the War. But, as Jane Robinson says in her social history *In the Family Way*, the all-pervasive post-war thrust had been to return to 'an image of perfect family life'. The media was full of visions of a 'bright new Britain' populated by conventional married couples with a 'sturdy son' and a 'frilly daughter' and perhaps a 'dear little Scottie dog'. Who can blame my mother if she saw my father's status as a divorced man as being in opposition to this idealised future?

Perhaps Bea and her family were even thinking back to the Abdication Crisis of 1936, when the king's desire to marry a divorcée had led him to renounce the throne? Certainly, my mother never had a good word to say about Edward VIII, nor would she mention Mrs Simpson without some condemnatory remark. There is also the case of Princess Margaret's thwarted desire to marry Group Captain Peter Townsend, a divorced man. Although that particular crisis took place three years after my parents' marriage, it is indicative of the attitudes of the time.

But these British instances of antipathy to divorce would have cut no ice with my transatlantic-raised sister. While in Canada there had always been a certain shyness about mentioning that her parents were divorced, but this faded rapidly when she moved to Texas. There she was living in a culture where, while it wasn't an everyday occurrence, divorce was neither as uncommon nor as frowned upon as it was in Great Britain. She must have been perplexed by my mother's obduracy in those early years of contact with her father. It is easy to see how she would have regarded Bea's decision, and her subsequent actions, as not merely objectionable, but as entirely unjustified.

For my mother, I doubt her insistence on maintaining secrecy was solely down to the social consequences of revealing that she was marrying a divorced man. My suspicion is that her concerns were more self-centred in nature, more driven by fear and an innate sense of self-protection. This is the very fear that John Lanchester identifies in his memoir *Family Romance* – the awful 'psychic disrobing' he sees as 'an irreversible baring of the self'. What is feared is not so much the uncovering of a single stone, a single mystery, but the avalanche of ignominy that will follow on inevitably from that first stone turned over. And, of course, in my mother's eyes there was at least one other stone teetering on the brink of the precipice down which she must have been desperate to keep it from falling. In this way, as it surely must have done in Bea's case, antipathy towards the disclosure of long held secrets turns into an almost visceral terror. This, I feel sure, is the way the situation must have festered in my mother's mind.

Despite it being a love match, my mother would have regarded marrying my father as, to some extent, a step down in the social hierarchy she so fervently believed in. She was the daughter of a man who had risen to the top of his profession as a vintner, distiller and company director. My father, on the other hand, was a more lowly commercial traveller – 'only' a salesman, as I feel instinctively Mum's family would have put it. Over his working life though, he was to do her proud, rising to become Scottish Manager of his company, even for a period managing the Northern Ireland department on their behalf. Childhood memories of meeting Gilbert at Turnhouse Airport, and my pride in having a father who travelled by plane in an era when few did, underline his rising importance in business. But at the time of their betrothal, I can only feel that my mother would have been conscious of their differences in class background as, of course, would her family. This would have made her even more disinclined to admit to his being divorced as well.

Bea had told me, during one of our many discussions of these revelations, that she would not have wanted anyone to know she was marrying a 'second-hand man' – that stock phrase she would often return to. An absurd notion. But, given my mother's subscribing to it, it may well have been a prevalent notion at the time. At least, it could have been current amongst the circles in which she moved, and so might be another of those received opinions she was so ready to adopt as her own.

You can almost hear such a line in the mouth of a Noel Coward or Terence Rattigan character: 'My dear, you'll never guess who she's marrying... a second-hand man! Can you believe it? How *too, too* awful for her.'

Slowly, the accretion of the years would have begun to bury all that Bea had so arbitrarily, even casually, concealed. It would almost become a given that no such secrets had ever been kept. That no such occurrences had ever been hidden away. It's so simple to forget about family confidences, to mislay them like some old abandoned garments at the back of a wardrobe. Packed away for some occasion that never happened, they begin to rot and fray, the fabric breaking down until they hardly resemble what they were in the first place. Everyone forgets where they've been secreted. But one day, someone raking through the past turns them up – and they're there, still recognisable, still identifiable for what they were.

By the time I was a teenager in the '60s, topics like failed marriage, though still regarded as shameful, were no longer shut out from immature ears. Thinking back to remarks commonly made then, it seemed to be the general belief that one party in a divorce was always exclusively to blame. In those days, the currently accepted causes – marital breakdown, incompatibility, shifting affections or divergence of ambition – never seemed to be mentioned. There *had* to be a villain or a villainess. There *had* to be an element of deceit. Marriages didn't 'fall apart' or 'hit the rocks'. No, someone 'ran off' with someone else or 'betrayed' their presumably 'wronged' spouse.

In fact, this view came up on one of the very few occasions my father's divorce was discussed following the initial revelation. Thinking back, Bea had said that, as far as she and her contemporaries believed, there was *always* a guilty party in *any* instance of divorce.

'People tend to think it's always the man's fault,' she said. 'But, in this case, *we* know that it wasn't.'

'People', in my mother's parlance, always meant the better sort of people, the right class. The ones whose opinions counted for something. For once she was stepping out of her comfort zone – but in her husband's defence.

★ ★ ★

There are many 'what ifs' in this story.

If Catherine Mary had never returned to Britain, had never made contact with my father, what would we have ever known of his past? Would my brother and I have found out that Gilbert had been married before? Would we have discovered that we had a half-sister? Would those secrets – the whole deception – have died with my mother? Was there any way we could have stumbled on it when Gilbert died, or even when Bea died over twenty years later?

This is unlikely. My mother, who had worked as a legal secretary for some time before her marriage, did all the paperwork when our father died. At twenty-five, I wouldn't have known where to start and was never asked. My brother, at almost three years younger, was even less qualified to assist. And both being in a state of profound grief at losing our father so young, we were in no fit state to be of any help. In all likelihood, we would have remained in the dark at that time, at least.

We did jointly manage the various administrative tasks when our mother died in the '90s. But we came upon no evidence of anything that had been concealed, nor anything relating to our father's hidden past.

It is true that there were photographs of Gilbert from his wartime days as well as some with his daughter and with his first wife and her family. But we recognised no-one in his wartime snaps and, without the background knowledge my sister had provided us with, we would have recognised no-one in the family photos either. It is more than likely we would have read nothing into any unidentified persons in Gilbert's other photos, such aged images generally being peopled by unknown figures. There was no sign of a wedding photograph from Gilbert's first marriage, so equally there would have been no clue there.

The sole available clue would have been unmistakeable, however. This is my parents' marriage certificate which, with her usual efficiency, my mother had filed away in a Legal & General Assurance envelope printed with the legend 'Your Birth & Marriage Certificates'. To this she had added in bold biro '& Death Certificate', it also containing notice of my father's decease.

Had my brother and I examined this, having remained ignorant of our father's earlier marriage, we would have been shocked to see him described as 'divorced' in the status column. While we might well have resented never being told about this, we would have known nothing of the back story and been unable to people it and bring it to life. It is conceivable, of course, that one or other of us might have embarked on a genealogical search. We could have uncovered a few bare facts about Gilbert's first wife; we could even have found out that we had a half-sister; we could have discovered her name and the details of her birth. But it seems unlikely that we could have gone further.

Despite any such facts being uncovered at that late stage, we would have remained – in our own imaginations – the nuclear family we had always imagined ourselves to be.

But, we would have lost a lot as well.

* * *

Double Exposure

From certain standpoints it has been fashionable, even seen as politically correct, to denigrate the nuclear family. At times, it has been derided as hermetic, stifling, blinkered and repressive. It has been seen as a means of chaining women to the kitchen sink, of limiting the horizons of its offspring, of encouraging male wage slavery.

A looser, extended family has often been characterised as a healthier environment in which to grow up. Its wider network of siblings and diversity of relations have been lauded as psychologically more supportive. All this *can* be true, but there is no gainsaying the stability that, in the best of circumstances, a close-knit nuclear family can provide.

None of which is to deny any of the nuclear family's inherent problems. We had those, for sure. Both my brother and I were rebellious teenagers – it *was* the '60s after all. We were always straining at the leash of our parents' authority. Our father too was always pushing for us to mature, to be less irresponsible. 'Grow up' was another of his stock phrases, applied when we had done anything particularly juvenile or childish. But he wouldn't have long to wait.

THE LAST POST

This army has beaten its last retreat,
lost the whole battlefield too. Gone west

are the pasteboard walls of the fort, the toy box
forsaken in one quick strike

as a father's urge to gee up his boys
takes hold on the fate of their men. Not one

to fall back on: no kilties, no cavalry,
paint chipped from the sibling wars, not one

of those battle-scarred troops. Though solid
as lead, they're cast out in their prime,

betrayed to the bin, parade ground turned over
to less peaceful ends, the wars

of toy soldiers being nothing to those
of teenage guerrillas, tooled up and letting it show.

Any such rebellion largely took the form of child/parent arguments. These were over the usual teen concerns of clothes – 'You're not going out dressed like that!' Or haircuts – 'You look just like a girl with your hair that long.' Or pop songs – 'I can't hear a word they're singing.' Or rock music – 'Turn that racket down!' I remember being amazed when Dad suggested that the only music of the period he liked was that of the particularly hippy-dippy Incredible String Band.

Puzzled, I asked him why. 'They're nice and quiet,' was all he said. I should have seen that coming.

Our friends too caused dissention between our parents and us brothers. Hairy and unkempt, for the most part studiedly scruffy, these boys went under a series of bizarre nicknames – Space, Neutral, Scuddy, Grease – which must have given our parents pause. The girls too – Snooks, Radish, Misty – were often bizarrely monikered. They would have begun to worry though, when we dropped the likes of Dan the Boar, Acid Alf and Freddy the Tuinal King into our self-consciously hip conversation. Our father, in particular, was openly critical of their appearance – 'Look at the state of that!' Or their presumed inactivity – 'A bunch of layabouts!' Not to mention their girlfriends – 'Like a long drink of water'. But neither Bea nor Gilbert ever attempted to forbid us from mixing with these shady sounding, but mainly harmless, characters.

These adolescent arguments would, on occasion, stray into politics and even religion – but such rebellions as there were never got beyond the stage of shouting matches. My father was particularly irked when I dragged others into this – the uncle I challenged about attending a South Africa rugby international because of my opposition to apartheid;

the cousin I accused of warmongering because he refused to join the CND; the teacher I described as a Fascist because of his pragmatic acceptance of Franco.

My father was not the most even-tempered of men. He would angrily dismiss what I considered principled moral stances – my embarrassing him by publicly resigning from my Church of Scotland bible class in a fit of agnosticism; my refusing to shake the Prime Minister's hand during his visit to an exhibition where I had a summer job. Where a smoothing over of our intergenerational jostling for position might have worked better, his approach was often provokingly confrontational. But he *had* been a sergeant. He *had* issued orders throughout the War. How our insubordination must have vexed him.

One particular incident sticks in my mind. Having just indulged in one of my not infrequent verbal spats with my father, who had been laying down the law on some matter long since forgotten, I stormed off to my room hissing, in what I thought was the clincher, that he was no better than Hitler. What astonished me, and pulled the rug from under my feet, was that this, to my mind, justified, even cutting comparison, caused Gilbert to burst out laughing. Self-obsessed adolescent that I was, I had been unable to take into account the implications of my parents having living through the War. They were only too aware of what a ridiculous comparison I'd just made.

But hindsight is easy. Not having the layers of experience their elders have built up over time, teenagers can resort to malice with such ease. It just comes tripping off the tongue, without a thought for the pain and anguish it can cause. It is fortunate for me that my attempts at malice – or at least my spiteful remarks – while they must have vexed and wounded my parents, never went so far as to alienate them.

* * *

We were, nonetheless, a strong, self-contained unit. We supported each other when the need came. My mother, despite her obvious disappointment that I showed no interest in sport, was always encouraging of my youthful interests in books, art and music, although anxious that these stay on the right side of respectability. My father, while not as inclined to indulge such 'airy-fairy' excesses, was always kind and supportive to me in many ways, teaching me to drive and, later, lending me his car – a great boon when it came to girlfriends.

His support was particularly evident when my fiancée's parents objected to my forthcoming marriage to their daughter. Gilbert went out of his way to plead my case and attempt to allay their fears. So much so, that they began to suspect he was not who he said he was; that their worries I came from a 'bad background' were true; that Gilbert, in claiming to be a kirk elder, was an imposter. Although this was all subsequently cleared up, the irony is that I now know that Gilbert was *not* the man he said he was – or at least led us to think he was. But not in the way my parents-in-law imagined.

Again ironically, they were right in thinking that I *did* come from some sort of a 'bad background' – one whose veneer of respectability was covering a hard knot of secrets. But that was unknown to me at the time and would not be revealed for years to come.

7

Letters Sent & Unsent

THE LONDON TO Aberdeen train pulled into the station of the Fife market town of Cupar one winter morning in late 1977. Waiting under the shelter of the overhanging roof, I was standing apprehensively by the side of my equally apprehensive wife. It was one of those days described in Scotland as dreich, not the ideal weather to welcome a new family member to the country. I don't recall anyone else being out in the damp chilly air, but we had a very special reason to be there. We had to be seen.

Cupar station bears no particular resemblance to a film set. But it felt like one to me that day. I was clutching a photograph my mother had given me of my recently discovered half-sister, my late father's only daughter. Standing at an open window in the train as it drew to a halt, she was scanning the platform for a sight of the brother she had long hoped to meet. All the makings of a drama were there.

While curiosity was uppermost in my mind, confusion and no little amount of trepidation were also present. Although I wasn't thinking about it then, being still more focused on my own shock at my mother's recent revelation, Catherine Mary's relief at finally meeting the elder of her two half-brothers must have been much overshadowed by her sadness that she had had to lose her father before this could be accomplished. That sadness would have been all the more sharp due to the way she had been obstructed and kept at arm's length by my mother following my father's death. It would also have been amplified by what she saw as an inexplicable delay in either brother getting in touch.

That delay was largely down to me.

At the close of the family meeting my mother had called the previous year, I had offered to make the initial contact. By letter, I thought was best. For over a year Catherine had been awaiting such a letter's arrival. She had initially endured a delay of six months – the time it took my mother to steel herself sufficiently to tell her sons of our half-sister's existence. Bea and Catherine had been in correspondence over this delay. In one of several letters, Bea explained her reasons for holding back on the exposé.

> I'm afraid I still haven't told the boys about you, Catherine. I would like to have them all together which has been difficult to achieve with Brian not in Edinburgh and at the moment holidays are on. There is so much still to do with the wedding that the time I feel is not ripe at the moment, but I will get round to it some time I promise you.

Rather tactlessly, Bea had cited my brother's forthcoming wedding as one of her excuses, drawing Catherine's attention to a family event in which she could play no part. In a similarly insensitive way, she had gone on to tell Catherine about her sons missing their father, the father Catherine had so longed to meet in their company. And more so to dwell on her own recent injuries at a time when his daughter would have been feeling almost as much frustration as grief.

> The boys both miss their dad a lot and often say I wish I could show that to Dad or ask him something. I had a chapter of accidents after your dear dad died, firstly injuring my back then spraining my wrist rather badly. Fortunately I can now play golf which is wonderful therapy that I require badly. I still miss your dear dad such a lot. It is wonderful though that I have so many happy memories of our life together.

And Catherine cannot have been much consoled by my mother's reference to holding on to happy memories of her father – she who had been denied many of those for years.

'What on earth is the hold up?' she must have wondered.

The delay over, and the revelation made, Bea had written again to tell Catherine that my brother and I were now apprised of all the facts. We knew of her existence; we knew of our father's first marriage; we knew of the divorce. And I had promised to get in touch. Understandably, Catherine couldn't grasp why no-one had written to her right away.

'Bea let me know she had at last told you about me,' Catherine explained later, 'and I was chagrined not to have heard from you – especially having waited so long.'

For my part, I was still very much grieving for my father. None of us had ever considered him dying in his sixties and his survival of his second heart attack – a major one – had reassured us he was going to be around at least for a while yet. We knew his health would be precarious, but such an immediate recurrence of cardiac arrest was a severe shock. While there is much glib talk of 'clean breaks' and 'swift exits' attached to heart attacks, the hollow they leave in a settled life is much harder to accept for being unanticipated and unprepared for. The further shock of my mother's revelation about his past life was disconcerting to say the least, further unsettling the equilibrium of my family background.

Once the concealed facts of Gilbert's past had been revealed to me, I was effectively also grieving for my nuclear family – the 'four of a family' Dad had always referred to and I had accepted as fact. Indeed, had always been led to believe *was* fact. Although I had kicked against its strictures in my own desultory, adolescent fashion, I had never known it to be other than the sole truth of my upbringing. Like an Eastern Bloc citizen, in the post-1990 aftermath of the Cold War, examining a previously doctored photograph to discover that an individual whose presence had long been denied – proscribed, even – was in actual fact a main player in some historical event, I was finding it difficult to 'get my head round' the very existence of my half-sister.

On top of that, I was feeling a great deal of resentment towards my mother – on several counts.

'How could she have treated my father so cruelly?' I asked my brother, though really musing to myself. 'How could she have put "bourgeois convention" before his personal happiness?' That's how I self-righteously saw it.

'You know, I just can't understand how she could've been so inconsiderate' was my brother's take on this. 'All our half-sister wanted to do was to meet us.'

Catherine Mary's aspiration was entirely reasonable, we thought, and only to be expected. How, after her own refusals to do so, could our mother now insist that we 'owed it' to our father to get in touch immediately with this half-sister whose existence we had never so much as suspected? Mum herself had delayed for six months before letting us into the secret. She had even waited until after my brother's recent wedding which, despite her pleas of having 'so much to do', must have been to ensure that no invitation was sent to Catherine.

'She'd not have wanted to explain the presence of some unknown family member to all the relatives at the wedding,' my brother suggested.

'And on top of that she's leaning on *me* to get a letter written! She could've resolved the whole sorry affair herself years back,' I said, 'with just one simple change of heart.' I was unable to get these resentful thoughts out of my mind and focus on my promise to write.

The initial six months delay over, and having finally heard from my mother that my brother and I were now in receipt of the facts, our half-sister had written to her again to ask what was causing this further delay. Understandably anxious to hear from her half-brothers at last, she couldn't think why we had not yet got in touch. Catherine wasn't to know it, but the effect on me was immediate. My mother upped the level of her moral blackmail – making more and more insistent demands, more and more frequent attempts to spur me to write. And more and more citing of what I *had* to do 'for Dad's sake'. All of which made me, in turn, dig my heels in still further.

'Why should I go out of my way to make my mother's moral anguish any easier?' was how I saw it. I had a brother to whom I felt close and, apart from the usual childhood spats, had always got on well with. I had been on the verge of forging an adult relationship with a father whom I had just tragically lost. Our family unit had already been fractured.

'Why do I need this further disruption to the family right now?' I thought.

Although I had left home eight years earlier and had been married for five, at twenty-five I had not really grown up. I hadn't reached the state of adulthood that the poet Kevin Crossley-Holland defines in his memoir as the ability 'to understand and not to blame'. I was unable – or disinclined – to see the situation from all points of view and, indeed, didn't even particularly want to.

If truth be told, I would not be able to do so until twenty years later, when my phone rang and another unexpected revelation was delivered – left on that long discarded answerphone tape. Only then was I able to see through the maze of interconnections with a bit more clarity. Only with that subsequent discovery of a further unknown sibling did I fully engage with my half-sister about our earlier lives. Only then did we discover each other as adults.

★ ★ ★

Catherine Mary Johnstone had been working for the US Embassy in London at the time my father had taken his major heart attack. Despite the earlier glitch – the 'warning', as his doctor had described it – he had continued to lead a pretty active life.

Recently retired from his managerial position with a leading UK pharmaceutical company, Gilbert was still doing a bit of driving for a business colleague by way of a part-time occupation. He was playing golf most weeks and going for short but frequent walks. Having learned to swim late in life, he and a friend would also go for the occasional dip at a local pool. My abiding impression of him at this time is one particular visual memory I have retained: seeing him in soft focus through the net curtains of the kitchen window, while I sat at the table chatting with Bea and drinking a cup of tea. Arriving back from the golf club or the shops, my father would appear, framed by the sash casing, smiling cheerfully as he opened the back door to greet me and welcome me back to the old family home.

It is both a familiar image and a disconnected one, influenced in the latter case by my future knowledge of his imminent death. This was far from my mind at the time, though. Our father had gone on for ages and seemed likely to be with us for a good while yet – he was only in his sixties, after all. As with so many other things, we brothers had not been told about the 'warning' and so had no notion of any ill health. Gilbert was ageing, admittedly, but was as dapper and sprightly as he had ever been. The trilby of his earlier years had now been replaced by a smart tweed cap, offsetting the sports jacket, home-knitted cardigan and cavalry twills of his retirement. And always a carefully knotted tie whatever the occasion. His neatly trimmed moustache still gave him the air of a mature Clark Gable, though his get-up made him appear more of a countryman. But he was sleeping too much, I remember Bea worrying. Napping a lot during the day – never a good sign, she thought.

Of course, where else would his major heart attack occur but on the golf course? And where else there but on one of the most inaccessible holes, and the one farthest from the main road? But he was with a good friend and was got into an ambulance and off to hospital expeditiously. Although he had survived, he was gravely ill, we were informed.

Gilbert had been rushed straight to the Royal Infirmary, which was in the centre of the city in those days. There he had been stabilised and, when we visited him, he was in an intensive care ward. Seeing our father hooked up to a tangle of wires and tubes, with various monitors bleeping and flashing behind him, was a shock. But finding him so weak and debilitated was infinitely worse. He had always been a robustly healthy individual. Apart from the usual colds and flu, he had never been under the weather for long. Now he had aged twenty years since I'd last seen him only days before. He was lying prone on his bed and breathing with deliberation, his face sallow, his cheeks sunk in. But he was pleased to see us, that was clear.

We spent long periods just talking. The visiting hours must have been more flexible then, or else the staff made allowances for Gilbert's poor outlook. Bea would often leave my brother and me to chat with him – although I have little recollection of what we talked about – but we all spelled each other, so each had a chance to speak to Gilbert alone. I do remember lending him a book when he got sufficiently better to be able to read. An account of the Klondike Gold Rush – the only book I ever passed on to my father. But most of my memory is of reassuring Dad – who'd always been a figure of authority to me – that he had all the love a son could give him. I remember sitting for ages at his bedside, holding him by the hand and trying to stop myself from crying.

It is strange that it took a life-threatening illness to allow us to overcome the emotional reticence with which our upbringing endowed us – but I thank God it did. Our father knew how much we cared, even if only at the end of his life.

★ ★ ★

My father's illness had prevented what might have been an even more explosive resolution to this particular portion of family secrets. Some time before he had taken this second heart attack, Catherine had given up waiting and decided on her own move. Growing impatient with the endless delays and excuses, she began to despair of Gilbert ever being able to persuade my mother that it was wrong – or at least unreasonable – to conceal his daughter's existence any longer. Taking action on her own behalf, Catherine had written directly to my mother. Her letter asked Mum to reconsider her decision. My mother's reply was brief. She flatly refused. Adding insult to what was patently an injurious response, she coldly suggested that Catherine turn her attention to making a family of her own.

This response prompted further action on my half-sister's part, but not the action my mother had proposed. She decided to sidestep Bea completely. Working at the time for the American Embassy Cultural Affairs Office, she was on the verge of heading north in connection with a series of interviews she had to organise as part of her work. As she explained:

I decided to hold the interviews of candidates for an exchange programme in the Consulate in Edinburgh because I noticed that several were from the north of England or Scotland and I thought it would make sense. And then I had another thought... I was getting impatient with not being able to meet you both (because Bea wouldn't let Daddy tell you about me). So I decided to relieve him of that conflict and write to you direct as you were no longer kids.

So Catherine wrote another letter, this time directly to my brother and me. In this she explained her background and told us all about our father's first marriage and her early life. But write it was all she did. This self-same letter was signed, sealed and stamped, ready for the post on the very day my mother called to tell her Gilbert had suffered a major heart attack. So it was never posted. Catherine's immediate concern was now for her father's health. Naturally, this took precedence.

But her travelling to Edinburgh had another benefit. When my mother – after a few days of recalcitrance – had made that call to tell her Gilbert was seriously ill, she was able to visit him almost immediately. My mother must have been panicking that by some freak chance we'd run into each other in the hospital. But she must have co-ordinated the visits with care. I can remember no rushed exits or postponed arrivals. Thus, Catherine too was able to spend some private time with Gilbert as he slowly regained some of his health.

If my eventual meeting with my sister the following year had felt like a scene from a film, the concurrence of letter and heart attack, resulting in the thwarting of Catherine's resolution, are the stuff of high drama. But it was a drama averted. As she rightly thought, I'm sure the shock of a pre-emptive revelation on her part could only have made my father's health worse. It might well have had a similar effect on my mother's frame of mind, under severe pressure as it had been since the heart attack.

In fact, during their conversations in the hospital, Gilbert had strongly urged his daughter to help him bring his three children together – and to do so right away. She was in Edinburgh. It could have been done. But was he up to it? Was the time right? It says much for Catherine's selflessness and consideration that, out of concern for his fragile condition and the stress everyone was under, she persuaded him to delay.

Gilbert had not been aware that Catherine was planning to be in Edinburgh at the time. Lying in his hospital bed, having pulled through the initial trauma of the cardiac arrest, he would never have expected his daughter to visit. It was a welcome surprise for him. She later told me how his face had lit up with joy when she approached his bed. But that was to be their last meeting.

★ ★ ★

Gilbert did recover – at least partially – but, after those emotionally close hospital visits, I was also never to see him alive again. We spoke on the phone several times in the short period he had back in the family home. But I know that he was longing for another visit from me and I am sad that it never happened. My mother told me that whenever there was a knock on the door, Dad would say, 'I hope that's Brian down from Fife.' But it was not to be. Time was too short.

My brother was still living at home in the run-up to his marriage, so was able to keep up the closeness with our father, through further talks and supportive chats. Gilbert had similar conversations on the phone with his daughter. From what he told her when he was ill, I know how much the things we had said to each other had meant to him. And from what he said to me, I knew how glad he was that my wife and I were finding success and satisfaction in our nascent teaching careers and how pleased he had been that my brother and his girlfriend had got engaged.

Meeting the mourners at Dad's funeral, and shaking the hands of distant relatives I hadn't seen for years, I had no inkling that before the year was out I would be meeting his – to us at any rate – 'long-lost' daughter. That I would be meeting my own elder sister – shaking *her* by the hand. Meeting someone with whom I seemed to share many character traits and cultural interests – which was yet another unfamiliar experience since my character and my brother's are rather different and our interests rarely converge.

It was this sister I was holding out my hand to on the station platform on that dreich winter's morning. A sister who, as I had already noticed in her photograph, bore no resemblance whatsoever to our shared father.

And it was this sister who was introducing herself not as Catherine Mary, but as Catrina. This sister to whom I was giving a hesitant first hug, even – in a demonstrative un-Scottish way – a first kiss on the cheek. Wrapped in a fur coat against the east coast chill, an elegant silk scarf around her neck, she had a distinct air of American style about her. It's difficult to pin down, but fashion and dress sense, her neat short hairstyle, her manner even, all had a definite transatlantic feel to them.

She was strange to me then. As I must have been to her. But here we were, as our father had hoped, together.

We headed for home, out of town, in my old Morris Traveller. In twenty minutes we had covered the few miles over the north Fife hills and were heading up the long track to the remote estate cottage my wife and I were renting at the time. There, a brace of pheasants awaited us and a good few bottles of my home-brewed beer.

Drinks were taken, meals were eaten, walks were embarked upon. And the long process of filling in nigh on forty years of gaps was hesitantly begun.

★ ★ ★

Over the next couple of days we pottered about in the shelter of the greenhouse, sowing seeds for the summer to come. It was only then that all three of Gilbert's children would eventually meet up. Why my brother wasn't able to join us for Catrina's first visit that winter has long been forgotten, but the photographs my wife took show only my sister and me happed up against the cold, the bleak and empty fields of winter stretching away behind us.

But the visit was a success. Catrina returned the following year during what the next batch of photographs show to be a warm and sunny period of summer weather. This time both of us brothers are lined up with our sister, the three of us united as our father had wanted. Time would be the agent of our growing closer as he had hoped, anticipated, even.

There is a poem I wrote for my sister years later. It is about taking new steps, embracing change with an open heart, about the present transforming the future. Looking at it again in the light of this narrative, I feel it is about more than that. I think it is also about the transform-ative power of time, the unlocking of possibilities. As such, I think it speaks also to Catrina's reconnecting with her father many decades ago; but it equally echoes the understanding between the two of us that has been achieved by opening up about the past.

A DEFINITION OF SPACE

Perhaps it is enough to walk along
these edges, gather stones
and send them skimming over water

till each ripple copies and recopies,
spreads still further from your gaze
and the stone sinks deeper,

out of reach. At these places
where the meeting and the parting
are the same, the sands run smoothest;

shores are banked with rushes
whose singularity of line stands sheer
and pencil thin against the space

each interrupts. Until they flower:
a seed head budding from the stems
whose starkness seemed exact

before the breeze got up, the light changed
in that way you'd often heard about
that brings the distance close to shore;

and you began to notice how things were.
How rush stems paired and danced
in moving air, formed geometries

inclining to each other, held space
the way a pair of hands cups time.
It is enough to know this, see how right

can be the bending of a line,
how integral the angle of these stems
to their perfection. They hold your eye

as, from the shore, you take the gift
you've chanced upon; thinking simply
that the stone, which rests a moment

cool against your palm, must be
as perfect too; that it will find the water
fitting to its temper, move across the surface,

will not cease. And in the endless light
of June, you crouch down at the lakeside,
make the throw. It goes and goes.

★ ★ ★

The sort of closeness I share with my brother is what my sister had felt
she lacked. For most of her childhood and youth she had lived alone

with what we would now refer to as a 'single mother'. The two of them had been close – perhaps too close. The relationship had changed as Catrina grew up. It had become oppressive, claustrophobic almost. As Catrina said to me in a later letter:

> I just wanted to know you all – Daddy and you two boys especially – almost my only relations anywhere and the nearest by blood. I was pretty unhappy at the time as my mother was making me feel very guilty about leaving her and leading an independent life, so in a sense I was seeking understanding and support from Daddy, to ease my guilt and balance the equation somewhat. Does that make sense?

It did then – and it does now. My sister has expanded on that over the years. She had a real emotional need to get back in touch with Gilbert. Her own mother was far from stable and she needed the security of a parental relationship which she knew she would never have if she stayed in the States. My only hope is that Catrina wasn't made more unhappy by the fraught nature of getting to know her brothers – and by the convoluted nature of making eventual contact with us.

While I would have been happy to have had the opportunity for the closer interaction of a shared upbringing with my sister – even had it started at a later age – circumstances prevented it. There is another strange irony. Catrina and I actually have a great many interests in common, substantially more than I have with my brother. Culturally curious, we are both followers of the arts, avid travellers and voracious readers. One of the earliest things we discovered we had in common, during that very first meeting in 1977, was a shared love of Greece. Poetry too soon emerged as a bond and through my sister I have discovered several American poets who have become favourites.

Much of this is the basis of our current happy relationship. It *has* to be, as so much of our formative experience – the experience that shaped us as children and in our youth – was *not* shared. Wishing that it had been, does not make it so – can never make it so.

Sharing an upbringing with my brother has left us as adults with an almost intuitive understanding of each other, despite the only-to-be-expected scrapping and jockeying for position of two boys growing up in close proximity. Although we share few specific interests, we are close to each other emotionally. My brother is 'always there for me', in contemporary terms. It is not simply a case of that old cliché 'blood is thicker than water' – a notion I do not subscribe to – but rather one of shared experience of long duration moulding and extending our relationship.

Nothing can take the place of a shared life, and nothing can replicate it. Every long year of my marriage convinces me of this, as does the long history of life events I have shared with my brother. To me it seems impossible that any 'lost' sibling emerging of a sudden into one's life, could ever have as strong a bond as a sibling who has been a constant through the years.

That, I feel, is the simple truth – even if a sad truth – but one with which we must live. Though it is one on which we can build as well.

8

Mum's the Word

M Y AUTUMN HOLIDAY in 1998 – the year of my mother's death – did not prove very restful. It was coloured by the content of the phone message I had received only 36 hours before we set off. Coloured too by the knowledge that we had been through an almost identical episode before. Nothing had been resolved, and nothing confirmed before we left. I spent my fortnight in the sun back in that state of confusion and disquiet I remembered from twenty years before.

It was fortunate, given the circumstances, that I had that good friend who worked as a professional genealogist. With my brother's blessing, I had decided before leaving on holiday to turn to this friend for advice. Her reaction to the revelation proved helpful to my peace of mind.

Caught up in such a highly charged personal situation, it is tempting to react in a 'why me' frame of mind. To see oneself as somehow singled out for a unique emotional shakedown. My friend though, was able to reassure me. Far from being rare, such stories verge on the commonplace. Even the rather crass means of relaying the news was not unfamiliar to her.

So while I had flown off to the Greek islands, my friend and her genealogical colleagues, furnished with the basic details of the persons involved, had set to work. They would discover whether, in truth, my brother and I did have another unknown half-sister, this time the child of our mother. Born before we were even thought of? We presumed so. Born before her marriage to Gilbert? Surely? Before our father came on the scene? Before the War? Before she left home? We would see.

We returned from holiday to find that the genealogists had been busy. Far from being any sort of scam, this half-sister – this *other* half-sister – was real. Our friend had even spoken to her on the phone and had got a note of her home address so I could write. Meanwhile, a genealogist colleague in England had traced the birth to Newcastle upon Tyne and had got me a copy of the birth certificate. A girl – named Patricia Mary – had been born in June 1941. It verified that my mother was the parent. And so the revelation was confirmed. It was now definite.

Beyond any doubt it was clear that I did have a second half-sister. It seemed like I was beginning to build up a collection.

★ ★ ★

Newcastle proved to be the key. My mother's case was beginning to gel. The northern English city was the hub around which revolved the mystery of that phone message. It was a city, my genealogist friend explained, that was often the first resort of women from north of the border seeking to bury the secret of an unmarried birth. In many of her own cases it had also been the key.

A brace of genealogists, north and south of the border, pieced together at least the first part of the puzzle. My friend had passed on what I had told her to an associate in England, asking for the English records to be searched. This had turned up the address at which my mother was staying at the time of the birth. That done, it was possible to make a check of official records to discover in whose house she had been a temporary resident. We really had no idea where this might have been. Was my mother secreted in a boarding house, fending for herself? Was it a private nursing home or an establishment specifically for unwed mothers? Was she staying with a friend, a landlord, a private home owner? Or, given family connections, with a relative even?

Numerous establishments existed for the care – or at least the secreting away – of unmarried mothers at the time. Ranging from Salvation Army Mother and Baby Homes to Church of England hostels, these could be found throughout the country. General hospitals, of course, continued to admit mothers-to-be – married or not. In fact, during the War, locally-based maternity services had complained that the number of women in the forces falling pregnant and taking up much needed bed space was causing them severe problems; so much so that in 1943 a new care regime was instituted by the Ministry of Health. But at the bottom end of the range, for potentially disgraced, out-of-wedlock mothers, there remained privately run, dubious-sounding hideaways, one of whose 'matrons' was even convicted of baby farming as late as the 1960s. In addition to this, the remnants of the workhouse system were still admitting 'fallen women' in some local council areas right into the '40s.

But it seemed obvious that my mother's social background would have spared her from such indignities. More likely she would have spent time in one of the private nursing homes for professional women that guaranteed comfort and discretion – but for a price. What seemed unlikely, though, was that she would have been in any way in the care of family members, given the inevitability of the scandal attendant on her condition being revealed.

My brother and I were aware of a family link with Newcastle, albeit a distant one. My mother's cousin, by then in her late eighties and whom we had seen nothing of for twenty years, had her roots in the city. And her late brother, also a cousin, had spent the best part of his life there, living in the same house all his days. Perhaps we shouldn't have been surprised. Perhaps we should have recognised that, in the circumstances, a family would have pulled together. But in some ways it was a relief to discover that the address my mother gave at the time of her daughter's birth turned out to be that very one – the home of Bea's late cousin Jack and his wife Netty. It was this cousin, by then a widower, to whom Bea had been particularly close in the last decade of her life. It would seem there was more than just mutual support behind their affection. A shared secret? A hidden past? A small domestic conspiracy?

By sheer happenstance, my second-cousin Lil was my oldest living relative. Might this close connection mean that Cousin Lil would at least *know* of Bea's wartime baby? The War itself meant that Lil might have been anywhere but Newcastle in 1941. She might not even have been in the country. But I had no idea what she had done during the War. There was still a possibility that she would have stayed in her home town. There was still a chance she could throw light on the mystery.

But not for a minute did I suspect precisely *how* close Lil had been to the circumstances of the birth.

In November of 1998 I wrote to Cousin Lil. Out of the blue. Poor woman. We hadn't had any contact for upwards of twenty years. Even when we had, such contact had been sporadic. And here I was writing to her with a question dating back to before I was even born. A question centred on a staggering revelation. On a mystery I couldn't even be certain she was aware of. And one that had prompted a strong desire in another relative to whom I had spoken to keep the whole matter as hidden away and unresolved as it was before.

Of the few other relatives to whom I had mentioned the secret, some had been decidedly cool in their response. There was no understanding of my need to delve further; no seeing that this wasn't based on prurience but on a desire to somehow relieve my mother of a burden, albeit posthumously. Only one relative had any inkling of what we had discovered, and then only the vaguest notion. Others had no knowledge of it whatsoever. And one, of course, had advised me to keep it all secret as it had been in the past.

How, I wondered, would Lil react?

★ ★ ★

I have a few memories of Cousin Lil visiting the family home during my childhood. The fact that she stayed in London, and led a busy professional life meant that, as with so many of my extended family, I saw little of her as a child. A retired professional pianist, she had made her living latterly as a music teacher in a girls' school in Kensington. She had been an acclaimed classical recitalist and sometime composer before the War, frequently broadcasting to the Home Nations and the Empire. In line with the formality of the day, whatever might be the hour, BBC regulations had required her to wear full evening dress. This regardless of the fact that she was on the radio – or wireless, as it was universally known then – and out of sight to all but the studio engineers. Her career had also taken her all over the country and even abroad to give solo recitals and perform concertos with leading orchestras. She had been in the WRNS for the duration of the War, Lil told me later, and, once peace was declared, had not been able to regain sufficient technique to return to the concert platform.

'Mr Hitler put paid to that career – like so many others,' she told me years later, 'but at least I survived.'

My strongest memory of Cousin Lil had been of a visit she made to the family home in Edinburgh when I had just entered my teens. At that time, I was an enthusiast for the canon of nineteenth century popular classics, one particular favourite being the Grieg piano concerto. The prospect of her visit – given her former profession – excited me greatly. I can remember asking her to play a section of the Grieg on the beat-up piano my parents kept in the study – the same one on which my uncle vamped out show tunes when he visited. The last use I'd made of the piano was to hide in its interior the James Bond paperbacks I was reading when I was supposed to be swotting for my school exams. But despite the all apparent poor quality of the piano, Cousin Lil stoutly agreed to my request and the opening bars of a favourite concerto, live in my own home, thrilled my imagination.

But Lil fades from my life after that. Apart from her brief appearance at my brother's wedding in the late '70s, I had seen nothing of her on reaching adulthood. Happily for me, when we met again the following year after our exchange of letters, Lil proved to be someone with whom I shared many interests. She had even published a few poems in her youth. And she could recall that visit which had been so memorable to me at the start of my teens. She even remembered playing those few bars of the Grieg.

* * *

Mum's the Word

It didn't take Lil long to respond to my letter. On receipt of her reply, only four days later, it was immediately clear why. 'Poor woman,' I had thought, thinking of her possible alarm at the contents of my letter. Much poorer, though, for the burden she explained she had been bound to carry for over fifty years.

> Your letter yesterday came as a shock, bringing back so vividly the past, but I am very glad you wrote to me. I have kept this secret faithfully ever since. Yes, you do indeed have a half-sister – I doubt I can be of much help but at least I can give you the facts as I knew them personally which, if nothing else, is perhaps better than cold statistics on paper. All this must have come as a shock to you but to Bea it was the past and I'm sure she never expected it would come to light, nobody knowing except Jack, Netty and me and not one of us ever spoke of it to anybody.

Far from knowing only a few vague details of the mystery and being able to flesh it out a bit as I'd hoped, Cousin Lil astonished me with what she said next. She had actually encountered the baby, the new born Patricia Mary, as she had been named by her mother – *my* mother – in the early years of the War.

And so the story came out. My grandmother, Lil's Aunt Emily, had written to her early in 1941. She had been, as Lil explained in her letter, terribly upset to discover her daughter had fallen pregnant. This was nothing less than an out-and-out scandal according to the standards of the day. As Lil said:

> You'll understand, I'm sure, the older generation at that time saw things very differently and Aunt Emily asked me to destroy her letter and to tell nobody – not even my own father. I have often wondered through the years about that lovely baby but Aunt Emily had made me promise to say nothing to anybody, ever – a promise I have kept. As far as I know, no Edinburgh relations ever knew anything at all. So many questions remain – and one can only remember the feelings and reactions at the time, so little was ever said. So much was kept from us.

This was all particularly scandalous in the context of my mother's class and family background. Respectability demanded that it be covered up, as respectability would also demand that no mention be made of it ever again. Whatever the circumstances of her pregnancy, my mother would have been held to be entirely blameworthy – the 'fallen woman' of popular imagination. Had her condition been revealed she would have been shunned by 'polite society', her family would have been regarded as pariahs and her career would have been finished.

Attitudes to extramarital pregnancy had changed little even by as late as my own adolescence in the so-called 'swinging sixties'. When my wife and I were married in the early '70s it was without her parents' approval. It is significant that nine months had to elapse before there was any renewed parental contact. Clearly the suspicion was that we 'had to' get married. In the years immediately before we met, we had both encountered instances of the stigma evoked by illegitimacy continuing to operate – in my case, a student friend who had been forced to resort to an abortion in order to complete her university course; in my wife's case, a pregnant student room-mate who was obliged to abandon her degree and give birth in secret. This puts my mother's predicament in historical context. As late as 1940, the powers that be went so far as to arrest a doctor on obscenity charges for no more than publishing a guide to birth control. And the stories are legion of women of all classes stigmatised, banished from their families, exiled from their homes, or forced into contorted relationships through falsifying a baby's parent-hood. Society was not prepared to countenance anything approaching the more liberal morality that pertains today. It was not really until the '80s or '90s that illegitimacy lost its attendant shame. Only then, and only in certain quarters, did unmarried parenthood begin to be socially acceptable.

The baby boomers – the generation born after the War – were brought up in families who generally aspired to a respectable lifestyle. With the return of peace, the desire to conform to the conventional image of a perfect family was extreme. Jane Robinson's *In the Family Way* puts this across emphatically. 'Social reconstruction' she says, wasn't simply a case of restoring public services, it had 'moral implications' as well. A shiny new post-war country was on the make with a 'bright new public face', populated by 'hygienic-looking husbands' and wives decked out in 'hand-knitted woollies and tweeds'. Everything was to be back to normal – but some sort of idealised normal handed down from on high.

In the '50s, and even the '60s, any idea that physical urges had not been held in check by convention needed to be hidden at all costs. As Jenny Diski points out in her cultural commentary *The Sixties,* it was essential that the body was under 'the strict control of the civilized mind'. Shame and embarrassment – 'the great weapons', Diski calls them – were constantly brought into play to achieve this end. The mores of the time dictated that it was nothing short of a disgrace to become pregnant outside of, or even prior to, marriage. It was far more important to hide any pregnancy than to acknowledge it. The remedies were there if one looked – 'shotgun weddings' with a reluctant groom 'marched to the altar'; grandparents transposed into parents, with the actual mother in the role of elder sister; babies abandoned in hospital doorways or church steps; shady operatives able to 'get rid' of unwanted babies. It was the time portrayed in the Mike Leigh film *Vera Drake,* the time of the 'wise woman' who looked after girls 'in trouble' and the last resort of the backstreet abortionist. Small wonder then, that a whole generation previous to this, my mother's condition caused nothing less than panic on the part of my grandmother.

In that letter, her Aunt Emily had explained the state of affairs to Cousin Lil. She told her that she was arranging for her daughter Beattie to travel down to Newcastle before the pregnancy became obvious. She explained that she had asked Lil's brother and sister-in-law to put her up for the duration. My grandmother went on to swear Lil to complete and absolute secrecy. No-one – particularly of the older generation – was ever to find out about this disgrace.

Thickening the plot, my grandmother further explained that my mother's absence was being ascribed to the prospect of a better job. The story given out was that this meant her working in Newcastle for a while. This was an entirely plausible circumstance with all the shifting about of personnel necessitated by the War. As my mother was working in Edinburgh for the government Air Ministry at the time, she would already have been forbidden, or at least discouraged, from talking about her work to anyone. Those 'careless talk costs lives' posters spring to mind. It is unlikely in the extreme that anyone would have been irresponsible enough to probe her for details of this new post or question her about the nature of this special job south of the border.

Had anybody tried this with any wartime official worker, a simple 'mum's the word' would have been the general response.

'It's classified. I need to keep it under my hat,' from Bea would have done the trick in such an event.

Lil went on to fill in a few more details of my mother's time in Newcastle in what proved to be the first of many letters.

Bea came to stay with my brother, Jack and his wife, Netty, at his home in Gosforth and they took care of her for several months and made arrangements for her to go into hospital when the baby was due. In spite of everything, Bea was happy with Jack and Netty and they, I assure you, did all they could for her. Bea went back to Jack's on leaving hospital and stayed with them a few weeks before finally going home to Edinburgh. She was her old self when we three eventually saw her off at Newcastle, not knowing then to what was to be a much happier life with your dad and her family-to-be.

It is easy, though, to imagine the difficulties my mother must have been under, even removed a hundred miles to the south. Despite the rise in births out of wedlock during the War, I suspect she would have worn a fake wedding ring and used an alias to conceal her true status. As so many women's husbands were away in the services, a woman alone and pregnant would have caused little or no speculation. And it is equally likely that any who did suspect would have been indulgent, given the desperation of the times.

The subterfuge was made more awkward by the stringent level of secrecy Lil was sworn to by her Aunt Emily. She was not even able to tell her own father about the situation. The fact that he also lived in Newcastle, only a few streets away from Lil's brother's home, made things even more fraught. Fortunately, it was her brother's habit to visit his father at the latter's house, rather than vice versa. So nothing was uncovered. And Bea was able to spend some time with Lil herself who goes on:

> I was in the Wrens, but serving as a 'plotter' in Newcastle and saw Bea often at Jack's. If not on watch, I would meet her in town at times and we'd go places together. As I remember, the hospital at that time was called the General and was in Rye Hill. But it wasn't too difficult to get to and I visited Bea there a few times.

But how would Lil and my mother have coped when out and about? Lil recounted how they had had to duck into shop doorways or back alleys in the city centre if ever they saw her father approaching in the distance. It's astonishing they even risked leaving the house, especially as she told me there were a number of near misses when he hove into view. But their luck held and an encounter was avoided. It would all have been very tense – adding to the tenseness of wartime. But any assessment of risk would have been coloured by the dangers of living in a city that was being regularly threatened by bombs.

Thus was Bea looked after in secret by her Cousin Jack and his wife Netty until it was time for her confinement. All the arrangements for her admission to hospital for the birth were made on her behalf by this cousin. My grandmother had made a good choice in her confidants.

★ ★ ★

The baby was born in June 1941, a birth Cousin Lil was prevented from ever revealing by the promise she had made to her Aunt Emily. Obviously, she could have discussed the secret with her brother and sister-in-law in later years. She could also have done so in private moments with my mother. But, this is to discount the attitudes of the time, and the need to be ever vigilant in maintaining appearances. My guess is that it was never even spoken of again. It had never taken place, being the implication. All Bea told Lil was that the baby was being adopted direct from the hospital. That was an end to the matter.

'She'll be going to a new life, well and happy,' she had said to Lil at the time. The break would be final.

TAKING A LETTER
The best upper sets do it
Cole Porter

Missing from work, she explained it away
as a family affair. To the family, work was to blame,
wartime posting her south, her stenography skills
just what the doctor ordered.

But not what he said, probing so deep
that it hurt, blaming the thing
on the war, the bad faith it induced. But love
had induced her to do it, just like it said in the song.

Relations all said it was wrong, against every code,
but still booked a hospital bed, kept her hidden
when truth swelled the lie. All those letters
she'd taken, bar one, left unread.

The shorthand for 'ward' was *for good;* for 'adopted'
it was *for best*. The letter made it all plain: she won't see
that baby again. It's back to pounding the keys.
The bell rings – the line ends. Understood?

Mother and baby were caught in the inevitability Sylvia Plath evokes in the metaphors of her poem 'Three Women'. The sleeping baby is a small, peaceful island. But the mother is a lone vessel sounding 'goodbye, goodbye' on the ship's klaxon.

Lil closes her thoughts on the adoption by saying, 'There was nothing else Bea could do – wartime and no way she could keep her.'

★ ★ ★

Lil wrote in her letter to me that she never did know the names of the adoptive parents. She had often wondered about how the baby's life developed. But she was definite in assuring me that she had never broken her promise to my grandmother. She had never revealed the secret to a soul.

That, though, is not the most poignant part of Lil's letter. Only two days after the birth she had visited my mother.

> I went to see Bea in hospital when the baby was born and actually held your little half-sister in my arms when she was two days old. She was the most beautiful baby I had ever seen. I loved her for herself and Bea, who would only say she was being adopted. I'm sure it makes no difference to your love and memory of Bea now – it didn't to us then – or after.

A sentiment that was echoed by every one of the relatives with whom I discussed this revelation. As is by me.

Somewhat strangely, Lil was very clear on one thing. Bea was adamant at that time – underlined in Lil's letter – that she had no intention of marrying anyone. Had she been deserted or abandoned by the father? Was it a casual wartime affair she immediately regretted? Had she been seduced with a promise of marriage and subsequently betrayed? Whichever it was, Lil's reporting of these remarks does make my mother sound bitter.

One sentence from Cousin Lil's letter sums up my mother's whole position. She was a twenty-seven year old living through the fears and uncertainties of the War. She had, even by that relatively early date in its duration, already lost friends and family members who had been killed arbitrarily and in horrible circumstances. Is it any wonder she seized – as did so many other women at the time – a chance of love or a moment of happiness, even if it might only have been fleeting?

As Lil said, 'Wartime is very hard – emotions are stronger and one didn't know if one would ever see tomorrow.'

9

Twice Shy

I HAD BEGUN to take it in. For a second time, a sudden and shocking revelation had exposed a family secret. For a second time a bolt from the blue had revealed a half-sister about whom I had no prior knowledge. Once again an adjustment in the family line-up was necessary, another changing of places in the game of musical chairs.

I have never been one for gambling, and have little understanding of probability, but the odds against two such coincidental exposés must be pretty high. What's more, the odds against both occurring after the respective parent was no longer around to explain the circumstances must be at least above average. And even higher that each should be exposed after exactly the same amount of time had elapsed after each parent's demise. Not to mention the odds of both newly revealed siblings bearing the exact same relationship to me, albeit from different sides of the family. No, the whole thing was uncanny, too weird to fully take in.

★ ★ ★

What neither Lil's letter nor the birth certificate had revealed was the identity of the father – a blank was left in the space allotted for the other parent's name. Unlike Gilbert's daughter Catherine, this half-sister was not the offspring of an earlier marriage. She was an illegitimate child, born to my mother out of wedlock, fathered by an unidentified lover. It is much easier to see why the existence of this particular daughter had been concealed.

But one thing was clear – and it was a relief. This was not any sort of false identity fraud. From the start there had been confusion as to who this person might be. When I had called my brother to inform him about the shock phone message, he had initially thought I was referring to Catrina.

'But why would she need to leave a message like that?' he asked. 'And who is this husband anyway? Has she got married?'

'No, no, this is an entirely different person,' I explained. 'It's not Catrina at all. It looks like we've got another half-sister.'

'I don't believe it! It's too much of a coincidence! Who in God's name is she anyway?' he responded.

'It seems this one's Mum's daughter, not Dad's. Let me play you the answerphone tape again and you'll see.' And so we had continued until we were both able to accept the revelation as fact.

Our genealogist was also able to allay my brother's more practical concerns that this might some sort of attempt to make a claim on our mother's legacy. As this half-sister had been adopted at birth, she had, our friend told us, no legal claim on Bea's estate. It seemed that the particular timing of the phone message, and hence of this disclosure, had been purely coincidental. Thus from the start, give or take a couple of weeks, all our concerns were dealt with. The opening gambits had been made. It was time for the more serious moves.

★ ★ ★

In the passage of a fortnight a further development had taken place. While my wife and I had been away on holiday, a letter had arrived in which my new half-sister introduced herself. Using a variation on the Christian name entered on her birth certificate, as Maria she wrote:

I was very distressed, and could not believe it, when I found out that my mother had died in March this year. It was so sad and it was too late. I do feel for you losing your mother. Please accept my sympathy, you must have been very close. I only found out that you were my half-brother, after reading the death certificate. I was meant to find you, there was some meaning to it all.

Dated a couple of days after the initial phone message, the letter was presumably a response to my not having returned her husband's call. It confirmed the details on the birth certificate we had received and told me that she was on holiday near Aberdeen. She hoped to meet me while she was in Scotland. She reiterated the phone number left in the answerphone message and let me know how long she would be up north. Unfortunately – although in retrospect, possibly for the best – she had already returned home to the south of England by the time I got back from our holiday and received the letter.

At this point though, my brother became increasingly eager to meet up with Maria. This was not my preferred course of action.

'The sooner the better,' my brother thought. 'We could get a flight next week. I'm dying to meet her.'

'But why?' I asked. 'I think it'd be better to take this cannily. Don't you?'

'It's an amazing opportunity. She might look just like Mum.'

As he explained, he was convinced she would closely resemble Bea. This seemed to be the principal reason he wished to arrange a meeting. He was, I now realise, channelling his sense of loss at the death of our mother into a desire to meet someone who could be some sort of surrogate. This was understandable, the death of our only surviving parent having been followed by a revelation so startlingly similar to the one that had occurred after the death of our other parent. All of which may well have motivated him in his impulse to meet Maria – and to meet her right away. Strangely, he is the brother less frequently in touch with our sister Catrina, but I have no reason to doubt his sincerity in wishing for a meeting with Maria at the earliest possible juncture.

But I preferred a more measured approach, as I had too with Catrina in the '70s. Since my wife and my brother's wife, both of whom were as wrapped up in this state of affairs as we were, also favoured holding off for at least a while, this course of action was agreed upon. Caution had prevailed. My brother rapidly dropped the idea of an immediate flight down to the south of England, avoiding what we all thought was likely to be an even greater emotional upheaval had he met our new half-sister while his feelings were so raw. A letter first, it was agreed. So, having got hold of an address, my role was once again to write and make the initial contact.

★ ★ ★

There was a long wait for a reply, nearly two months. But this was a relief to me as the time elapsed gave me the opportunity to consider the situation and get used to it and its implications – 'to get my head round it'. Having experienced a similar, though not as shocking, exposé once before, I was well aware of the fragility such an experience could induce. Tracing and being traced, in the context of an earlier adoption, is an increasingly common experience. The poet and writer Jackie Kay, who herself has located 'lost' family members, is only too aware of this. 'Tracing suddenly asks someone who has had one life to have two,' she says in *Red Dust Road*, 'and you can't have two lives; you can only have one.' I was feeling as if I was being asked to have three.

Maria's reply, when it came in late December, began by clearing up one of my concerns – why the revelation had been made via what I considered to be the inappropriate method of a phone message. In fact, the message had been left in the belief that I would already know about this half-sister. As Maria wrote:

The first thing to say is that I am so sorry to have given you such a shock. I had built up this story in my head that Mother had told you about me in her later years and that she was hoping I would make contact. I am afraid it was a big shock to me to find out that you did not know. I had just assumed that you knew of my existence.

It puzzles me to this day that Maria should have been so convinced that I was aware of her existence. But that certainty draws me back to contemporary understanding of how thought processes can turn impression into memory, assumption into certainty. In an *Observer* article on amnesia, Tim Adams wrote of 'fascinating, unsettling impulses … that sense of [our] identity being a bundle of all of the stories we tell ourselves'. Maria had evidently built up a picture in her head of her continued presence in her birth mother's life, and it was a blow to her to find that this did not match reality.

She had already spoken to my friend the genealogist on the phone but at that stage had still not grasped the situation fully. She continued:

> When I spoke to your friend on the phone, I thought it was a 'bolt from the blue' because I had got in touch <u>after</u> Mother had died. I thought you had given up hope after all these years and now it was too late. It was a shock <u>to me</u> to find out that you didn't even know of my existence.

My letter though had explained our total lack of knowledge and Maria now realised that Bea had never breathed a word about her birth. I feel for Maria in this – it is almost a denial of her very existence to find that her birth mother should have told absolutely no-one. But Maria could not have been aware of the circumstances of her birth, nor of the reasons for her adoption. The rest of her letter was replete with details of her childhood and upbringing.

Maria told me she had been adopted by a childless couple. They had also adopted a boy who became her brother. They had lived on the south coast of England where she had had a secure and happy childhood. Although her adoptive father had died when she was five, a relative of her adoptive mother had moved in with the family and the two children had been brought up in a safe and loving environment. They had lived in an old rambling house surrounded by a wild garden and only a few miles from the sea, which made for a wonderful child-hood. She described her adoptive mother as a 'kind and sweet person' who gave her and her brother 'a lot of love'.

Maria had known for a long time that she had been adopted as a baby. She had acquired a copy of her birth certificate a good while before making contact with me, though nothing had come of that then. She began to fill in the details:

> I was born in Newcastle upon Tyne in 1941. I was adopted, but my adopted parents are no longer alive. About 2 months ago I had a very strong urge to find out about my birth family. I had not attempted to try and find Mother before. I sent for a copy of my birth certificate 9 years ago but did not go further, I kept meaning to, but something kept stopping me, and the time did not seem right.

In her letter she told me that she had been very close to her adoptive mother and was greatly distressed at her death some years previously. Whether it was because of this or not, I don't know, but she had only very recently made up her mind to look for her birth mother. Living so far away from Scotland had been partly the cause of the long wait but, as she said, she felt the time was not right. These feelings, she stressed, I should take into account.

On top of this, there are many deep-seated emotions attendant on adoption also to take into account. There is what Adam Mars-Jones, writing in the *London Review of Books*, describes as the 'negative algebra' of adoption to consider. Life in a world consisting largely of families with their own children is difficult to accommodate for the adopted child. It is possibly even more complicated for such a child than it is for the birth mother and for the adoptive parents. The whole condition can be a maelstrom of conflicting feelings and interactions.

Adoption never operates by a simple formula. It is not a case of one baby extra filling a gap neatly created by the lack of one baby elsewhere. The emotions involved rarely add up, rarely come to a neat solution. It is easy to recognise, even expect, that an adopted child can feel abandoned by a birth parent. But for those without direct experience of adoption, it is seldom understood that such negative feelings can be replicated in the child's attitude to the adoptive parents. After all, the child they have got is not the child they actually wanted – a child born of their own union. The baby they've got is just the baby they have settled for – almost the best of a bad job. Happily, this seems not to be the case in Maria's upbringing.

In extreme instances, such as those quoted in Jane Robinson's *In the Family Way*, adopted children could be made to feel almost responsible for the act – perceived by the self-righteous as sinful – through which they had arrived in the world. There are examples of children having the fact that their parents weren't married constantly rammed down their throats; others of them being regarded as a sort of 'trophy owned by the adoptive mother.' There is even one instance of a child never being referred to as the family's son, but always being introduced as 'my adopted son'. As Robinson says, such terminology is 'redolent of detachment and the sort of qualification no "real" child would ever be subjected to.' Even in less strained relationships, there are always instances of adoptive parents more taken with the idea of having a baby, than with the often messy reality of the situation. And from the adopted child's point of view, on being made aware of their status, there must often be a fear that they could be 'un-adopted', sent back as not up to snuff.

While my half-sister's letter told me of a happy childhood, one can never be sure. In her circumstances, there could have been further factors in play, particularly in relation to her adoptive parents. The death of her adoptive father when she was very young; the more recent death of her adoptive mother which she had taken several years to get over. Her resolution to wait for what she felt to be the right time to look for her birth mother could also have had an impact. This delay may well have been governed by her closeness to her adoptive mother, and by the sense of betrayal that such a search could well have induced. Or it could equally have been a result of over-dependence on the adoptive mother and a fear of letting her go. We can speculate, but who can say what was working its way through her mind, what internal pressures she was under?

* * *

Maria stressed that the moment to make contact with her birth mother had at last seemed right when she and her husband came up to

Aberdeenshire on holiday. Such emotionally charged things often do seem to have their own specific correct time and the visit to Scotland would have reinforced this. But is it possible to argue that this feeling of 'rightness' had any connection with my mother's almost simultaneous death? I'll have to leave that open to the reader to decide. But, whether it did or not, being in the country of her mother's birth enabled Maria and her husband to do the necessary research in the National Archives here. They soon picked up the trail of my mum as her birth mother.

My half-sister's long letter to me expressed both surprise and sadness that Bea had died. Maria had been convinced – again through the stories she had told herself – that, while Bea would have been of relatively advanced years, she would still be alive.

> I imagined Mother had given birth to me when she was a young girl of 17 or 18, so thought there was a good chance that she would still be alive. In fact, I was convinced of it, especially after feeling strange and restless earlier this year and then having a feeling of urgency. I thought at last the time had come.

This conviction, she said, was based on her assumption that the bearer of an illegitimate child in 1941 – during the War, and its attendant loosening of morals – was more than likely to be a young girl.

Far from being the case, it would appear that all age groups had, understandably, been freer with their affections amongst the stresses induced by wartime conditions. My mother – her mother – had, in fact, been twenty-eight at the time she had given birth and so the calculations behind Maria's conviction had let her down. Let her down badly. It was doubly sad for her that her birth mother had died so recently, only a matter of months before she had begun to seek her out.

Maria told me she had only learned of my own existence during her search in the archives. As the elder brother, I had signed my mother's death certificate, entering my address as the signatory. So, it was a simple matter for Maria to look me up in the phone book and for her husband to make that call.

As to meeting up, Maria's letter suggested, to my relief, that we take things slowly. While both my brother and I had agreed that we would arrange a meeting if one was suggested, I was particularly relieved that this did not need to be any time soon. Reeling from the coincidence of discovering, at almost exactly the same interval after the death of each parent, that each of them had been a parent previous to our births, we were too stunned to think straight about the situation.

The Venn diagram that had expanded in 1976 to include a new name in my father's field had now expanded symmetrically on my mother's side to include another new name there. The old security of our 'family of four', which had been so unexpectedly knocked off its pedestal once before had now been further challenged. While my brother and I had made a good attempt to bring our sister Catrina into some sort of close relationship with the family circle, here now was another 'person unknown' with whom it seemed likely we'd have to make a similar accommodation. The old game of musical chairs I had evoked back then had truly started up again.

To be honest about how I was viewing this, I must return to the expression 'once bitten, twice shy'. But in this case with reference to myself, not to Gilbert. In saying that, I have to be absolutely clear that it was the occurrence itself, the shock of the unexpected disclosure, that made me shy of taking any precipitate action this second time round. I wouldn't wish my citing of the proverb to seem as if I was being unfair on my sister Catrina. She is entirely innocent in this matter. No, what was exercising me was the unforeseen and coincidental nature of these two revelations, all of twenty years apart. The jolt they induced in me – that was the 'bite' I was fighting shy of second time around. The proverb is apt. As my father must have been shy of putting his second marriage at risk by defying Bea in revealing his 'long-lost' daughter, so I was shy of putting my relationship with Catrina – that very daughter – at risk by contacting this new half-sister.

* * *

Maria and I exchanged a few more letters over the next couple of years but never got any closer to fixing up an occasion to meet. Eventually she sent me a request for a brief outline of our mother's background and some photographs of her in her younger days. This was a request that could easily be acceded to but, due to circumstances that my brother and I had inadvertently caused, proved a bit more laborious than I'd anticipated.

Unlike my father's youth, my mother's is extensively documented in photographs. Partly this is a result of my grandfather's cousin being an enthusiastic amateur photographer, and a film-maker to boot. Though it is to be lamented that none of his film work survives, I have a number of his stills which engagingly document the goings-on in his and my mother's families. The immediacy and relaxed feel of his shots sets his work very much apart from the stiff, posed images from the early part of the century and distinguishes it from the often random and arbitrary snap shots of other family members.

Bea's well-off, solidly middle-class family was one to take snaps of each other on almost any occasion of note. While not approaching today's smartphone levels of photography, the images are there in considerable quantities. This plethora of holiday shots further documented Bea's life – in particular the carefree times she spent on her annual summer holidays and on the round of social gatherings she attended. At least, that's the tale they appear to tell.

There are, of course, other stories, darker stories, absent from the happy scenes these photographs portray. Other scenes that lie hidden like badly exposed shots, their images barely discernible. Or like that now virtually obsolete occurrence, the double exposure – where the ghost of something not quite revealed is lurking in the background of a different image, compromising its validity, freighting it with disquiet.

The constant reference points such photographs provide for Bea's life – and, in particular, her youth – make the discovery of a roll of film, still in place within the Box Brownie unearthed after her death, emblematic of the personal discoveries made six months later. That film, which I accidentally exposed to light in my eagerness to check out the workings of the camera, has come to symbolise the secret Bea hoped to take to her grave. What had been on that film, I'll never know. In all probability, some banal late family snap shots – if indeed it had even been exposed.

Double Exposure

But the secret that came to light – and I use that phrase deliberately – was an exposure of a different sort. One that doubtless would have shocked so many of the douce matrons and stolid father figures in all the early snaps of Bea's life; one that would have sent a worrying thrill, a caution, through the younger family members – an exposure she had done so much to prevent, to keep tightly wrapped in its light-proof roll.

Opening the back of the old box camera was not our only mistake. Bea had kept large numbers of family photographs – from her childhood right up to ours. Aware that adding dates and locations to the back of the prints could damage the image, she had catalogued them all neatly in dated chemist's envelopes. However, the over-excited carelessness with which my brother and I had approached them after her death, made the task of making a selection for Maria somewhat harder.

SNAP SHOTS

Knowing you'd best not write on the backs – despite
that enticing space – in case of making indents in the image,
ink leeching through to cloud the black and white,

you took the time to sort each summer to a separate pack,
mark them up with year and place, ready to pass on, the way
your old Box Brownie would be passed on too,

left on its allotted shelf, the only missing element:
yourself. Two things conspired against your careful plan
and we confess them now. One son, too keen on cameras

by half, undid the back, finding not an empty spool
but unexpected roll film still in place – ruined by his action,
lost to light. The second damned this gaffe, and loaded up

the snaps, life story for the telling, so he thought. Forgetting
to secure the box was his mistake. Back home, he found the lot
slid out, undated, rearranged – a car boot sale

of jumbled histories – as random as the memories
we somehow try to save, the present always just too bright,
its glare obscuring everything we thought was black and white.

But, despite this mishap, we managed to reorder the snaps as best we could. Before long I was able to send off a series of old black and white prints, of which I had duplicates, so Maria could build up her own picture of Bea's life.

The photos allowed me to go right back to my mother's rather privileged upbringing – to her school days, through her youth of sport and parties – then up to her late marriage and the arrival of her two boys. I was conscious that these snaps, at least the early ones, would present a rather glamorous image to Bea's 'long-lost' daughter. But I sent them off. Then it all went quiet.

Having had no acknowledgement of the parcel of mementos, I was reduced to wondering why for over a year. Eventually, I began to worry that it had got lost in the post and so wrote again to Maria to ask whether or not the package had arrived. My thoughts as to Maria's reply are principally ones of sadness for her sake. She wrote back in the end, saying that the whole thing had been just too overwhelming for her.

> I have been having great difficulty coming to terms with the fact that
> Mother never said anything about my existence to you or your brother.
> I more or less put your letters and photos away and tried to forget about
> the whole thing and get on with my life. I should have written to you
> before but every time I thought about doing this, and facing up to the
> past situation, I found it too distressing.

While she didn't rule out a possible meeting at some unspecified time in the future, she seemed to prefer that our correspondence should lapse. Despite replying to that letter, I have heard nothing from her since.

Double Exposure

This is an ending I am inclined to regret, but now feel I might have played a part in precipitating myself. Why did I not see that a lifetime of photographs would be too much for her to bear? Was it not the shock of seeing a whole life that, if attitudes had been different, she *could* have known, *could* have been part of, that caused Maria to stop writing? Could Bea's patently privileged upbringing have made any such sense of regret even more poignant – induced a feeling of jealousy, of envy? Thinking about it now, I can't help wondering whether a single snap shot – or just a brief selection – would have been enough? A studio portrait maybe? Or a few shots of Bea as a girl?

But at the same time, Maria had built up her own idiosyncratic notion of her birth mother's situation, her own story as to how she thought she *must* have been present in Bea's life. Her discovery that this in no way matched the actuality must have been a harsh blow to her. The fact – of which I am now aware – that my mother had done everything in her power to conceal Maria's existence would have been an even crueller blow. Looked at from that perspective, I doubt whether there is anything more my brother and I could have done. Even had we met up in the immediate follow-on to her initial contact, I suspect the end result would have been the same. As a person who believed in destiny, perhaps Maria is now consoled by believing that we were never destined to meet.

It is well over a dozen years since we were last in touch and still we have not met. Nor does it look likely that we ever will. So, why did the letters cease? Once again, here is another mystery, albeit a small one. Once again, something I'll never know.

★ ★ ★

Time has produced a more realistic take on this. I doubt whether any meeting with Maria could ever be based on anything other than a sort of genetically inspired, but nonetheless idle, curiosity. Maria had never known her mother – never known my mum. Barring the genetic coincidence of us both having shared the same birth parent, what was there connecting us? Apart from the likelihood of some physical resemblance and the possibility of some shared character traits, what would be the basis of any relationship?

To me, it's not the ties of blood that count. Families work not because they are related to each other – at least, not *just* because they are related. There are plenty of instances of the exact opposite being the case; Maria's own adopted family seeming to be such a one. My own belief is that if a family sets about creating an identity for itself, inventing its own reality, that – rather than any genetic link – will put it on the road to cohesion, to success. This can be worked at. But there is always a large element of luck about it.

With my sister Catrina, on the other hand, I had Gilbert in common. She could be – she *is* – my sister in that context. We had both known our father as an individual at different and at overlapping times in his life. Although this was independently of each other, we could still fill in gaps in each other's knowledge of the man. Together we could empathise with his joys and worries throughout his sixty-eight years. We knew our father as a real person, not as just a genetic link, and on that we have built a relationship, a warmth and a love for what we saw of our father in each other. Each of us can illuminate and expand that period of our father's life to which the other was not a party. We can add flesh to the bones of supposition and guesswork. My writing this memoir and discussing its content with Catrina has brought us, I sense, closer than ever before. Although we never knew each other before Gilbert's death, we have connections that can span his place in both our lives, can even at the best of times almost seem to abolish that death.

While blood patently *is* thicker than water, it is not as dense as flesh. As the poet Vicki Feaver says, 'care is not for the flesh of our flesh / but flesh itself.' And it is flesh that makes contact – flesh that hugs and supports, that grasps hands, that puts an arm round a shoulder, gives a pat on the back – flesh that binds heart to heart. Every time I embrace my sister Catrina – as I do with my brother – I embrace not only my father's flesh, but the flesh that knew him, that held him by the hand, that hugged him, enfolded him.

In the case of Maria, my more recently discovered half-sister, there is no such link at all. Any similar empathy would seem to have been impossible. While my father had expressly wished for – pleaded for – his children to be brought together, in my new half-sister's case, it was abundantly clear that my mother hadn't wanted anyone to know about her child. She had, indeed, done everything in her power in order to keep the existence of her illegitimate daughter hidden. Perhaps Maria herself realised this and decided to cease communications. Perhaps it became clear to her that, while the mother who gave birth to her was someone she could have bonded with, a pair of brothers connected to her by no more than genetic chance weren't worth the upheaval any direct contact might have caused.

But, while I have never felt the draw of blood relationships to be paramount, I cannot for a minute deny that others will not take the opposite view. What, of course, I can never refute is that my thinking here 'has form'. I am every bit as much a product of my upbringing as the next man. My own hands-off childhood, coupled with the stiff-upper-lip mores of the time, is bound to have influenced my thinking. Equally so, the many enduring friendships I have been privileged to enjoy throughout my adult years have inclined me in *their* favour, rather than towards family ties. Others have had different experiences, different upbringings, different family interaction. It is inevitable that their conclusions – their instincts even – will differ.

It is clearer to me in retrospect than it was at the time that my half-sister Catrina had a real need for a family connection. Her dissatisfaction with the state of her relationship with her mother – indeed her alienation from it – was a prime driving force in her seeking out her father. It drove her too in her hopes of being welcomed into a family. Vain hopes, as it turned out, but hopes nonetheless firmly predicated on blood relationships.

That my half-sister Maria waited so long before seeking out her mother is an indication of her closeness to her adoptive mother, a deeply founded but clearly non-genetic relationship. But she *did* search for her birth mother. And she also thought long and hard about it over many years. The blood relationship was clearly working away at the back of her mind. While I am still not clear about what exactly she hoped would be the outcome of the connection she was too late to make, she was obviously driven to attempt to make it. *And* had a sufficiently strong belief in it to gamble on a positive result.

As the numerous and often anguished personal histories that proliferate in memoirs, biographies, tv series, articles and blogs all seem to tell, that urge to seek out and connect with a blood relative – especially a parent – is an enormously powerful one. Am I deficient in not responding to it? Is there something in my make-up that holds me back from its pull? I am, of course, privileged in my background – a stable, two-parent family, a secure and largely steady middle class life. So the need – the sheer craving – for a missing blood relation is one I have never felt. But undeniably, others have.

It would be completely crass of me to reject their experience out of hand. The numerous accounts I have read in researching the background to this narrative, and to other stories of a similar nature, have convinced me that the genuine need for a blood relationship is only too real.

But not for me. That's all I am saying really. That it just doesn't do it for me. And the irony of that is clear.

It was my own family background, its hands-off, get-on-with-it nature, that formed that opinion. My own extended family, its distant and remote relatives, seen rarely if at all, that contributed to my point of view. My own parents' twin objectives of keeping each of their secrets – at least initially – that threw up an invisible barrier to deeper affection, closer ties. *It's* in *my* blood. I cannot escape that.

I still feel, therefore, that neither my brother nor I are in any way constrained to pursue further contact with my second half-sister. The circumstances differ hugely from my father's case. While I don't deny that there was dragging of feet and much wasting of time in making initial contact with Catrina, and that I was resentful of my mother's insistence that we 'owe it to Dad' to get in touch, ultimately we did meet up and have kept in touch to this day.

In my mother's case there is no-one telling us that we 'owe it' to them, no-one insisting that a duty must be done. My brother and I are not under any obligation to a parent to make a connection with Maria. The precise opposite, in actual fact. Were we to exactly honour

our mother's efforts during her lifetime, there should be no contact whatsoever. Nor, if I am honest, am I sufficiently inquisitive to initiate a meeting with Maria. Had she been eager for such a meeting, things would surely have been different. But it seems clear she was not.

Circumstances *do* change, of course. One day a letter may arrive. One day another phone call may be made. Maria *could* change her mind. Sadly, she seemed to be more troubled than consoled by what little contact we did have. But nonetheless, the possibility that she may wish to revisit her decision and take steps towards renewed contact is always at the back of my mind. But for now it seems unlikely.

It was Maria's choice to let things lie. It was my decision not to force the pace. She still has my address; I'm still in the same house. I still have hers; assuming she is too. Maybe one day she *will* write again; maybe one day I will. We *do* share a parent – I can never forget that. But maybe one half-sister – one *sister*, as I think of her – with whom I share a parent we *both* knew and *both* loved, is all I should wish for.

10

Most Unusual

IN THE 1980s I had become seriously engaged with photography. A regular for a number of years at my local camera club, I was even elected society president for a while. With a few competition wins, some inclusions in group shows and a couple of solo exhibitions to my name, I was becoming a regular at various clubs around the area. There I would talk about my photographic work and show audio-visual presentations, often including poetry to accompany the slides. It wouldn't last, but for a time I reckoned this was where my creative impulses would take me.

Perhaps it was my competition wins, but more likely it was my being elevated to the post of president, even if only of a photographic society, that sparked my mother's interest. She had always been frustrated by my lack of promotion in my teaching career, never able to understand why my background – private school, serial prize-winner, university graduate – hadn't immediately ensured my appointment as Director of Education. After all, she had made many sacrifices to ensure my future. But in truth the heart of her concern was her own ambition for me; she could never grasp why I had not been promoted to head teacher, or at least assistant head, not appreciating that pedigree counted for little with the local council education committee.

Now, though, Bea began to show an interest in my photography

– perhaps she was envisaging me as some sort of nascent Lichfield or Snowdon. Having seen a few of my prints, and even having accepted the gift of one which she regarded highly enough to hang in the lounge – only the second framed work in there – she decided she'd like to take a look at one of my AV presentations.

At that time I was drawn more and more to taking abstract shots featuring strong colours and patterns, picked out either in close up, or at a distance through the isolation of elements using a long lens. As the slides clicked one after the other through the projector, I could tell that Bea was getting increasingly baffled by my compositional approach. Where were the misty mountains in the glen, the Highland castle at sunset, the fishing trawler beating up The Minch? Where was the artfully arranged vase of flowers or the view of a burgeoning garden in spring? Where were the portraits, the still lives, the glorious landscapes? There was nothing to compare with the Peter Scott *Flight of Geese* she had on her dining room wall, or the Vernon Ward flower print that hung above the settee in the lounge. But, more particularly, why was there a total lack of any conventional 'view' in even one of my shots?

It was then that she resorted to one of her stock comments. 'Most unusual,' came the response to slide after slide.

Even – '*Most* unusual!' to those shots of a more rigorously abstract nature, which she must have been struggling to comprehend, even to see what the point of taking them was.

She intended each remark as a compliment, I'm sure, but it was one couched in her own bafflement at something she saw as well beyond her ken. This was so typical of her approach to life. To be usual, normal, conventional – to live the sort of life expected of one –was of paramount importance for Bea. Although I had realised this long ago, it is an attitude I would like to say I do not share. Still, I loved her no less for having this particular approach to life. I had come to take it for granted. But it always made me laugh silently or groan inwardly.

Thinking of another occasion entirely reveals a similar aspect of her approach to life. My mother was beginning to find certain more strenuous outdoor jobs too taxing, and I was doing some pruning for her in the garden of the family home. Trying to assuage the boredom of working alone on a repetitive task, I had balanced her transistor radio on the garden wall and tuned in to a Radio 3 jazz show. On I went, wielding the secateurs to be-bop and boogie-woogie. But after only a short while Bea rushed out of the back door and insisted I turn the radio off.

When I asked why, her response – which really I should have expected – was, 'What on earth would the neighbours think?'

'What does that matter?' I snapped back, not wanting to miss a favourite programme, 'Who cares what the neighbours think?'

'Well, *I* care,' she said, in a quiet indignant tone. '*That's* the most important thing of all – what other people think of you.'

* * *

There's no doubt that my mother had a privileged upbringing and had absorbed many of the conventional attitudes of her class and her time. With a father in the upper echelons of a prosperous business, she had been used to life in a large and comfortable house. The family had a live-in servant right up until the War – their parlour maid Hannah, of whom my mother had been really fond. As well as employing a maid, my mother would have regarded as quite normal living in a large detached family home with rooms ranging from drawing room to morning room with a brace of bathrooms besides; enjoying a size-able garden sporting its own badminton court and stocked with deck chairs, swings and other paraphernalia; and taking at least a month's summer holiday, with the family renting a villa on the coast. All this at a time when the majority of the population would have had no inside toilet, a point I remember her disputing with me in her old age.

Bea always regarded the fact that she had been alive at any period under discussion as trumping whatever historical knowledge I might have. But the reality is that she had woefully little understanding of how anyone lived, apart from her own class. Tim Jeal, writing of the same era in his memoir *Swimming with my Father,* refers to his mother admitting that, until she was married, she had always believed that

131

people received their gas and electricity for free. I would not have been surprised had my mother been similarly deluded in her youth. Her class just didn't mix with the *hoi polloi* in those days before the War. The classes were as segregated from each other as they had been for at least a century previously. With a closed social circle and no television to show how 'the other half' lived, it would have taken a conscious effort for Bea to explore the experience of the 'lower orders'. It is an effort I can't see her even thinking of making.

Having taken only the one foreign holiday in her lifetime, Bea was equally unaware of how other nationalities lived and was cheerfully 'gung-ho' about the superior values of British life. All inherited from her kin, of course. Reading over family diaries and journals of the time, it is often difficult to square attitudes recorded and terms used – which today would be deemed deliberately offensive – with the kindly nature I remember of the person who wrote them. A classic example of this is a '20s travel journal reference, in my grandmother's well-remembered handwriting, to a carriage driver encountered in Lisbon as being 'very pleasant – for a dago'. It is clear that Bea's private education from infancy, her inward-looking, extended family and her class's lack of experience of working class lives would only have encouraged her to regard her own hermetic world as *the* world.

Revealingly, she used to tell a story from her childhood in Aberdeen. Having fallen off her bike and hurt herself, she was sitting crying in the gutter when a local grocer's boy, passing on his delivery bike, had offered to help her.

'Far dae ye bide, quinie?' he had asked, needing her address to see her home.

Bea recounted how this had reduced her to even more tears. Despite living in Aberdeen from birth until her teens, she had no Doric and hadn't a clue what he was saying. In relating the story, she never implied that she ought to have understood her would-be rescuer, but rather that she could not understand why he was unable to address her in 'proper English'. And that he was somehow primitive or, at best, quaint for not being able to do so.

All of these other lives – both native and foreign – all of these other lifestyles, I feel sure she would have described with that choice phrase of hers, as being 'most unusual'.

Bea had 'married down', of course. It only takes a glance at her brother's wartime rank − major − and my father's − sergeant − to underline how she would have seen it. But then, knowing what I know now, it is clear that she − and anyone in the family who knew her secret − would have regarded herself as 'damaged goods'. The phrase crops up again and again in testimonies from mothers of illegitimate babies right up to the '60s. While her situation wasn't common knowledge, such attitudes would have been bound to undermine her confidence. I can only think that by the age of thirty-seven she must have been getting a little bit desperate. Remarks in letters to her brother hint as much. But this is not in any way to demean her relationship with Gilbert. I am convinced theirs was a genuine love match.

The joy of their relationship shines out of so many photographs I have of my parents. Early ones, taken in the late '40s before their marriage, show them arm in arm; my mother beaming out of the picture fit to dazzle the viewer; my father visibly 'over the moon' with his 'best girl'. Gilbert does have a somewhat rakish air in one or two of these snaps, his hat at a jaunty angle, a rather louche smile hovering below his moustache, but he looks delighted all the same. Later pictures, often taken at dinner dances or business functions, capture their evident pride in one another, each glowing with the fullness of it.

In my mother's case, I am particularly sure she would have been thrilled to have found a husband, despite all her past had put her through. Not long beforehand she had remarked to her brother − quoted back to her in one of his letters − that she would need to find a husband pretty soon. Tellingly, her brother reminded her of this when he wrote with his congratulations on her engagement:

I am sure you will be feeling very thrilled, Beattie. I don't say I was not surprised because it is, of course, very much out of the blue and sudden - but you did make fairly frequent mentions of Gilbert at Xmas. And when you were speaking of wives getting double & treble presents, you said, 'I shall have to get me a husband,' which caused me to ponder.

It is clear. Bea and Gilbert were happy – probably even rather relieved – that they'd both been able to make a new and better start after the miss-taken steps of their previous relationships.

★ ★ ★

To my mother's credit – even although I don't agree with the thinking behind it – she did attempt to pass on much of the privilege of her own upbringing to her sons. Ambitious for our social standing, she enrolled both my brother and me in one of Edinburgh's many mid-range fee-paying schools. A former pupil of that establishment's sister school for girls, it was her choice, one which I doubt my father had much say in.

From the age of five we were taught to look up to higher-ranking establishments, to look down on other private colleges lower in the pecking order, and to disparage everything to do with state schools as being irrelevant to our lives. So rigid was the city's educational hierarchy that I can remember my mother making only two exceptions in her disdain of the capital's many state schools. These exceptions were made on the unarguable grounds – to her, anyway – that the two in question also charged fees, albeit more modest ones than our private college, and therefore must be a cut above the base quality she assumed was characteristic of run-of-the-mill, free-for-all state schools.

While I too had precious little experience of any class other than my own, as I got older I was insistent on my self-professed egalitarianism. This inclined me to despise the inherent snobbery I saw in the attitudes tied up with my school, and in my mother's deference towards it. Osbert Lancaster, the newspaper cartoonist renowned in this period for his satirical take on society, talks in his autobiography about the 'snobbish shame' felt by most adolescents at what they see as the inadequacy of their families. In Lancaster's case this led to 'an uncritical rejection of all the artistic values which my parents upheld'. While I did suffer from this, in my case it was a reversed snobbery based on the conviction that, while my mother might profess to respect and admire culture, this was no more than lip service. My own growing interest in the arts placed me, I haughtily used to suppose, on a different plane from my parents. My 'shame' at my parents, and at my mother's values in particular, was also coupled with a wholehearted dismissal of the social standing she sought to secure for me through her choice of school. And an equally emphatic rejection of the 'sacrifices' both my parents had made in order to send me there.

'I never asked to go to that bloody school,' was my general response, one that was guaranteed to annoy.

Self-proclaimed radical that I was, I affected to despise all of that class-based ambition for the best part of my teenage years.

My mother's social ambition for both of her boys extended well beyond the sort of education we received. Throughout our childhood she did her best for us in the only way she knew how. Our school uniform had always to be bought in the cream of George Street's academic outfitters. At Christmas time it was always the better sort of Santa Claus – the one in Jenner's, high-class department store – on whose knees we were placed. Such a polite old man! As an occasional treat I remember being dressed in my best school blazer and taken for afternoon tea in Small's – William Small & Sons of Princes Street – another of the city's better class of stores. While sipping tea out of fine china cups and nibbling delicate cakes and pastries, we were able to watch the parade of mannequins and admire the models' poise and grace.

Always influenced by fashion and style, Bea was keen to pass on this attribute to her children, even if both were male. On achieving the great age of fourteen, my first sports jacket, essential wear to accompany my first long trousers – grey flannels, of course – should be bought nowhere but in R W Forsyth's of – where else? – Princes Street. Appearances were everything.

Looking at old photographs of her now, years after she has gone, it is easy to trace the development of her style and glamour – the glamour that appealed so strongly to my father, judging by the battered print of Bea looking absolutely ravishing that he carried in his wallet all his days. Early snaps of my mother show her in pigtails, plain and slightly chubby, clearly the tomboy she always said she was as a kid;

later photographs, however, show an immaculately groomed young woman, dressed in very much the latest fashion – the '40s shots being particularly stylish. With her long blonde hair bound up in a version of the Barbara Stanwyck look, she could even have been one of those glamorous mannequins we had so admired.

When not being taken out for treats or for a trip down town, like all kids of the period we were expected to go off and amuse ourselves playing outside. However, Bea expressly forbade us from venturing as far as one particular street. Situated a few blocks to the north of the family home, this street was made up largely of down-at-heel tenements. Despite my brother and I spending the first years of our lives living in a tenement flat ourselves, my mother felt that we had sufficiently gone up in the world to put 'that sort of thing' behind us. The street we had moved up to consisted exclusively of Edwardian terraced villas with a few semi-detached houses on the other side of the adjoining main road. This difference must have induced my mother's belief that the people who lived in the forbidden tenemented street were beneath us. We were emphatically instructed to shun this street and the 'rougher sort of boy' who was assumed to live there.

I can still remember the first swear word my brother ever uttered, when one day out of the blue he dramatically told me to 'bugger off!' My mother was horrified. She immediately assumed he had picked up this 'language' by trespassing into that very forbidden street. There he must have associated with playmates who had led him – or his vocabulary – astray.

'Where did you hear such a rude word?' Bea demanded, threatening the age-old remedy of a mouthwash with soap.

'Nowhere,' came the stock reply. The reply that never worked.

Eventually she managed to get his friend's name out of him. But she was proved wrong about the swear word's origin. Its source was a terrace much like our own. But since the boy responsible lived in a house that actually backed onto the forbidden street, she declared that this must be the reason for his objectionable turn of phrase.

My father was little better in his attempts to fight swearing. At one point, reacting to a particularly fruity mouthful of my own, he declared that he had never heard such language in all his life. I admit now, I find that hard to believe from a man who was a sergeant in the RAF throughout the War.

But the fact of the matter is that, while there were raised voices and arguments on occasion in our family, there was never any 'bad language' from either parent. All of 'that sort of thing' came from my brother and me and was rapidly quashed on its appearance. So it is easy to understand my total incredulity, when taking my first ever holiday job in a hospital laundry, at the language of the full-time employees on the shop floor. This was a revelation of a different sort. That every single noun and verb could be qualified by an obscenity was a plunge into the deep end from which my parents had been so assiduously protecting me.

★ ★ ★

It was quite straightforward – we needed constantly to shore up the image of a polite, conventional family, discreet and self-contained, well-bred and restrained. A family who attended church regularly; whose children went to Sunday school; whose *pater familias* was an elder of the Kirk; whose lady of the house was a caring mother and a punctilious housewife; whose parents were respected members of the local golf club. All true, of course, but all concealing so much more that has come out since.

Hide it, you can; pretend it was different, you might be able to do; but 'no-one forgets the truth' as Richard Yates says in *Revolutionary Road*, they just 'get better at lying.' Both of my parents were a party to at least one deception. But my mother, definitely a party to two, must have been especially desperate to keep the past hidden.

How sad it must have made my father never to be able to talk to his sons about his early life; never to be able to see *all* of his children spending time together, getting on, bonding. How frightened my mother would have been – even come the more relaxed attitudes of the '60s and '70s – that someone would reveal what I am convinced she saw as her terrible secret. Indeed, why did Bea frequently say to me as a boy – even say to my wife more than once – that she'd always wanted a daughter? When she already had one. Would that remark not just have added to her heartache? But, of course, adoption at the time when she had consented to it meant total severance. There would have been no contact whatsoever between the adopted child and its birth mother. So, effectively – and presumably in the resolution of her own mind – Bea had never *had* a daughter.

My mother's terror of the first of the secrets – my father's divorce – being discovered, went as far as to delay her informing Catrina when Gilbert died in 1978. She put off and put off phoning her, using the stress of bereavement and the pressure of making funeral arrangements as her excuse. In the end she called her only a matter of hours before the funeral. Catrina takes up the story:

> I only heard that Daddy had died when Bea phoned me at about 10pm on the eve of the funeral – with apologies of course, but effectively ensuring that I could not be there. Though I did dash around packing for a few minutes, I eventually accepted the futility of it.

However she disguised this, it is obvious Bea knew full well that the late notice would make it impossible for Catrina to get up from London to attend her father's memorial service. I found that deliberate prevention very hard to forgive – to excuse even – and I still do.

Similarly, despite her promise to my father, my mother put off informing anyone of Catrina's existence until well after my brother's wedding, hence the delay of six months before we were let in on the secret. As I suggested, this can only have been to ensure that Catrina would not be able to attend the ceremony, that her presence wouldn't reveal the secret of the divorce to the assembled relatives and family friends.

As I discovered later, relatives who were aware of Bea's secret daughter, and others who knew my father to have been divorced, were amongst the wedding guests. I even have a photograph of Bea, done up in the height of '70s 'woman of a certain age' fashion, chatting to the very cousins – Lil and Jack – whom I discovered she had been in contact with when she was pregnant. Presumably Bea's fear of my father's secret getting out was tied up in her mind with the possibility that one revelation would inevitably have led to another. She must have been convinced that a mysterious young woman attending my father's funeral or my brother's wedding – or, worse, both – would lead inevitably to the discovery of Gilbert's divorce. And that secret being out, what other secrets might also get out of the bag?

We will never know if our father was aware of his wife's secret – her wartime illegitimate daughter given up for adoption. I am almost certain from the evidence of later letters that he was not. The social opprobrium attached to illegitimate births at the time makes it infinitely more probable that Bea would have kept very quiet indeed about this 'shameful' episode. One piece of evidence dramatically backs this up. In Daisy Asquith's BBC4 documentary *My Mother the Secret Baby*, the story is told of the eponymous character's birth mother having the secret of her previous illegitimate child accidentally revealed. Taking place right after this woman had been married to a man who knew nothing of her previous child, the relationship turned from love to hate in an instant. Since the story took place in Catholic Ireland, divorce was out of the question. The couple were doomed to a lifetime of hatred from which neither could escape. While my parents lived in the less constrained culture of Scotland, I cannot see my mother risking even a scrap of such opprobrium by confessing her past to Gilbert.

As we were to discover through later correspondence, putting something behind one in those days meant more than just brushing it under the carpet. It involved a complete papering over of the cracks brought about by past errors. But like those scribbled messages left on a wall, revealed later when layers of wallpaper are stripped, my mother's secret had come to light over half a century after the event. Just as a new generation redecorating a house can discover, pencilled on the bare plaster decades before, the identity of the man who first papered the room or painted the woodwork, so the identity of an unknown and unguessed-at sibling had emerged, hidden all the while behind the respectable exterior of the past.

Did my mother have to carry the burden of that secret all on her own? Would she have been doubly terrified that, if my father *had* found out, she would have lost his love, lost his respect? If so, the fear must have eaten into her, worn away her sense of assurance, put her constantly on edge.

* * *

I am thinking back to a poem I wrote during the last few years of my mother's life. I acknowledge that it was very much prompted by her reactions as together we worked our way through the random accumulations of what felt like aeons in the old family house. On writing it, the piece seemed to me to be inspired by my own stressed-out reaction – not a terribly charitable one – to my mother's struggle to cope with old age and ill health. It seemed then to focus on the anger and frustration she felt at the way in which this loss of fitness had impinged on her active life.

However, while the poem predated by over a year the exposé of Bea's illegitimate daughter's existence, revealed to us six months after my mother's death, I am tempted to view what I wrote as verging on the prophetic.

CLEARANCE

You do this. Place your anger in a box,
pack tissue paper round it, cosset it
with more than fifty years of indecision
waiting for that moment you have lost.

I find it deep within a cupboard's reckoning,
labelled with a biro's printed marks
and tied with string. A folly cracked with age,
a half remembered urge, now half forgotten.

No need to spell it out. The baggage
that we carry is enough. Those faces ache
with nothing more than resignation, disbelief.

Climb out. The dark recess I find you in belies
a trust in life. A grubby handprint hovers
at the hemline of your dress.

I should stress that this poem was completed well before my mother's death, and has not been rewritten in any way since – this is how the final draft came out. Could it perhaps embody some sort of premonition, a forewarning of revelations to come? That is another thing I must leave to the reader to decide. But I am not alone in thinking this might be plausible, possible even.

In her memoir *Ghosting* Jennie Erdal writes that 'in some sense you also write in advance of what you know.' What you are consciously aware of at any given time, Erdal suggests, may be underlain by what you know 'at a subliminal level' which might not be fully appreciated 'in the normal sense' until some time has elapsed. Could I have picked up subconsciously the unease and disquiet that underlay what, at the time, I regarded simply as a consequence of Bea's deep unhappiness? Her resentment at age and ill health forcing her to leave the family home? Was I subliminally latching on to a deeper distress – a sort of moral anguish that has somehow leeched into the poem? That closing image seems to me now to be utterly startling, given subsequent revelations. Where did it come from? It wasn't, as far as I remember, an observed circumstance that I turned into a descriptive metaphor. And anyway, as readers will have realised by now, my mother would never have been seen in a marked dress, even had she worn dresses more than infrequently. The fact that I arrived at a handprint as the crux of the image haunts me too. It is almost as if I was somehow aware of the existence of another unguessed-at individual having some sort of hold on Bea's emotions. I cannot help feeling that the image must have arisen from my own subconscious, driven by some sixth sense perception of much more than was discernible on the surface at the time.

Reading the poem now – in the light of the bombshell phone

message in 1998 and the unanticipated facts I subsequently discovered – it is very hard *not* to see it as containing at least an element of foresight.

★ ★ ★

The sadness of the whole situation was – indeed is – almost too difficult to bear. All I want to be able to do is to tell both my parents how much I loved them – and how I would have loved them no less had I known what I know now. I long to be able to convince them – and my mother most of all – that it truly *doesn't* matter what others think. It just doesn't. Love doesn't work like that.

Neither of them – in their youthful follies or in the mistaken choices of their early years – had done anything remotely wrong. Both have been victims of overbearing convention and received attitudes, nothing more. I long to be able to break the horrible web of secrets in which their lives were bound up.

But it is all too late. Far too late.

11

In Love or Otherwise

MANY THINGS HAVE come out of the revelations that prompted this book. Many have come out of the phone message that started me off on this journey through the maze. And many more may yet be to come. But the most important by far, was that an elderly lady approaching her nineties, who had carried another's secret for all of fifty-seven years, was at last able to unburden herself. My second cousin Lil, the woman in question, emphasised in every letter she sent to me that she had never breathed a word to a soul. She had never raised the matter again, even with anyone who was a party to the secret. A burden indeed.

Such restraint is almost alien to us now; such propriety seen as bizarre. The atmosphere that prevails in the present day is one of rampant disclosure, gushing confession and often toe-curling self-exposure. All this is largely thanks to media advocated prurience, and the online abjuring of privacy. Such a culture may be uncomfortable, its output repellent. The impulse to 'share' may result in outpourings of a demeaning, cringe-worthy nature in overwhelming quantities. Its encouragement of anyone with the slightest grievance to assume victim status may be depressing. But the current climate of openness is preferable to the reticence, obfuscation and denial that gave rise to the burden Cousin Lil had to carry for so long.

Of course, she was not the only one. Lil's brother and sister-in-law were similarly constrained. Both Jack and Netty have passed away with the secret intact. As has my grandmother, who had the same burden to carry. As did my mother's sister whom, we discovered later, my grandmother had taken into her confidence. It is hardly surprising that she did. As Lil was emphatic that my grandfather had no inkling of my mother's pregnancy, my grandmother would have needed at least one sympathetic person she could confide in. We know nothing of this sister's attitude to the situation, but that could be the reason behind what I always sensed was a certain brittleness between my mother and her bookish elder sister. It could be the true reason for the infrequency of our family visits to my aunt and uncle in Glasgow.

Although I never knew my grandfather, I was always told by Mum – a fact reiterated by Lil – that he was a strict disciplinarian. While he was a kindly man, he adhered to Victorian values. In her letters, Lil was certain he would never have been told anything about my mother's illegitimate pregnancy.

> Bea, I'm sure, only told her mother she was pregnant – whether she told her who was responsible, remained their secret, but I think she refused to tell anybody that. I'm sure she never expected it would come to light, nobody else knowing except Jack, Netty and me, and not one of us ever spoke of it to anybody. Aunt Emily likely told [her daughter] Betsy – she must have needed somebody to confide in at that time, I felt, and still do – but she dared not tell [her husband] Uncle John.

Lil felt this was borne out by my grandmother being so frantic when she had written both to her and her brother. Had my grandfather been made aware of the situation, she felt sure that would have resulted in very dire consequences for my mother. This underlines still further the strain everyone was subjected to by this secret. No-one more so than my mother herself, would seem to be the case. But a further disclosure has convinced me that there was more to it than that.

While I was aware I might uncover further family secrets during my research for this memoir, the last thing I expected was to discover one that had direct bearing on my mother's situation at the time of her illegitimate pregnancy. The first person she told about this pregnancy was her mother, Cousin Lil's Aunt Emily, my own grandmother. The fact is, Grandma herself had been born illegitimate· This is late evidence I only discovered recently on downloading her marriage certificate. The space labelled 'name, surname and rank or profession of father' is left blank, as it was on the birth certificate of my mother's daughter half a century later. Although the certificate includes the fact that Grandma's mother had later married − and gives the name of her husband − the conclusion is inescapable.

The shock nature of such a discovery has not completely faded with changes in attitudes over the years. I will admit to a sudden rush of sadness on making this discovery. Not because I felt any differently about my grandmother. But I was saddened in retrospect that the lovely old lady of whom I had been so fond should have had to cope with the shame attached to a situation for which she bore no responsibility. Given the more judgmental social attitudes of the period, her own illegitimacy must have made Grandma absolutely petrified that her husband might discover Bea's secret.

At the time, illegitimacy was still regarded as evidence of 'bad blood', a taint that could − indeed would − be passed down through the generations. Jane Robinson's book *In the Family Way* provides plenty of evidence of this. She quotes an 1895 pamphlet − one published well within my grandmother's lifetime − that suggests 'children of immoral parents are no less to be shunned and suspected than the children of diseased, deranged, drunken or low-caste parents.' Thousands of years old, the concept of 'bad blood', Robinson shows, implied 'an inherent defect in the moral and mental faculties of bastards and their mothers.' My grandmother must have been horribly exercised in case her husband regarded her as having passed on the 'taint' of illegitimacy to my mother, leading directly to Bea's own illegitimate pregnancy. This makes it doubly clear why it had to be concealed from Bea's father at *all* costs. And doubly clear what a climate of fear and foreboding the pregnancy must have brought about. A double exposure to social ostracism was a risk Bea's mother could not countenance.

The secret of Bea's pregnancy, the birth and subsequent adoption of her baby was more than enough to keep. But my grandmother had also concocted a cover story whose elements had to be kept in play. It would have been necessary to maintain the subterfuge of Bea's phantom job in Newcastle, the prospects of the even better job it was supposed to lead to, and the reasons for my mother's subsequent return without appearing to have secured that better job. There were endless possibilities for her to be caught out.

Yet, as Lil said, 'None of the Edinburgh relatives ever knew.'

It *was* wartime. There were rules. People were instructed not to make any unnecessary enquiries. And those instructions were obeyed.

It is easy to imagine Bea, or anyone else an enquiry was directed to saying simply, 'Oh, the job was classified – it's all very hush-hush.'

This would have satisfied anyone then. And my mother could have breathed a sigh of relief. Her secret would remain intact.

★ ★ ★

In the '90s, we were not so easily fobbed off. Moving on from our shock at the initial revelation, my brother and I were curious. Naturally eager for more details, we were thinking back to the '70s when we had discovered the first of our now double ration of half-sisters. Getting to grips with the backstory then had helped us in understanding the whole situation, in not holding any grudges or harbouring ill will. We wanted this new story to be equally resolved, or at least to have its details as complete as possible. Principally, we wondered if there was some way we could solve the mystery of who the father was. The birth certificate my genealogist friend had acquired for us was left blank in the space assigned for the father's name, so we had literally nothing to go on.

On this question, Lil had been unable even to hazard a guess. She had never been told, nor it would seem had anyone else.

I'm sorry I can't help at all with regard to who the father was and that is probably what you are most anxious to know. Bea never mentioned any names. She would not allow herself to dwell on what had happened, though privately, she must have felt it very much. There is more than we know in all this.

Aware now that my aunt had been a party to the secret, I was able to speak to another cousin, that aunt's youngest daughter. She too knew nothing of the father's identity and even less about the secret than I did. Every path we were following led to a dead end in the maze.

Bea had always been a great storyteller and had often spoken about various times in her past, long before she met my father. On occasion she had waxed lyrical about a 'lovely weekend' she and her best friend had spent by the seaside with two boyfriends during the War. One, she had recalled, savouring the glamour of it, had been a trumpeter in a dance band. Could this have been the occasion on which Maria was conceived? Had it been, and given the consequences, would she have described that time as 'lovely'? Given her predicament, and her mother's reaction to it, that would seem unlikely.

We were still going through Bea's photos in the aftermath of her recent death, attempting to restore each to its correct era after the mix-up described in my poem 'Snap Shots'. Bea – or Beattie as she would still have been in most of them – was there in almost every conceivable aspect. Girlish snaps from the '20s of picnics in the countryside, the names of chums pencilled on the back. School photographs from earlier – sports teams lined up and classmates in uniform – or pictures of her as an infant playing in the garden with her mother in Aberdeen. Snap shots from the '40s had her dolled up for parties or posing in her swimming costume on the beach, in the company of brothers, cousins and family friends, all familiar, if distant, faces. Group photos of golf parties and tennis tournaments, action shots of badminton in her back garden; portraits on horseback at her uncle's stables, of riders cantering along the sands at Gullane. Even an enlargement of a press print with her as one of a troop of performers all got up in sailor suits for an ice dance show. All were there.

Amongst these photographs, there were two intriguingly unexplained snaps from around the right time for our purposes. Both showed someone neither my brother nor I recognised. This was a man in army uniform: one snap with him holding a horse by the bridle, another with him alone. But neither had any identification written on the back of the print and he bore no physical resemblance to any of Mum's family. Could this be her mysterious lover? Neither Cousin Lil, nor any other relative to whom we showed this picture, had any notion of who this man might be – nor did he even look familiar to anyone. Given her attitude to the man responsible for her pregnancy, as later described by Cousin Lil, does it seem credible that she'd have kept his picture? But still…

A few years previously I had taken my mother out for a drive into the hills to the south of Edinburgh. Stopping off in Tweeddale, at the Borders town of Peebles, Bea had asked to have a look at the war memorial. She spent some time there searching for a name. The person she was looking for, she explained – naming someone I had never heard of – was a man she had been very fond of during the War. She had almost been engaged to him, she said, before he was killed, or died of a tropical disease – she told me she couldn't now remember which it was. A strange thing to have forgotten. At any rate, his name was not on the memorial and the matter was dropped. Never suspecting any of the subsequent revelations, I never thought to ask her more. It was, I now realise, an opportunity missed.

Knowing all that was revealed after my mother's death, I naturally wondered if the man she had been looking for in Peebles had been the father of her daughter. Had his death been the reason that no marriage had taken place? Remembering the name, I later found this individual's address in an old city directory from the 1930s. But, not knowing any more, nor able to find out anything else, I had reached another dead end in the labyrinth of possibilities.

★ ★ ★

Does all this not amount to the same sort of prurient curiosity I have objected to earlier? I hope not. My brother and I were intrigued and perplexed by the state of affairs. At this stage, we assumed a meeting with our half-sister Maria would eventually take place. Before that, we wished to be in possession of as much of the story as was possible.

In addition, I felt that it was only access to the facts – or as many of them as possible – that would set me back on my equilibrium. The whole experience, oddly symmetrical as it was with the revelations of twenty years previously, was worrying. I find my feelings echoed by Terri Apter in *The Sister Knot* where she suggests that making 'a claim on my family story is telling me I'm not who I think I am'. This, she goes on to say, can be 'very disconcerting'. My brother and I were unquestionably both unnerved by the discoveries themselves but also by the uncertainties they presented.

There is another aspect to take into account. Equally naturally, we hoped that the circumstance through which my mother had become pregnant had not been distressing to her in itself. Given her consequent attitude to men, as recounted by Cousin Lil in later letters, we realised it might have been.

Well aware of the romantically charged, hothouse sexuality of wartime, we imagined some sort of 'Moonlight Serenade'–inspired affair. The allure of the moment would have seen it consummated, all caution abandoned. No-one then knew if they were going to be alive on the morrow. Young couples in their twenties – in love or otherwise – would have been even more conscious of that.

'Why wait?' would have been the prevailing thought.

'We may never meet again. We may never live to see another day,' was the mood of the moment.

My mother was not alone in this. The increased independence of young women and their detachment from their communities due to war work gave an enormous boost to their sense of personal freedom. The shared danger and the unpredictability of the future was something everyone was prey to. Companionship and mutual support – leading often inexorably to physical relationships – are only to be expected. The huge increase in illegitimate births during wartime speaks for itself. The rates virtually doubled over the six years of the War and in 1945 were almost treble the pre-war rate. While much of this would have resulted from intended husbands failing to survive the War, a large proportion *must* have been from the very sort of wartime romance or casual affair I've evoked.

Had such a romance happened and the worst fate possible befallen my mother's lover – being killed in action or succumbing to an air raid – she would have been left alone and pregnant with no possibility of marriage, despite what promises might have been made beforehand. Very many women were in that situation at the time. Making the best of the possible scenarios, we hoped that this had been my mother's position – a predicament brought about by the widely experienced tragedies of war, rather than anything pertaining solely to her actions and whose outcome she would have been forced to ascribe to her own situation. But hoping so does not make it the case. It was equally possible that Bea had been betrayed by some initially plausible man who had made all sorts of promises to her that he had no intention of keeping.

My mother had been single all her adult years. She had lived the life of a career girl in a busy and bustling city. She had numerous friends of both sexes and had told lots of stories of lively and carefree times in their company. She had holidayed apart from her family on numerous occasions: in the Highlands, in the Lake District, in the Channel Islands and once in Switzerland. In private homes and sophisticated hotels around the capital, at dances and ceilidhs on holiday up north, she and her closest friend Joan had been real party girls. She had told many stories of time spent with previous boyfriends: driving through the country in an open sports car singing at the tops of their voices; ice dancing at midnight on Happy Valley Pond to the tunes of a swing combo; swimming in summer at the beaches of East Lothian; and cocktail 'dos' at private clubs in the city centre.

Is it likely that she lived a life of innocence until the age of twenty-eight? Is it likely that her falling pregnant was the result of a first encounter? Her many boyfriends and her liberated approach to male company would seem to deny this, as would all of the gay social whirl I've just described. Is it not more probable that she had long been discreetly enjoying the sexual freedom of an unattached young woman? Is she not likely to have indulged in affairs and liaisons for at least a number of years?

In the previous chapter I included the poem 'Clearance', written when my mother was in the distressing final phase of her long life. It is a piece of writing I considered to be unsettlingly prophetic of the secrets discovered after her death. Of course, I never showed that poem to my mother. But I did show her others – and one in particular.

This was a poem where I tried to capture her in the flower of youth. In it I try to evoke the carefree enjoyment she described experiencing in the period immediately before the War. It was personally dedicated to her and was published in my first collection; the only one Mum lived to see.

SKATING ON HAPPY VALLEY POND

On nights of chill but little frost
they would flood the tennis courts
allowing a film of ice to form.

A small band played. You danced,
a hand-made dress of turquoise and black
swirling, like dreams, about you.

And came the greater chill,
the harder frost to freeze the pond,
a happy valley opened at your feet.

The chance support of water in a skin
snapped wings upon your heels, gave grace
its romance, space its sporting chance.

A flash of blades, the lifelines
turned across the ice, opposing, crossing,
merging at your will.

And later, when the fires were lit,
you sat between the knees of men and boys,
held briefly in the slow suspense of time.

My mother never appeared to appreciate either the verse or the dedication. This may well be because of her resistance to the lack of rhyme or meter, her view that only moon/June, 'dum-de-dum' type verse could claim to be poetry.

But I still wonder whether there might be more to it than that. She seemed to be put out by the poem's narrative. Did she think I had somehow intuitively 'blown her cover', revealed her to be more of a 'good time girl' than her later respectability demanded? Might one of these same 'men and boys' from her skating parties have been the individual with whom she had had a wartime affair? Could that reference have led her to think that I'd somehow guessed something of her secret – and that its following on from 'when the fires were lit', my metaphor for the start of the War, had correctly located that secret in time. Unlikely, but conceivable. Or was she worried that, if she did respond to the content of the poem, she might reveal something that I had no inkling of at the time. That she might say too much, hint at an affair, or more.

What then if such an affair had gone wrong? What if her pregnancy was an 'unhappy accident' – the converse of the 'happy accident', as she described my own conception, nearly ten years later? Given the mores of the time, she would have expected her lover to stand by her and make the birth legitimate. Had he not 'done the decent thing', this alone would have been sufficient to produce antipathy towards him – even a rejection of all men. Lil reports as much in her letter describing Mum's attitude after the birth.

> Bea gave me the impression that she'd be glad never to see the father again. I remember her attitude well because I was worried for her and didn't quite know what to do. I wanted to comfort her but there was to be no sharing of feelings.

Of the likely scenarios, subsequent letters from Cousin Lil bear out the betrayal theory. She went on, in the course of our correspondence, to point up my mother's emphatic opposition to marriage and her feelings of bitterness – at the time, that is – towards *all* men. She had no interest in marrying *any* man. She had made that clear, in no uncertain terms, to Lil:

> I can tell you when Bea said to me she had 'no intention of being married to anybody', she was more angry than anything else. She made it plain she wanted no further involvement and marriage was the last consideration – in fact, no consideration. It was not, I'm sure, a passionate war-time affair, but something which happened which Bea, later, devoutly wished had never happened.

This seems to indicate that she had indeed been betrayed – or at least badly let down – either as a result of promises broken or from the failure of the man to stand by his pregnant lover. Other details in Lil's letters back this up. She talks about my mother exhibiting anger more than any other emotion. She writes of her not wanting to dwell on what had taken place. Had the pregnancy been the result of a casual affair, in which contraception had failed, there would seem to be little reason for the anger. Disappointment, yes; irritation even; but anger at what seems to be *all* men – there was more in this than a mere 'mistake'. But there was to be no sharing of feelings, no woman-to-woman empathy. Lil felt sure that Bea very much regretted what had happened. She had made it very clear she never wanted to see her former lover ever again.

★ ★ ★

Making her first visit to the maternity ward two days after the birth, Lil had been surprised that the baby was not in the room with her mother. When she asked to see the new-born girl, a nurse was summoned to bring her along from the nursery.

> When I held the little one in my arms Bea ignored us both and soon called the nurse to take the baby back. As soon as the nurse had gone, and taken the baby away, Bea started to talk to me of 'riding again soon if I can get into my habit' – which I understand perhaps better now.

With the baby gone, Bea was able to focus on other matters with Lil, matters relating to the life she was returning to, rather than to the new-born life her circumstances were forcing her to abandon. Pondering how soon she'd be able to get back to riding, and whether she'd be able to fit into her kit, was no more than a defence mechanism against the heartache she must have been going through – Bea who was to say repeatedly in later life how she had always wanted a daughter.

While Bea's actions may seem heartless – even cruel – it is clear to me that my mother was doing her best to protect herself emotionally. At least, that's how we'd describe her actions in contemporary terms. She knew she would never be able to keep the baby – even if she wanted to – without bringing complete social disgrace down on herself and her family. That's an outcome she would have been unable to contemplate. She would already have made arrangements for the baby to be adopted and knew there was no going back on that. All she was trying to do was ensure as little bonding as was possible took place.

There were three approaches open to mothers in her situation: they could relinquish their babies immediately at birth; or after ten days; or after six weeks. Even though such babies were already destined for adoption, the legal papers could not be signed until those six weeks had elapsed. This could be the reason behind my mother remaining in Newcastle for a period after the birth. But either way, she had chosen the first option and that was that. There are numerous stories of mothers becoming so attached to babies already put up for adoption that they were unable to go through with the process. One such occurrence, returning to an account from Robinson's *In the Family Way,* tells of a woman who had taken the same option as my mother but, being shown her baby by mistake three days after giving birth, completely lost her resolve and was unable to part with the child. The adoption agreement could only be signed at that later date to guard against such an eventuality. Bea was clearly steeling herself against any weakening of her resolve.

However, it is clear that Bea *did* care about her new-born child. In what may be another reason for her protracted stay in Newcastle, she arranged for the baby to be christened before she went to her adoptive family, A sincere, if somewhat literal Christian, and as long as I remember a life-long church goer, my mother would have considered failure to do so a risk to the child's soul. Those of a non-religious frame of mind may not consider this to be of any real significance. But, having experienced the doctrinal anguish my mother went through when later family members decided against Christian baptisms for their children, I am certain that having baby Patricia Mary christened is paramount proof of her care for her daughter. She mattered to her, even if she was never going to see her again.

★ ★ ★

Several years on from this revelation, in the last letter I received from Maria, my half-sister told me that she had known the name of her father all along. Our speculative peering into my mother's past had been both fruitless and, we now discovered, pointless. The man in question had been born in 1914 and so was roughly a year younger than my mother. His name, as Maria told us, had been included in her adoption certificate. This was a standard arrangement I was not aware of then. As I subsequently discovered, all mothers offering children for adoption were required to complete forms giving the details – if they were able – of the father's height, weight, eye and hair colour, general health and so on. They were also asked to name the man. Knowing this, Maria had gone so far as to try and trace her father only to discover that he had died in 1980. (That was, coincidentally, at a very similar age to my own father at *his* death.)

Not a single person in my extended family had ever heard of this man. Given my mother's attitude as explained in Cousin Lil's letters, it is probably just as well that no-one had – and even more fortunate that no-one else was a party to his identity, to the information that my mother had had to include on that form. But the fact that he was named in the adoption papers allows me to discount the most unpleasant theory of all. Happily, given she had freely named the father when required, it would seem that my mother was not a victim of any criminal assault.

No, the most plausible conclusion is that my mother succumbed to the highly emotional atmosphere induced by living through the War. At least, that is the story I tell myself. She was involved with a man who was so persuasively silver-tongued as to be irresistible but who, for whatever reason, failed to stand by her when the time came. Either that or, in the worst case scenario I will allow, the man was a 'bounder', a 'cad' who made her promises of marriage he never had any intention of keeping. But 'the jigsaw can never, ever be completed,' says Jackie Kay in *Red Dust Road*, her own memoir of adoption searches. 'There will always be missing parts, or the pieces will be too large or clumsy to fit.'

Whichever it was, my mother was very badly let down. She was literally left holding the baby. That this baby went on to have a happy childhood and a stable upbringing with her adoptive family would have been a real consolation to her. To her mother – *my* mother.

12

Dates Changed & Unchanged

SOMETIME IN THE late '70s, I discovered that I was a half-bastard. A minor discovery in the light of the others contained in this book. But an intriguing, and perhaps significant one, nonetheless.

It had always been my mother's practice to remove her engagement ring when doing the washing up. I was used to seeing it lying on the mantelshelf in the kitchen, amongst dog-eared family snaps, old postcards and handy bits of string. But I would never give it a second thought. However, one evening when I was drying the dishes, for some reason Bea removed her wedding ring as well. Carrying the crockery through from what she always referred to as the kitchenette, to put it away in the kitchen cupboard, I noticed that, unusually, her engagement ring had a companion resting by its side.

I don't know what prompted me – idle curiosity, a moment's respite in the parade of plates needing dried, or just plain nosiness – but I picked up the wedding ring for a closer look. It was an object I'd always been familiar with and to which I had never paid any particular attention. But I had never known her to take it off in the past. Mum was still fully aproned, rubber gloved and up to her wrists in suds so, even if she'd noticed me picking up the ring, she would not have been able to stop me examining it in time. In the event, she can't have noticed. Turning her wedding band around in my fingers, I took a quick look before getting back to the plates and dishtowel.

The inscription round the inside of the ring gave me pause. It commemorated the date of my parents' wedding in April, 1950. As they had never celebrated their wedding anniversary, all I was aware of was the year of the marriage, but neither the month nor the date. With such occasions being outwith the radar of a young boy, especially one in a largely male household, it had never occurred to me as odd that the date wasn't a cause for celebration.

Since I was born in the September of the same year, it immediately dawned on me that my parents could not have been married when I was conceived. At the time, this was intriguing, but I let it lie. It was not something I broached with my mother until many years later. I never once raised it with my father, who died not long afterwards. The information was stored away in the back of my mind until, with the revelation of my father's previous marriage, the circumstances and timing of my conception became more relevant, began to take on a feeling of importance to me.

To one who was a teenager in the '60s, there was nothing shocking about an out-of-wedlock conception. My generation grew up with the increasing ubiquity of 'the pill' and the spread of a culture that aspired, or at least pretended, to 'free love' – albeit rather skewed to the advantage of the male libido. At the same time I was amused that my parents' relationship hadn't differed so far from my own. I wondered if my efforts to conceal the fact that my wife and I had been living together for a time before we were married had been at all necessary. Remembering a surprise visit Dad had made to the student house we had been sharing, perhaps I could now understand why he had made no enquiries whatsoever about our living arrangements and had seemed not at all put out by my wife-to-be's presence there. So very different from my future in-laws from whom it had been vital to keep the nature of our relationship undisclosed. Dad's relaxed attitude certainly contrasts with my wife's parents' outrage when they arrived unannounced at our cottage some years later only to find us out, but – scandal of scandals – an unmarried couple of friends in bed together in our spare room.

Being relatively newly married when I noticed the discrepancy of dates revealed by Bea's ring, I remember thinking how romantic the circumstances of my conception must have been. A decade or so before I would have tried to pretend that such a thing had never happened. At any earlier age, to have imagined my parents indulging in such intimate physical activities would have been an image I would have cringed to conjure up. And as an adolescent, I firmly accepted Philip Larkin's assertion in his poem 'Annus Mirabilis' that sex had only been invented in 1963, 'between the end of the Chatterley ban', as he put it, and 'the Beatles' first LP'. To have realised that this was far from the case would have undermined the naïve illusion I held to of sexual liberation dawning only with the advent of '60s youth culture and later 'flower power'. However, by my twenties, when that tell-tale inscription was spotted, I was happy to take all that it implied on board. And, perversely, I was equally happy to take on board the rather rakish notion that I was, if not a whole one, at least half a bastard.

The term 'bastard' was, of course, ubiquitous. A common swear word, even in the supposedly refined halls of my fee-paying school, it was bandied about with alacrity. It was not always so. In earlier times it was a term of genuine degradation. Applied to all illegitimate children, it even had gradations of shame. 'Natural bastards' were those whose parents could have married, but for some reason chose not to; 'sacrilegious bastards' were those where at least one parent had been in celibate holy orders; 'spurious bastards' were those whose fathers couldn't be identified due to them 'doing a bunk' or to the mother having had several simultaneous lovers. Further categories, whose natures can easily be imagined, included 'abandoned', 'adulterine' and 'incestuous' bastards. So sensitive could the term's application be that there is a case from as late as 1952 where a man was murdered for insulting another by calling him a bastard – the individual so addressed turning out actually to *be* one. His loathing of the term so incensed him that he straight away did his verbal abuser to death. That was the world into which my mother's secret daughter had been born in 1941, and the very same in which, had circumstances differed, I might have been similarly categorised at my birth.

All this was far – very far – from the flippant attitude we took in the 'liberated' era of the '60s and '70s. Then, we of a certain age thought we had changed morality. The word 'bastard' took on an almost comic aspect, laughed at in sketches from *Monty Python's Flying Circus* and the like; meaningless to those who favoured the term 'love child'. The disgrace attached to the 'taint of illegitimacy' had so exercised previous generations that it had been seen as something almost able to be inherited, the 'bad blood' that families were desperate to protect future generations from. Even this was now a topic for humour. The Bonzo Dog Doo-Dah Band did this so well in a number from their 1972 album *Let's Make Up and Be Friendly*. In a spoof western ballad, lyricist Vivian Stanshall captures both the outmoded notion of an ineradicable taint and the ridiculousness of such an idea. Bad blood, the song says, is like some egg stuck to your chin – 'you can lick it but it still won't go away'.

I had long been particularly amused by a laconic quip that closes a Lee Marvin western of the period. Perhaps this goes some way to explaining my fascination with my new found birth status. In the movie, Marvin's character finally bests the main villain of the piece and prepares to take to the trail.

'You bastard!' the baddie hisses, through gritted teeth.

Not lost for words, Marvin turns in the saddle and snaps back at him, 'Yes, sir! In my case an accident of birth. But *you* are a self-made man!' Then off he gallops into the distance in a cloud of – surely contemptuous – dust.

Sadly, no-one has ever – at least since then – called me a bastard to my face. All my fantasies of a similarly pithy riposte have remained just that – fantasies. But there's time yet.

★ ★ ★

At the time I discovered it, I had said nothing about the discrepancies in dates that Bea's wedding ring inscription indicated. I preferred to dwell on the various romantic scenarios my imagination provided. It was only many years after my father's death that I decided I'd like to know more. Considering that my mother might be put out by a direct and potentially embarrassing question, I felt she couldn't really object to a tentative enquiry. I had nothing to lose. But rather than confront her with a direct question, I decided I would just bring up, in a casual manner, the inscription I had noticed on her ring back then.

'Is it possible that I've got the date wrong?' I went on to ask her. 'I might have misread it all those years ago.'

'Actually, you haven't,' Mum said, not at all put out. 'It's perfectly correct.'

The wedding, she went on to explain, had originally been planned for July. But, discovering that she was pregnant, my parents had brought the date forward to April. On my probing further, she was insistent that they hadn't decided to get married as a consequence of my conception. When they got engaged in the first weeks of 1950, they had not even known she was pregnant. I was, it seemed, what Bea described as a 'happy accident.'

Ages on from this, when I found a cache of letters after my mother's death, her whole plan for a 'proper' church wedding was revealed. In a letter from her brother down south, dated from mid-January 1950, he congratulates her on her engagement and promises to get a copy of *The Scotsman* newspaper – always tricky in London – so he can see the announcement.

We were very much excited over the news in your letter of this morning which has been practically the sole topic of conversation here all day! We have already said so on the phone, but once again, my very best wishes to both of you & I hope you will be very happy. I am sure you will be feeling very thrilled. Please convey to Gilbert my congratulations & best wishes & tell him that I look forward very much to meeting him. I believe it is not considered the correct procedure to congratulate the lady, but I most assuredly wish you all the very best both now & after 1st July.

The date mentioned at the end of that passage is, of course, the date on which my parents had originally intended to be married – in a ceremony that would have been very different from the one to which the pregnancy obliged them to resort.

My mother had written to all of her immediate family with the happy news of her engagement and her elder – and favourite – brother, living in London at the time, had been the first to reply. Many of her numerous and widespread relations would have been invited to the wedding. Since her father had died in 1947, she had asked her brother to 'give her away'. He went on to respond to this in his letter:

> Well, Beattie, as I've said I shall be very happy to do the honours. It is, of course, the elder brother's place to give the bride away and if you had not asked me I should have pushed myself forward! Seriously, however, if Dad had still been with us, he would have been taking you up the aisle, and I feel, apart from the fact that I shall be more than pleased to do it for you, that he would have liked to know that I would take his place on such an occasion.

Had it taken place as planned, the whole affair would have put my mother, given her competitive streak, on a par with her older sister whose large church wedding had been celebrated some years previously.

Her pregnancy made this impossible. For her to have walked down the aisle obviously pregnant – as she would have been by July – would have caused a scandal. The wedding had to be moved forward. Its location had to be changed to a registry office. And it had to be converted into a small-scale, discreet affair. At last I had the story behind those differences I had noticed as a child between my uncle's and my parents' wedding photographs, why there was no church step shot of my mum and dad. It was now obvious why my grandmother had seemed so reticent about them.

Knowing the effect it would have on her plans, my mother must have been disappointed when she discovered that she was pregnant, so it was doubly reassuring that she had described my conception as happy. But she must also have been happy – though secretly so, given all that was concealed – that she was now going to have a child that she would keep, the child of her pending marriage.

I vividly remember the moment I asked Bea my next question. My wife, who was visiting the family home with me at the time, immediately shot one of her classic 'old-fashioned looks' in my direction. Unable to imagine ever asking her own mother such a question, she was visibly uneasy at my doing so with mine. I had mentioned that I was going to ask Bea about the date of her marriage in order to clear up – at least in my own mind – what had happened and when, back in 1950. But I hadn't told her what else I planned to ask.

To my mind, the next question – asking Bea *where* I was conceived – was even more significant. If my birth had been the conventional nine months or so after the wedding, I would have just assumed my conception was on the honeymoon. But this was not the case.

Still – good for her – Mum took it all in the spirit I had intended. Her answer, and the details she provided, proved to me that my romantic notion had not been wide of the mark. Far from it, in fact.

★ ★ ★

My mother and father had met in the late '40s at Ratho Park Golf Club just outside Edinburgh. They had initially been part of a large and fluid group of friends, so they didn't constitute a couple from the outset. My father had a rather impressive list of Christian names to choose from. Although he had been known as Tom Johnstone in the RAF during the War, by this time he had reverted to the name by which his parents had known him – Gilbert, his third forename – which was in fact his mother's maiden name.

I can imagine that this rather distinguished name would have appealed to my mother, always one for a touch of class. Oddly, she must have misheard it at first, probably in the general chatter of conversation. Her recounting of the incident has stuck in my mind. Bea had thought my father was called Gordon. Whether it was that misunderstanding that brought them together, I'll never know, but amongst the many stories Bea told was one of her first addressing my father as 'Gordon' and him emphatically correcting her. She would have remembered the correct name after that. And soon Gilbert and Bea became a couple.

Living not far from each other, in Edinburgh's inner suburbs – my father in 'digs' in the Shandon area and my mother still living at home in Merchiston – they spent their time going for runs in Gilbert's car. They would motor out to the Hillend Roadhouse for games of skittles or further to their favourite hotel, The Open Arms in Dirleton for lunch or afternoon tea. They would head along the coast to the beaches or golf courses at Gullane and North Berwick or down to South Queensferry to watch the ferries from Fife come in. In town, they'd meet their friends in the cafés and cocktail bars of the city centre, going on to dinner dances and balls. But whenever they had the opportunity, they'd be playing golf and relaxing afterwards in the clubhouse bar. This sport was to be their abiding interest throughout their lives. Despite continued encouragement, I never took to it. I myself am what might be called a 'golf orphan'.

My father must have been introduced to my grandmother around this time. She had been widowed not long after the end of the War and Bea – her younger daughter – was still living with her. Mother and daughter were shortly to move into a compact main door flat – as apartments opening directly onto the street are known in Edinburgh – but at this time, they were still rattling around in the large family home in Merchiston. My uncle's letter shows concern that their mother will be left on her own, but, as he says:

> Mother will be very pleased & happy to know that you will have a husband to look after you, and although she can not do other than miss you a great deal, at least you will, I gather, still be in Edinburgh & no doubt you'll be popping in to see her every other day or so, to say nothing of ringing her up on the phone.

But my uncle needn't have worried. Both of my father's parents were long dead by this time. He hit it off with my grandmother right away. This is perhaps why he was every bit as devoted to her, for the rest of her life, as my mother was.

Dates Changed & Unchanged

When the time came for the move to the smaller flat, Gilbert – then my mother's fiancée – was there to help with the packing and the heavy lifting, assisting my grandmother in her dealings with the removal men. In later years, he would do all sorts of odd jobs at her new home; cutting the grass and looking after her garden, even spending time renovating the sub-basement in the flat so Grandma could rent the rooms out for a bit of extra income.

Gilbert would take his mother-in-law for trips in the car and was always happy to have her along on the annual family holiday until, in the early '60s, she became too frail to travel. He also played a great part in helping Bea care for her mother in the old lady's twilight years. Initially this was in Grandma's own home but, becoming increasingly incapacitated, she stayed with the family in Morningside for a while, up to her death in 1966.

★ ★ ★

This bonding with Grandma would have helped cement my father's relationship with my mother. Their shared interests were pulling them closer together. In their early snaps as a couple, their strong physical attraction is almost palpable. Each looks delighted with the other.

Clearly my parents were falling in love. When the actual proposal of marriage came, and where that took place, is one thing I never got round to asking either of them. But whenever that was, it was not before Hogmanay of 1949. And it may even have occurred in the wee small hours of the following New Year's Day.

That evening, my parents – or Gilbert and Bea, as I *must* call them in this part of the story – were out at a dinner dance, bringing in the New Year in convivial company. Perhaps it was the very one at which we have them captured in a photograph of the time. They are in a group with another couple I can remember visiting us at home when my brother and I were small. Everyone is beaming, but no-one more than my mother. Behind them, a white-suited barman is serving drinks from a generously stocked bar. Gilbert, like the other men, is spruce in his dinner jacket and black tie. Bea is wearing an elegantly cut evening gown, its sweetheart neckline and cap sleeves offset by a triple strand of pearls at her neck. Cigarettes and drinks in their hands, they are clearly having a fine time.

It was the start of a new decade and a step in time away from the decade that was synonymous, in the minds of their generation, with the War. Both had lost many friends then, and both would be hoping to leave some of that sadness behind in their new-found love for each other. It doesn't take much imagination to see how, later that night, they would have fallen into each other's arms; how they'd have wanted to make the New Year unique with their love.

And so, it turned out – as Bea told me many years later when I asked her the question. Her response convinces me that it *was* the romantic occasion I imagined. That was the very night on which I was conceived, on the sofa in my grandmother's front parlour as the first hours of the new decade moved in and the mid-point of the century slipped into the past.

Turning the Page

He's the air force sergeant
likely man about the house,
sweeps her off her feet, she tells him,
smiles to break her heart.

But doesn't do that this time,
says she's the one he'll keep.
Proposes, swears he loves her, so
he's never out of step.

All that and now the '50s,
the war's the past decade –
hope will seize her one more time,
he'll help her turn the page.

Dates Changed & Unchanged

He dances in the new year,
she's counting down the days.
He's handsome in his DJ,
she's dolled up in lace.

Lying in his arms hours later
she knows what they have made.
Nine months till the boy is born.
Four months till they're wed.

On the first night of their honeymoon, those four months later, Gilbert would take Bea in his arms again. Mum told me what Dad had whispered to her then.

'This time, it's for good,' he had said.

And for twenty-six years – long enough to celebrate their silver wedding in 1975 – it was.

13

Maintaining the Fiction

WHEN MY PARENTS wed in 1950, the last thing my mother would have expected was the reappearance of my father's 'long-lost' daughter. Catrina and her mother had been living on another continent for a good number of years. He had been divorced from his estranged wife. Father and daughter had long lost touch. To be fair to Bea, how likely can it have been that Gilbert would ever see the child again? Surely that's what she must have thought. How likely is it, they'd both have reasoned, that Catrina would ever return to Britain?

Nonetheless, the situation in which my father and his daughter came to be trapped was undoubtedly down to my mother's reaction to Catrina's later reappearance. It is not my mother's insistence on the original decision to hide my father's divorce that troubles me. Rather, it is her subsequent rejection of any possibility whatsoever of Gilbert revealing his past and introducing Catrina to his sons. This is the real knot at the heart of the whole tangled state of affairs. Of course, Bea had her own secret to keep, of which we knew nothing at the time. Without doubt, the maintenance of that secret would have informed her insistence on my father keeping his own past a secret.

We will never have any idea whether my mother ever let my father in on her own secret – the birth of her illegitimate child during the War. The more I think about this, the more I am inclined to think she did not, *could not* have done so. Cousin Lil bore this out in one of her letters when she said:

> Whether your father knew anything, I can't possibly know but I always felt he didn't. But if he had, it wouldn't have made the slightest difference to him, I believe. We can never know definitely, but their relationship was strong enough to withstand any revelations.

However strong their relationship, we can never be sure how such an admission might have panned out. But what we should really consider is not what might have happened in that event, but what my mother thought *could* happen, and how those thoughts would have troubled her. If Bea had never told Gilbert about the existence of this child, she would have been that much more exercised about his own daughter. This could have manifested itself psychologically in two ways. She would have been unable to avoid feelings of jealously and envy that Gilbert and Catrina had been reunited, that he had been able to meet and bond with his daughter, something she believed she'd never be able to do with hers. And she would have been worried that any opening up about Catrina's existence could affect the keeping of her own secret. Both of these feelings would have nagged away at her psyche and tied her up still further in knots.

Bea would also have had a considerable emotional response to Catrina's eventual reappearance. Despite the fact that it is a daughter we are speaking of, not anyone like a former lover or an ex-wife, I think the circumstances must have undermined my mother's feeling of being my father's sole partner. Had Gilbert 'gone public', this undermining would almost inevitably have been seen by Bea as a humiliation – a psychological blow. She would have felt threatened – and felt the integrity of her family to be threatened.

Despite my own belief in the likelihood of my brother and I being able to accept my father's situation, Bea must also have worried as to how it might have affected us. We had no inkling of our father's previous marriage, nor of his daughter's existence. Bea was right to be worried. It was an entirely unknown quantity. At only sixteen and fourteen at the time Catrina first made a return visit to Britain, my brother and I were pretty sheltered and immature for our age. Remember, we were an uncommunicative and emotionally bottled-up family. Who is to say how we would have reacted? Bea, and even Gilbert too, could well have been concerned lest my brother and I had rejected our half-sister out of hand. Far from resolving the situation, such a reaction would only have added further to its complications.

While it is a hurt that we were never brought together while Gilbert was alive, for which I *do* hold my mother responsible, I know in my heart that I was more than capable of causing hurt myself. Teenagers of that age, or even older, are unpredictable. Self-centred and self-important is how I remember it in my case. Giving any consideration to the feelings of my parents came very low down on my list of priorities. I am not one to dwell on regrets, but in my parents' case I do have one major regret, one thing I could have done for them that would have cost me nothing. But one thing I failed to do because of what I can now see was my own posturing.

On completing my university studies, I had the option of graduating in person or opting to receive my degree through the post. My parents were looking forward to attending my graduation and proudly watching their elder son – even now the only person in the family ever to do so – receiving a degree, and doing so in a suitably formal and dignified manner. My own petty objections to the 'bourgeois' traditions of the graduation ceremony denied them that pleasure. That I was so tied up in my own self-proclaimed and simplistic political standpoint as to prevent them from happily enjoying a ceremony I could have taken part in with ease, still saddens me.

Being capable of that level of self-centredness at twenty-two – no longer with the excuse of adolescence – has led me to realise that I could easily have taken some similarly 'pig-headed' position on my half-sister. It would be obtuse to pretend that such a consideration might not have been part of my mother's reluctance to reveal Catrina's existence to her half-brothers. She may have worried that, in one of my headstrong adolescent moods, I might have scorned Catrina as a family member and refused outright to accept her. That I might have influenced my younger brother to do the same. Such a reaction would have hurt Gilbert even more than having to maintain the secret. And, had Bea agreed to the secret coming out, *she* could also have feared such a response. It could have led to a rejection of *her*, on the back of a negative reaction to her supporting any decision of Gilbert's to introduce us to his daughter. How was she – how were they both – to know that their sons wouldn't merely round on them as liars and dissemblers?

In her earlier life Bea had, it seems clear, been rejected by the father of her daughter, who had abandoned her to face the consequences of the illegitimate birth on her own. This put her in the position where she had no option but to reject her daughter in turn. This memory, haunting her past, would have made her more wary of creating a state of affairs where she, and my father too, might be rejected by one or both of their sons.

There are other considerations. My mother might have felt that setting Gilbert's relationship with Catrina on a more open basis was a threat to the unity of our 'four of a family'. She had been deserted in one way or another at least once in a previous relationship. This could easily have been a background concern to her decision, even if it wasn't paramount. Revealing Catrina's existence to her sons, she might have felt, could mean that Gilbert's love for us would be compromised. But I do not think this would have been so. Our father would have found more love to extend to his daughter as well as his sons, as he must have done since Catrina re-entered his life. I had been living away from home since the very year she had moved back to the UK. My brother was on the verge of marrying and moving out too. Our formerly close-knit family was already undergoing a change in its dimensions.

But it is necessary to face facts. However charitable I attempt to be, I am forced to admit that propriety seems to have been my mother's principal consideration. Propriety required by other factors in her life – but propriety nonetheless. It drove her to keep our half-sister, Gilbert's cherished daughter Catrina, apart from us, the two sons he loved. *And* it drove her to maintain the fiction about my father's past. But it was propriety wrapped up in her need to maintain her own secret and her desire to avoid what she would have seen as social and personal humiliation. My mother must have suffered a great deal of moralising and criticism at the time of her illegitimate pregnancy. Secret discussions of her predicament would have been frequent. Whispered conversations about her 'lapse' would have begun to wear her down. Many value judgements must have been made and plans laid without her input – or even her consent. She must have genuinely feared any 'talk' that would have resulted from breaking with propriety and acknowledging her step-daughter's existence.

★ ★ ★

Is an individual's capacity for love finite? Could my parents have welcomed either of their 'lost' children into the family and offered them their love in that context? Is it always a case of dividing up a finite quantity of love between all those in receipt of it? I rather think not.

Is it not that one's capacity to give love is directly related to the number of individuals potentially in receipt of it? That the growth of love is relative to the extent to which it must be spread? One proof of this in my family is the fact that Bea and Gilbert showed a great deal of love for their daughters-in-law (or potential daughters-in-law, one being still a fiancée to my father, who died before my brother's wedding). Similar proof was my mother's love of her grandchildren, whom my father, regrettably, never lived to see. Both parents *could* have loved their opposite number's first child. Not quite as their own, it is true, but as a nevertheless welcome and cherished family member. The bleak fact is that circumstances, coupled with at least one previous and mistaken decision, conspired to prevent this.

It is easy to see that my father loved his daughter every bit as much as he loved my brother and me. I wouldn't expect otherwise. His intense desire to bring all three of his children together, which my mother opposed, suggests he might have been less concerned with propriety than she was. Did he set as much store by what people thought of him, how they judged his behaviour, as my mother clearly did?

I can easily see him, had my mother agreed, cheerfully sorting the situation out in the easy going, convivial manner I came to recognise as I grew up. This would have been all the simpler had he survived his heart attacks. The shock of the second of these, and its severe impact on his health, had resulted in an intense sharing of feelings. That would have 'reset' family relationships. I feel sure my brother and I would have reacted sympathetically to the introduction of our father's daughter as our own sister, given how much it meant to Gilbert. And how much his well-being would have meant to us both *had* he lived to accomplish this.

But whenever he had chosen to take that step, I think he would have been capable of making the original cover-up of his first marriage and his divorce seem an entirely reasonable reaction given the culture of the period in which it took place. Neither my brother nor I were completely ignorant of differing standards and mind-sets. He could have characterised his subsequent decision to open up about it as the obvious *and* right thing to do at that point in time, in contrast to the hidebound attitudes of the past. We would both have responded to this angle. I feel sure he could have carried it off.

Few would have been surprised. Gilbert could have presented the facts – how it had made sense not to mention his first marriage back 'in those days'; how attitudes to divorce that were prevalent in 1950 had stayed his hand. Our grandmother had died in 1966 and few of her generation were still around to be scandalised. Even if not everyone, most would have been happy for him that he had reclaimed his daughter and welcomed her into his life and his family circle. Everyone was aware by the time Catrina reappeared in the late '60s that social attitudes were changing. They were bound to go on changing, even in staid and straight-laced Morningside.

★ ★ ★

Certain clues to my father's less hidebound attitude should have been more obvious to me at the time. I have already mentioned Gilbert visiting a couple of times, while he was in Fife on business, during the year or so my wife and I were living together before we were married. We had never stated directly to my family that we had 'shacked up' in our student house, so I worried that these unannounced visits were likely to let several cats out of several bags. This was in the very early '70s. The judgemental term 'living in sin' was still employed freely and that state of affairs was still very much frowned upon. It had been vital for my wife-to-be to use a different address for her letters to go to, in order to conceal what the university authorities described as cohabitation from her parents. Landlords were known to ask student couples if they were married and refuse to rent accommodation to them were they not. It had only very recently become possible for unmarried women to be prescribed 'the pill', and only then if they assured the clinics offering this service that they were in a stable relationship.

I was, therefore, somewhat embarrassed when Gilbert, full of cheerful greetings, had arrived at our door. But, as I said, I need not have worried – his supportive approach was maintained. It must have been obvious we were living as a couple, both of us finding ourselves welcoming him to our flat in the student house. Gilbert never batted an eyelid, implying an open-mindedness I hadn't expected of him. But despite this, he never referred directly to the situation or acknowledged it in any way.

He was also hugely supportive of us when, to the emphatic opposition of my wife's parents, we decided to get married. My father backed us up in every way, refusing to accept the objections of my future parents-in-law. Both Gilbert and Bea were happy for us to get married, despite our young ages, and went out of their way to be sympathetic. Despite their obvious disappointment at not being able to host the traditional family wedding, due to my wife's parents flatly refusing to have anything to do with our union, they invited relatives from my extended family, and those prepared to be tolerant from my wife's family, to a formal dinner they arranged for us. Gilbert even made a long trip down to the Borders to plead our case with my parents-in-law to be. Fruitlessly, it turned out. Given the nine months it took them to resume contact with their daughter, it's clear they had considered our marriage to be one of necessity, rather than love and commitment.

Who knows – perhaps Gilbert thought the same to be the case? Perhaps his own past made him more sympathetic to what he

– erroneously – might have seen as an awkward predicament we had found ourselves in. But I hope he simply believed his elder son when I told him I had found the love of my life. As indeed I had, and still have over forty years later. At any rate, I'll always be particularly grateful to Dad for all he tried to do for us. And for generously stepping out of the more rigid social attitudes that still held sway at the time.

* * *

Knowing my mother – who died when I was in my late forties – over the twenty-plus years of her time as a widow, and having grown up under her care as a middle class boy in Edinburgh, only reinforces my belief that, to her, keeping up appearances was paramount. The usual minor things from our childhood are evidence of this – her forbidding us to eat in the street, her objection to us wearing jeans, her banning of vernacular in our speech, her horror at 'bad language'. This even went as far as an incident I remember with amusement – her claiming to be outraged at my first use of the word 'sexy'. And I was only using it to describe my fashionable new sunglasses. So unmentionable was the word 'sex' that I remember deciding it was better to lose a game of scrabble I was playing with my mother rather than play *that* word to get the higher score the large number of points would have given me.

In my early teenage years it was through working for our local newsagent that I discovered sex – but at the same time, unfortunately – suicide. We had been with the same newsagent's as long as I could remember, having first been customers there when back in our tenement flat in the '50s. We had *The Edinburgh Evening Dispatch* delivered every teatime, *The Weekend Scotsman* on a Saturday and *The Sunday Post* on the Sabbath. Taking a job there as a paper boy, delivering a round of evening papers after school, I found I was carrying hot property. The Profumo scandal broke in 1963, when I was twelve, and I would prolong my round by sitting in the dim light of a common stair and lapping up the salacious details of the case. Although euphemisms such as 'call girls' and 'hostesses' were used for the principal female characters, it rapidly became clear to me, reading between the lines, what was going on. The subsequent demise of one of the main male players also made me conscious of the reality of suicide in a way that no amount of mentions overheard in *sotto voce* adult conversations had ever done.

What had happened to the newspapers my parents had at home? Would these stories not have been covered? Hidden from youthful eyes, I suspect, like the brown-paper-covered gynaecological handbook my brother and I had discovered hidden behind the Walter Scott novels. But my parents' preferred newspapers were nothing like the more sensationalist rags that I was delivering on some of my round. These filled me in on enough of the goings-on of Christine Keeler and Mandy Rice-Davis to fuel many a teenage fantasy. Years later, when I heard Morningside referred to as 'all fur coat and nae knickers', it would remind me forcefully of those furtive reads in the close of some tenement, while indoors, customers were doubtless wondering why their evening papers were so late.

* * *

There were many, many things my mother couldn't abide. Stickiness was one of them. She always had a damp cloth handy to wipe sticky fingers or jammy mouths, or to run over the Formica table-top in the kitchen after we'd finished eating. Condensation too she abhorred. This had an unfortunate effect on our enjoyment of bath times. She would insist that the bathroom skylight be kept open to ensure the egress of the damp air – not just while the bath was being run but while it was being taken and afterwards too. And this in an unheated room. We got used to frantically towelling ourselves dry before hypothermia set in. Likewise, grubby footprints on the carpet, drip marks on the lino from wet hands, fingerprints on the glass door to the front hall – all were to be avoided at all costs and any evidence of their occurrence was to be immediately removed lest it be thought by anyone that they were tolerated.

One unfortunate incident – strangely emblematic of the welter of family secrets – must have reduced my mother to despair. My brother and I were enthusiastic readers of the weekly *Fun Section* in *The Sunday Post*. Here was the safe side of the 'lower orders'. The characters may well speak in Scots vernacular, they may well be working class – but they 'kent their place' in the scheme of things. To this day I am an admirer of the cartoonist skills of Dudley D Watkins, but as boys it was the knock-about humour of *The Broons* and *Oor Wullie* that attracted us. Speaking a sort of cod Scots – almost, but not quite, the actual 'bad English' my mother railed against – the characters would get into hopeless scrapes in an environment that was immediately recognisable to us. My mother may have insulated us from 'such-like folk', but the Broon family and 'Oor Wullie, a'body's Wullie' brought us all the couthy humour of these salt-of-the-earth working class characters in the sanitised version publishers D C Thompson promulgated.

Such was my own devotion to the *Fun Section*, a detachable double-page spread in the newspaper, that I would race my brother to be first to extract it. In order to make the section more comic-like, I took to folding the pages and running them under a heavy weight to put in a proper crease. A leg of the kitchen table was my preferred means. This worked fine until one day my brother beat me to the doormat and grabbed the paper first. Having taken note of my convoluted folding routine, he went to do the same. What he had not reckoned with was the table being set for breakfast. Raising the nearest leg, he slipped the *Fun Section* below it. At the same time, four bowls of cereal, a jug of milk, a pot of tea, the butter and marmalade dishes, together with every single piece of crockery and cutlery slithered, in what seemed like slow motion, down the now sloping surface of the table. Hitting the wall against which the table stood, the entirety of our family breakfast dribbled slowly down its painted surface as I watched horror-struck. Corn Flakes, milk, marmalade, margarine, tea, sugar, butter and toast, all flowed over the skirting board and dripped onto the lino, where it joined the cutlery, the tea pot and the fragmented remains of the crockery.

This was the ultimate mess. My mother was more than furious. I was obviously the one to blame, she asserted, as I had given my brother the idea in the first place. Being the older, I should have realised this could happen. The family outing planned for that day was immediately cancelled. We were banished breakfastless to our room. And Bea began the hours-long task of restoring the kitchen to a state of calm and rectitude.

Despite buying my mother a new butter dish – out of my own pocket money too – she would refer to the incident, and my part in it, for ages to come. The marmalade dish, still usable since only part of its base was broken, stood on the breakfast table as a constant reproach until years later. The new butter dish, a cheap plastic one, went on for years as well. But it too was eventually broken. My mother was still using it, its two halves stuck back together with matching red insulating tape, when, quarter of a century later, we came to clear the family home for her move to sheltered housing.

* * *

A general belief in maintaining appearances was my mother's driving force. This was deferred to in many ways. During my father's brief period of unemployment in the late '50s, which resulted in a change of companies, she insisted that he leave the house daily at his usual early hour. It had to look as if he was off to work. Gilbert, she insisted, had to spend the day in the Central Library going through the adverts and making job applications. This did lead to success in finding a new post and my father must have been happy to go along with it. But it was surely also motivated by my mother's desire that the neighbours think he was still in work.

Even maintaining appearances within the house was absolutely paramount. Another incident is almost symbolic of her attitude to that. It has always stuck in my mind because of the classic remark it produced from my mother. Returning home after some sort of youthful accident – I forget what, a fall off my bike or something similar – I came into the kitchenette as usual through the back door. I was displaying an impressive collection of weeping grazes plus several dripping gashes to my legs. I got no further than the doorstep as Bea's never-to-be-forgotten words stopped me in my tracks.

'Don't bleed on the lino!' she cried out, hustling me out into the garden to be patched up. Appearances – this time of the precious kitchenette linoleum – winning out again.

Maintaining the Fiction

Propriety and that old 'what would the neighbours think' attitude were all wrapped up with this. I don't know how common in other Morningside households were the strange quirks I noticed in my mother. I had to guard myself against laughing at her attitudes on occasion for fear of hurting her unnecessarily. Some of her notions were just too ludicrous to be taken seriously. Things like her insistence on keeping the curtains partially drawn at either side of the windows since she insisted that, if her curtains weren't visible from the outside, people would think that she didn't actually have any; she preferred a dimmer room to being considered lacking in curtains. Things like her keeping an old unmatched teacup, which was reserved for any workmen doing jobs in the house, but was *never* used by any of the family or by guests. Bemused by this segregation of crockery, I cheekily tried moving the cup in the hopes that she'd have to use one of the day-to-day cups for the window cleaner or the gardener. But, as this poem shows, I didn't get away with that.

THE WORKING CLASS CUP

This is the working class cup. She takes it
from the cupboard where it rests, a lonely
afterthought upon the shelf, its only neighbours
anything she can not quite fit in space elsewhere.

I stand and stare. Can it be true that she has kept
this cup solely for tradesmen, as she says?
I cruelly taunt her with accusatory remarks but
can not dissuade her, cannot turn my wit,

show her this absurdity's completely out of date.
I hide the cup discreetly in a box, in hopes that
she'll forget it over time. Some chance. It knows
its place. Next visit – on the bottom shelf – replaced.

★ ★ ★

Lurking in the background, behind my mother's desperation to keep up appearances, was her own secret. A secret I believe my father was not aware of. Were the facts of Gilbert's earlier life to come out, Bea would have been worried that one revelation could lead to another. It is possible she believed that her own secret, in some coincidentally symmetrical way, would then come out as well. I'm inclined to think she would have felt humiliated if my father had decided to be open about *his* past. But I am certain that she'd have been distraught had her own secret been revealed. Rarely can the Gordian Knot of deception and counter-deception have been so tightly or painfully tied.

Because of this, I am relieved that Maria made contact with the family only after my mother's death. If Bea's illegitimate daughter *had* got in touch with her, especially if that had happened during the period of ill health towards the end of her life, I think the shock could have resulted in a severe mental breakdown, or even hastened her death. We are fortunate that contact was never made at that time. And, despite all I have said about secrets, my mother is fortunate she never had to face hers in public.

But there was another prospect. Suppose Maria had made contact while my father was still alive? By 1971 she would have been thirty. She might have been longing to know about her birth mother, as many people do at these milestone birthdays. So this *could* have happened. Would my mother have confessed all, revealed her secret to my father? It would have made her own stance on Catrina seem hypocritical, so I don't see it as likely. Any letter from Maria would have gone straight into the bin – almost certainly unanswered. If she *had* risked replying at all, I feel sure she would have instructed Maria never to make contact again.

Such outcomes have happened in similar cases. By no means all birth parents welcome contact out of the blue with a 'lost' offspring. This often depends on the parent's attitude to the child at birth. Should the baby be one that was given up reluctantly, the potential for a loving relationship, even many years later, is still there. However, returning to Jane Robinson's study, the author is unable to give a single example from her research of 'an aggrieved mother forgiving her child for being born.' This sounds not entirely different from Bea's rejection of both child and father at the time of Maria's birth. 'If a birth-parent was resentful at the time of the child's birth', Robinson explains, that attitude is unlikely to alter in any way.

This is my mother's situation, I feel. The rejection of all men – all marriage, even – which Cousin Lil reports, together with the unfortunate circumstances of the conception she suspects, would seem to support that. It is probable that my mother would have rejected out of hand any approach from Maria. In effect, had Bea been alive when contact was made, the situation would have been worse for her 'long-lost' daughter. Put simply, she'd have stayed 'lost'. She would never have had even the consolation of learning from her half-brother about her birth mother's life. Nor would she have been able to engage in the albeit brief correspondence with that same half-brother, nor receive the photographs she requested.

I may be completely wrong on all of this. Maria's appearance when my mother was still strong and fit *could* have been beneficial. It *is* conceivable that Bea might – just might – have welcomed her as the daughter she always said she'd wanted. That she *might* have seen this as an opportunity to unburden herself of a secret of half a century's duration; that she would have felt, as Cousin Lil had, some relief at that. But I doubt it. The facts of Bea's behaviour at Maria's birth and her comments to Lil at the time, coupled with the fact that she'd never breathed a word about her daughter to either of her sons, seem to prove that.

★ ★ ★

The consequence of this whole construct – this tangle of deception spun around our lives – seems to me to be no more than an accumulation of loss.

True, Catrina has gained. She has two brothers who are happy to have her in the family and who get on well with her even if, in a strange echo of the extended families on both our parents' sides, distance means we don't see her that often. She has one brother who shares many of her cultural interests. She has another who has a large and growing family to whom she is an aunt and a great-aunt. Plus, of course, she was able to spend time with her father in the last ten years of his life.

But Catrina has not gained anything approaching what she might have expected when she made her Atlantic voyage in 1969. She was not welcomed into a family. She was not received as a 'long-lost' daughter, except in secret. She did not become a valued and loved member of her father's social unit. These were high amongst her hopes as she moved back to Britain. And they are all hopes she has lost.

Perhaps Maria too has gained – to an extent. But exceedingly little, by comparison. What frustration and sadness she must have felt discovering that her mother had died only months before she decided to seek her out. She may even blame herself for the delay. Her failure to act in time may well be the underlying reason for her breaking off contact with her half-brothers. She is not to know what I consider would have been the outcome of contact with Bea being made during her lifetime, but that cannot reduce her sadness. Any hopes she had, she has lost too.

Loss, then, is the principal outcome of these deceptions. While popular tv portrayals of such 'long-lost' family reunions almost always stress the happy outcomes, I wonder what other dire results are deleted or edited out, never even getting as far as the viewing public. Could there be a whole world of counter-deceptions out there? It seems more than likely. The 'touchy-feely' telly programme approach will always go for the happy outcome – parents weeping with joy at being reunited with a child once lost; siblings separated at birth jumping into each other's arms; adopted children warmly embracing a mother forced to abandon them at birth. Without that, the programmes wouldn't be such reassuring viewing – we *have* to believe in the happy ending, to believe that wrongs *can* be righted. But for every one of those, there must be similar numbers of cases where, for the 'found' individual, the focus is still on the abandonment, on the giving up, on 'it would wreck my marriage to admit to this' or 'I have my own life to lead now' attitudes – cases where there is to be no healing of ancient wounds, no re-evaluation of the loss.

So, in this case, what exactly has been lost? Maria has lost a birth mother and, through our correspondence lapsing, any contact with her two siblings and one sibling's extended family. Catrina has lost a father in very difficult circumstances. She has also lost the welcome into my parents' family she hoped for, even expected.

But what of the older generation? Through my mother's secret, my grandmother lost the ability to share all of her worries with her husband. Her sister, my own aunt, lost the opportunity to be fully open with her brothers. And at least four of my mother's other relatives lost the peace of mind being able to share such secrets would have afforded them. Although I admit they may not all have seen it like that, duty and propriety being stronger impulses in the past.

My brother and I have lost the secure notion of the nuclear family we were brought up to. We have lost the self-containment and self-belief that family embodied. But, more disquieting still, we have essentially lost our father and our mother – or at least the honest face our father and mother presented to us – more particularly, of course, in Mum's case. While neither of them were directly dishonest, the smokescreen they erected has had the effect of proclaiming them so. Neither has turned out to be the person we believed they were – the individual we were led to believe each of them to be.

These twin deceptions, and the labyrinth of secrets, deceits and omissions that have grown up around them, have resulted ultimately in loss – almost entirely in loss.

14

Continental Drift

B Y 1966 MY sister Catrina was living in Boston, Massachusetts. She had left Texas and her mother's house and struck out on her own. She was twenty-six, close to the same age that I was when our father died. Having been away from the country of her birth for over twenty years, she decided to return to Britain for a brief holiday. At this stage she had yet to develop thoughts of returning on a permanent basis. But curiosity about her father – an impulse her mother signally failed to comprehend – must have been a strong motive. Her mother had always claimed to be baffled that she had any interest whatsoever in her father. But this only served to bolster her determination.

Still a child, she had left England in 1946. The six-year-old Catherine Mary, accompanied by her mother, had been lucky to find a place on a rare early peacetime flight to Canada. The pair had settled in Ottawa, where her mother had a brother. There Catrina had won a scholarship to a well-thought-of boarding school where she was a successful pupil for the six years the pair spent in the city. But when she was twelve she was uprooted again. This time the move took her to the United States, to Texas where she has told me she almost – but not quite – lived the life of a classic '50s American teenager. A bobby-soxer, even. It was there that Catrina would attend high school and graduate from university. But that was never enough. She had held onto many happy memories of the earliest stage of her life in the Lake District. The remote Cumberland village where she had lived in the early '40s still lingered on in her imagination.

For a time back then she and her parents had lived as a family, until her father was called up for wartime service and joined the RAF. Having missed an earlier round of conscription due to his age and his married status, leaving his family had now become unavoidable. Like so many other men, he never joined up as a volunteer, but the War inevitably took him away from home when his call-up papers came. After that, all his daughter had to remember him by, apart from her very early impressions, was a single photograph of him in uniform, taken in the African desert, and the little beaded bag he had sent her from Egypt.

Her father – my own father-to-be – went right through the North African campaign, over to Sicily with the Allied Armies and up through Italy as they slowly advanced. Although I never heard a thing from his own lips about this time in his life, my brother once – but only once – managed to coax some details out of him.

Both ill with the flu, they had been tucked up in bed together. My mother, doubtless wishing to save on heating, had put them in the one room for the duration. Whether it was the enforced closeness or just that there were no other distractions, my brother remembers tentatively asking Gilbert what he had done in the War.

'I was based in Tunisia,' he told him, 'as a corporal to begin with, then I was promoted to sergeant.'

'But what sort of planes did you fly, Dad?' my brother asked, imagining, as we both had, that being in the RAF meant at least being in a plane.

'I didn't fly,' he explained. 'I was an engineer looking after the mechanics of the fighters and bombers – you know, the flaps and tail fins, things like that. It was in the desert in Africa and really hot.'

'Were you just in Africa, then?'

'No – when the invasion started I was doing the same sort of stuff on captured airfields in Italy. Later on I even had a group of Italian prisoners of war under my command – getting them to do all the donkey work.'

We have photographs of him in his desert kit, hanging out his laundry or washing the dishes – 'dobbying up' as it's described on the back of the print; posed shots arm in arm with the Air Force mate who would go on to be best man at his wedding to my mother; some snaps of him and various forces friends posing in uniform, in conditions ranging from snow to desert heat; and one of two – probably taken against orders – of the engineers working on planes. There are bought photographs too: some of a few beauty spots in Italy and the buildings in Rome; and an alarming series of postcards, probably distributed by the Italian partisans, of the bodies of Mussolini and his mistress strung up on lampposts. But most significant are the pictures of graves newly dug, their cobbled-together crosses a powerful reminder of what Gilbert was lucky enough to avoid.

But these photographs were only found long after our father's death. Not once did he show them to either my brother or me, nor even so much as refer to their existence. Had they not surfaced when I was clearing out the family house, I might never have known of them at all.

Years later, my memory of that discovery transformed into a poem.

Opening up the Bag

The kind of bag your mother knocked up
for your plimsolls, is what this item is

but military khaki not the regulation
colours of your school. And inside

not the gym shoes PE staff demanded
for the wall bars and the ropes. Instead

a route through Africa and Italy, grainy
in the black and white of contact prints

that haven't seen the light, it seems,
for years. They track the course of war,

Continental Drift

and one man's ordered steps along it
on the road to home, to his own ration

of the nation's thanks. Though dog-eared,
creased and curled with age, each snap

is an assertion that he made it, while
each figure there in all the early frames,

but absent as the pile grows lower,
is proof that others fell by waysides

heaps of soil and crosses hammered up
from scavenged timber mark in maybe

half a dozen prints – the last memento
of a mate who bought it as the war

rolled on. But he's there, balding even
at that early age, moustache as clipped

and neat as ever, recognisably the father
he'd become by making it on through

this one-man Med campaign. Its images
unseen while he was just a dad, the war

simply a reference point, a presence
never more than back story, a given

all his generation understood but wouldn't,
couldn't speak of to the next. Till death,

his passing in his sixties, opened up
this story, loosed off the drawstrings

of the bag, let out that younger man,
sergeant in his thirties, to march the route

again, in picture after picture, the family
he lived to make, following his train.

Almost single-handedly, these images tell the story of Gilbert's wartime experience. We have found a few other documents – regimental booklets, a menu from an engineers' corps dinner and the like – but it is the snap shots discovered in that bag that speak most eloquently to me. They are so much more than just record or documentation. To me, they become what French artist Roger Grenier characterises as 'trampolines for the imagination' where 'the present is a foreign country' in which the writer 'lives in exile'. In his memoir *A Box of Photographs*, Grenier describes the effect of this approach to writing as being like 'those curious infra-red photos where…the film manages to record the image of someone who…is already swallowed by the past.'

And that is all we have to go on. For, apart from the brief moment of expansiveness when he and my brother were together in their sickbed, my father never said a word about how the War had gone for him. Far from this being uncommon, demobbed personnel were advised *not* to talk about what they had seen and done in the services. A 1946 article in the *Manchester Regiment Gazette* counsels 'don't try and tell civilians about your experiences, even if they ask.' You'll be talking a 'different language' it goes on to say. 'Going on about it' was seen as a barrier to reintegrating into 'civvy street'. Millions of servicemen – my father included – must have bottled up feelings and experiences, never explaining or even hinting at what they had been through.

★ ★ ★

It was while her father was serving in the forces that Catrina's parents' marriage broke down. Whether it was the appearance of another person in her mother's life or whether her father's absence was behind it, we are not clear. Most likely, a blend of the two. Many years later Catrina filled in the gaps for me with all that Gilbert had told her. Coldly informed by solicitor's letter that his wife wanted a divorce, he was shocked, hurt to the core. But he had not given up on his marriage. By this time, although still under RAF command, he was back in a post-VE Day Britain and was able to apply for compassionate leave.

Since early in the War the authorities had been aware of the stresses caused to marriages by absence on military service and had set up legal aid sections throughout the forces. 'It is important that no man take the irrevocable step of bringing his marriage to an end while there is a reasonable chance of being reconciled,' says the report of one such body. 'It is essential to advise every applicant of the consequences to his wife, himself and any child they may have.' While the genders were reversed in this case, Gilbert would have had a sympathetic ear in his quest to save his first marriage, particularly since he was the parent of a young child.

But the state of the country at the time presented further problems. Stationed at an airfield south of London, Gilbert had to get to a remote corner of the Lake District in a limited period. Travelling back up north on trains crowded with troops and displaced persons, he had such an exhausting and protracted journey that he had little time at home before he had to return to his base. It was too late to engineer a reconciliation, too late to change minds. Almost inevitably he failed.

Catrina remembers her mother taking her away from the Lakes, leaving everything she had known in her young life behind. But she remembers being excited at the prospect held out to her. It was a new life, she was told, a fresh start in Canada. At six, she accepted change and adapted to it. A willing emigrant, she would only miss her old life later on. Only miss her father when it dawned on her she would never see him again.

The pair stayed with friends in Oxford, and briefly with others in Surrey. At this point Gilbert managed to get a further period of leave. He arranged to meet his wife again, even more determined to plead his case. It was the last chance to save his marriage. But Catrina's mother was equally determined. She had made her move. The marriage was over – over and done with.

Somewhere in the back of her mind, Catrina has held on to a vivid image of her father at this time. He was in uniform, autumn leaves swirling around him. A look of dismay was on his face that has stayed with her down the years. She remembers him pleading with her mother and their voices echoing from another room. She remembers him being rebuffed. But she remembers little else.

She was six then. Six when they'd had that fleeting goodbye. The War was over. She and her mother were about to start their new life. It was the last time her father would see her as a child.

★ ★ ★

What Catrina remembers most is their quiet Lakeland village, the cottage they had lived in there, the kindness of the villagers and the fells she roamed as a child. She remembers particularly the two elderly neighbours – always known to her by affectionate nicknames – who had so cherished and indulged her. It was this village that drew her back on her first return to England in 1966.

It was exactly twenty years since she'd left Britain in the aftermath of the War. After a week seeing the sights in London and visiting her mother's family in Manchester, it was to the Lake District that she went. Her old neighbours were still there. They welcomed her as their own. They retold all the stories of her childhood, reinforcing her own memories, peopling her recollections. She was, she says, walking through 'the twice told fields' of her infant years – that notion Dylan Thomas captures so well. Although they had kept in touch by letter, this couple who had cared so much for her as a little girl must have thought they would never see her again. Now here she was at their door.

A long time later Catrina and I walked around her village. She talked of all the places and experiences she remembered. The cottage she had lived in with her parents; the pub her father used to drop into, now long closed; the post office where she had helped with the mail; and the school she attended for a year before she and her mother left the village. I was struck by how she talked about that time as an almost magical preamble to her later life in North America.

Knowing from her mother, that at some point her father had been living in Edinburgh, she had begun to think of travelling still farther north – out of curiosity, if nothing more. Her mother had passed on that information with considerable reluctance, unable to understand why Catrina was interested in him – in Daddy, as she always called him. That curiosity was more than rewarded. A purposeful leaf through the Edinburgh telephone directory was all it took. There, clear as day, was her father's name – A.T.G. Johnstone, as he always styled himself. Those distinctive initials leapt out at her.

It must have been an enormous temptation to make contact right away and a real wrench not to do so. But Catrina is clear, she had wanted to do this properly, in a sensitive, considerate way. As she said herself in a later letter:

> I knew very little about Daddy's early life and nothing about what happened to him after the divorce, except that Mother once mentioned that he had probably settled in Edinburgh. I must have given some thought to how his life had turned out and that there might be complications, and that's why I was tactful in my approach after I'd found his name and address in the city phone book.

After all, she could never be absolutely sure the person she had found in the directory was the right man. If he were, getting in touch again out of the blue would be a shock. Renewing contact with him might not be something he would even wish to happen – he might prefer to keep the past, and the evidence of his failed marriage, behind him. So it seemed kinder to both her father and herself to enlist the help of a third party. Noting the contact details would have to do for now.

It was back to Boston for the time being, and back to her job in the publishing trade.

★ ★ ★

One of Catrina's good friends was an Anglican minister whom she had known since their student days in Texas. It was this man who was to take on a crucial role. He was well aware of her story and her desire to be back in contact with her father. Catrina had talked the situation through with him and his wife on more than one occasion. Now she was able to tell them that she had found – or thought she had found – the person she had been looking for.

At the time, Catrina was not aware that Gilbert had remarried. The phone book only showed the name of the principal subscriber – himself. Although she had thought of that as a possibility, she could not have imagined that this might create so many difficulties. But it was clear to her that her father's life would have changed – maybe changed considerably – in the intervening twenty years. So she was cautious in making any approach.

With the credibility attendant on his job, her minister friend was ideally placed to be the first point of contact between her and the man she believed to be her father. The decision was taken that he should get in touch and pass on Catrina's own address in Boston so that he could write back direct. A letter was drafted with great care. Finalised, it was dispatched on Catrina's behalf. There wasn't long to wait.

It was indeed her father. And he replied immediately.

He was overjoyed to be in touch and even more so that his daughter had sought him out – that, despite the miles and the years, she had found him again.

★ ★ ★

It is difficult these days to imagine that it was common for parents – fathers in particular – to lose touch with their children on the break-up of their marriages. But think about the considerable impediments to communication in the '40s or even later – expensive and unreliable long-distance phone calls, limited travel opportunities, expensive journeys by sea and prohibitive ones by air – compared with the contemporary world of emails and Skype, social networks and budget flights. That, taken with the lack of current custody and access arrangements, makes it easy to see why many would resign themselves to never seeing their 'lost' children again.

Such had been my father's – her father's – position. Gilbert's ex-wife and daughter had vanished from his life. He had no means of contacting them, no means of even knowing where they had gone once they had left Canada. If he was even aware that they *had* left Canada.

Much of the back story came out later, its details gleaned from correspondence with my sister.

Mother and I were wandering around London unsuccessfully trying to find passage to start our new lives overseas. As it turned out I was the one who found a way. Displaying an early spirit of enterprise, I think! I spotted a model of a plane in the window of an agency and dashed through the door saying, 'There's a plane that could take us to Canada!' And so it was. On condition that we could leave on 24 hours' notice, our names were added to a list of people who could be offered places when a transport plane wasn't full. A few nights later we set off from Croydon Aerodrome aboard a converted Liberator bomber.

An early instance of my sister taking the initiative – and an explanation of how a flight in that immediate post-war time of shortages and rationing had been accomplished. Catrina remembered her mother giving her remaining ration coupons to the waitress in the cafe at the aerodrome, and they were off.

I was the only child on board and had a ball, helping the steward do the washing up and getting to join the pilots in the cockpit. We refuelled at Prestwick, and then Gander in Newfoundland in thick fog, before flying over the wilderness of pine forests in eastern Canada – dense green evergreens interspersed with brilliant splashes of red and yellow maples. We landed in Montreal, thence by train to my uncle's in Ottawa. The day we landed is always a memorable date in my year.

And that date too always gives me pause, being four years before I was born almost to the day.

Again, it feels like something from a film. All the stock elements are there. The gallant airman wronged. His wife seduced by a glamorous American. The husband's desperate pleading to try and save the marriage. The Yank proving to be a dissembler. The wife realising that, despite this, the marriage was over. The child's last sight of her father amid the swirling leaves of autumn. Then the search in post-war London for a passage across the Atlantic. The child's chance discovery of seats on a transport plane. The flight over the ocean to the mists of Newfoundland. The landing in Montreal and the first journey in a new country. It even went on to have the slayer of an ending. The child, presumed never to be seen again, making a sudden reappearance out of the blue.

It is easy to imagine how overjoyed my father would have been to receive that letter from his daughter's friend, the Boston minister. But I can imagine too how anguished my mother would have felt at this – to her – unwelcome and unexpected development. Bea too had evidently thought that this daughter was gone forever. While I'm sure she would have been sympathetic towards my father over the loss of his first-born, I'm equally sure that she'd have preferred it to stay that way.

That way, her subterfuge over my father's divorce would always hold. *That way,* she'd never have to deal with being disparaged for marrying a 'second-hand man'. *That way,* she could keep up appearances.

It is even possible Gilbert may have promised her, at the time they had decided to get married, that he would make no attempt to contact his daughter again. But this was different – his daughter had contacted him. While my sympathies are entirely with my father, I hate to think of the barrier this would have thrown up between my two parents.

★ ★ ★

For the next year or so, my father and his daughter exchanged letters and photographs until, in 1968, Catrina returned to the UK for another visit. The opportunity for the two to be reunited had arrived at last. Travelling up from London to Penrith, Catrina was met on the platform by the man she recognised as her father – a scene virtually echoed ten years later when I met her off the train in Cupar. Rather turning the emotional screws, he drove Catrina over to the very same Lake District hotel where he and her mother had spent their honeymoon thirty years before. There they had a happy but emotional reunion lunch. Preceded, Catrina tells me, by the stiff whisky my father felt he needed.

In another parallel across time, Catrina was almost exactly the same age her mother had been when she had last lived together with Gilbert as man and wife. Thinking about how *my* mother would have felt about this coincidence could explain some of her resistance to their continued contact. Catrina was single and unattached. She was attractive and personable. Although Bea would have known full well that he wasn't doing so, I suspect it must have *felt* to her almost as if her husband was having an affair. Though in this case the secrecy was imposed by the wife, not instigated by her husband, the atmosphere of subterfuge would have added to the illusion and a feeling of betrayal would not have been far behind.

All the elements of such an occurrence are there: the concealment, the furtive meetings, the archetypal age gap, the sudden and unexpected change in relationships. While rationally Bea would have understood that there was no threat to her relationship with her husband, emotionally and psychologically there must have been a mountain to climb. And her requirement that Catrina's existence be kept under wraps would only have added to the tension. Bea had been married for nearly twenty years, living in a settled manner in douce suburban Edinburgh, with every expectation that this would continue *ad infinitum*. And now this. How unsettling must it have been? How unbalancing even? But however it affected her, there is little doubt she deeply resented another female having a claim on her husband's affections.

If that indeed was how my mother felt, she must have longed for Catrina to return to the States. She would have been desperate for the whole thing to lapse – or, at least, revert to correspondence.

But she was not to get her way.

* * *

In the course of several visits to England in the latter half of the '60s, Catrina's sense of where she belonged shifted. It was an unhappy period in the history of the US, particularly for the young and progressively-minded, a contrast with the 'swinging sixties' atmosphere she had experienced in London. Late in 1969 she made the last of the big relocations in her life. Deciding to make a full break with America and settle in the UK, Catrina moved permanently to London. There she began to lead a sophisticated urban life in one of the world's great cities. By the '70s she was working in the Cultural Affairs Office of the US Embassy – but as a British employee.

Gilbert kept in touch, all the more so now Catrina was settled in the same country. But distance was still a problem. He would pay occasional visits while on business trips down south. He would do odd jobs around her flat – hanging cupboard doors, putting up shelves. Catrina remembers him showing her how to use a new saw and leaving it with her for her own DIY. From time to time he would bring her gifts – on one visit a Celtic charm bracelet, on another a specially requested LP. She still has the record of the Verdi Requiem he bought for her when she was performing it with an amateur choir. On one occasion they travelled round the Scottish Highlands together while Gilbert called on his pharmaceutical customers there. But, on my mother's insistence, their relationship was one that *had* to be kept secret, private to themselves.

Before long Catrina had settled into the rhythm of London life: going to theatre performances, concerts and exhibitions; making friends through her work in the Embassy and the social circles in which she moved; coming to love the capital city for itself. This was her home now. As her circle of friends grew, so her life developed, took on new aspects – changes in her career, new relationships, foreign travel – but always as a single woman, free and independent, and based after a few years in a larger, bright and airy flat in a busy central part of the city. Hers was a cosmopolitan life.

At some point she even got a new name. When my mother had first mentioned her existence to my brother and me, she was introduced to us by the names with which she was christened – Catherine Mary

Johnstone – but I have never known her by that name. To me she has always been Catrina. This was an enhancement with which she was dubbed while holidaying in Italy with a boyfriend. A man of taste and discernment. I have always felt that Catrina is the name that suits her best. As does the husband she married in 2001, also a man of taste and discernment, whose insights and understanding have contributed to our growing relationship.

★ ★ ★

My father was delighted just to be back in regular contact with his daughter in these first years of her return. But I imagine it wasn't too long before he began to hope for more. He must have craved an end to the subterfuge over his first marriage and longed to introduce Catrina at least to his immediate family. He must have dreamt of eventually being able to open up to our family friends and our dispersed relatives. But at the time a brief meeting with my mother was as far as Catrina's further integration went.

Catrina first met Bea when she and our father were in London for a company reception. This was the single occasion on which she was to encounter my parents as a couple. Gilbert must have hoped that his daughter's charm and intelligence would have won my mother over. That meeting Catrina in person would melt her obstinacy. But all my father's hopes were dashed. Bea was as inflexible as ever. She was adamant that any more overt contact was just too dangerous. Certainly no visit of Catrina to Edinburgh – let alone an introduction to her half-brothers – could in any way be risked.

Thus things continued, on an unsatisfactory basis for both Catrina and her father, until his ill heath intervened. The sticking plaster that had been slapped at random over my father's true status back in the late '40s stayed firmly where it was. It had needed replacing when things took a different turn in the '60s but no-one – least of all my mother – seemed to notice that the wound it was covering was beginning to fester. No thickness of plaster can prevent that.

And all this at a time when together they should have been

celebrating. At a time when Bea should have been happy for Gilbert at his undreamed of reunion with his 'long-lost' daughter. Hurt piled upon hurt, deception growing deception. How could anything cover sadness like that?

15

Shouting the Odds

POSSIBILITIES WERE WHAT the '60s were all about – artistic possibilities, political possibilities, interpersonal possibilities. Even, spiritual possibilities. This was particularly so with the blossoming of the hippie movement in the second half of the decade. But this was a movement whose impetus to achieve its ideals was seriously constrained by the quantities of hash, grass and acid ingested at the time. While I was only an observer of all this from way back in the crowd, I was strongly impelled to play at it, to pose just a bit.

In 1967, at the very time my father and his daughter were getting back in touch, I was emerging from childhood. I was more than ready to be seduced by the new and the trendy, but I was hampered by the date of my birthday. Being born in September meant that far from it being the summer, it was the autumn of love before 'At Seventeen', I made it to the significant age that gave the title to the song. But even having reached that age, like Janis Ian herself, I stayed put at home inventing girlfriends on the phone, while devising equally fanciful personas to inhabit, and lifestyles to emulate.

Already writing poetry, and performing it to anyone who would give me a platform or even the time of day, I was in danger of taking myself more seriously than any of my copious but derivative output warranted. Another songwriter, Loudon Wainwright III, captures this adolescent fame-fest perfectly. As a youth, he hungered for the romantic life of a poet, even like me, identifying himself with Keats and Blake. The song 'School Days', from his first album, seemed to completely deflate my 'calling'. 'How I made them turn their heads', he sang, skewering my affectations so markedly that a couple of friends even made up a spoof version specific to myself.

I was hampered much more though – or so I felt – by the environment in which I had to operate. A suburban family unit with little or no cultural interests – despite a fawning regard on my mother's part for culture as 'a good thing'. An education establishment hidebound by rigid rules and traditions – only happy to promote the 'safe' arts of school orchestra and amateur dramatics. Fellow pupils whose aspirations amounted to scoring tries and getting off with girls at parties – apart, of course, from *my* friends, fellow self-proclaimed artistic types. It is hardly necessary to say, but my group of like-minded school friends rapidly acquired a nickname – 'the pseuds'.

This was the era of outrageous happenings and provoking interventions guaranteed to offend the self-appointed guardians of public decency. Naturally, we 'young radical' artistic thinkers were right behind all such happenings. At the time, Edinburgh had its own version of Mary Whitehouse in the guise of one Councillor Kidd. So ready to take umbrage was this 'city father' that, when theatre box-office sales were sluggish, directors would anonymously phone him up urging him to complain about some disgusting and obscene play being performed. Press reports of Kidd's outrage would rapidly turn into a surge in ticket sales. But while Edinburgh had its moments during the Festival and the Fringe, to my young eyes there was little of a radical nature going on at other times of the year. There was not a lot to appeal to the hippie-inspired beat poet I aimed to be – no, *believed* I was. All the truly 'groovy' stuff that seemed to be happening with any regularity was down south, in London mainly. But even better stuff was going on over in America. That's where 'the scene' was. That's where it was really 'happening'.

The 'correct' stance on the US at that time, for those of my turn of mind, was a sort of fascinated ambivalence. Politically objectionable

– that was how the hip were supposed to view the country; its government and, in particular, its foreign policy being anathema. At the same time we fawned over its cultural life. This should, we all accepted, be held in the highest regard, unlike the faded imperial twilight of dead-end Britain. The US had the music, the art and the poetry we idolised – as embodied by that unassailable '60s trinity of Dylan, Warhol and Ginsberg. Perversely, my own personal transatlantic trinity differed, refusing to be constrained by the 49th parallel. My trinity consisted of Cohen, Rothko and, from a generation back, Carlos Williams.

But, for me, all were presided over by the omnipotent Miles Davis, who reigned supreme in my cultural universe. The effect his music had on me when first I heard it is still with me. It was an extraordinary opening out and loosening of constraints, coupled with a transporting lyricism I had encountered nowhere else. I was staggered to read, years later in the LRB, the writer Ian Penman describe a similar reaction. Like him, I had been brought up in a family where 'neither introspection nor exuberance were madly encouraged' and where home life could be 'a cramped and stifling affair'. I too felt, as Penman says of Miles, that this music was able to 'melt the inherited chip of ice in the heart.'

Thanks to copious teenage record buying and marathon listening sessions in Edinburgh's record shops, I had been 'turned on' to jazz in my mid-teens. My fascination with America and with music that 'blew me away' began in the decidedly unhip listening booths of Rae Mac's in George Street and James Thinn's of South Bridge where I would spend hours stacking up jazz LPs for buckshee plays of a dozen whole sides at a time.

In my earliest teenage years, pop and fashion barely impinged on my consciousness. I was a strange child – self-absorbed and self-contained. I would watch ballet and opera on our neighbours' television. I would stay behind after music classes at school and borrow records from the teacher. My music then was Beethoven, Bach, Sibelius, Handel – all of whom are with me to this day – though back then my main passion was Tchaikovsky, whose work I now find intolerable. Just how unhip was I back then? So much so that I can remember, on first being shown a picture of The Beatles that some older pupils were parading around the school, that I had no idea whatsoever who they were. But I consoled myself by reckoning that 'that lot' wouldn't have been able to recognise a picture of Beethoven or Tchaikovsky. And *I* would.

The cooler side of pop music, essential to being hip in the later '60s, came upon me all of a sudden. A friend, a fully paid-up Bob Dylan aficionado, had long attempted to draw me into his lyrical net and into the orbit of other music he believed to be more vital than the jazz I was fixed on. There was more to this new music than pop – had I listened to blues, he wondered. And how about R 'n' B? There were pop bands that played R 'n' B he was quick to point out – bands I might even have heard on the radio, bands I might actually like. But no, I resisted. I wouldn't listen. But he persevered and forced on me an EP he was sure I would like if I would only give it time. I wasn't in the state of ignorance I had been in on my first encounter with The Beatles – I had heard of The Rolling Stones, of course, but I couldn't have imagined the sudden force with which one of their tracks would hit me. So much so that by the next evening I was calling this friend up on the phone to play that very same track back to him as proof of my conversion. And as he rightly foresaw, from there on it was an easy step to Dylan, and to so much more.

By the time the 'summer of love' had caught up with suburban Scotland – sometime towards the end of 1968 – I had fully bought into the naïve optimism of the time. Listening nightly, in the sanctum of my loft-style bedroom, to John Peel's first BBC radio programmes, it was possible to feel part of something that was 'really happening'. Life was going to get better for everyone. Youth would see to it. Change was bound to come. It felt like it. Many of the kids I was mixing with then believed it too. But as Peel himself wrote later, 'Quite what this "better" entailed no-one seemed entirely certain'. Looking back from the cynical and irony-obsessed twenty-first century, I am happy that I was a part of that optimistic upsurge in my youth. Saddened, of course, that the optimism evaporated over time. But back then, I was not ashamed to say, 'I'm a believer'.

★ ★ ★

Considering the hippie movement had spread to Britain from the States, I wonder how I would have reacted to discover I had an American – as she still was then – for a sister. I think I would have been thrilled – it would have been 'far out', 'groovy', even 'something else'. But Catrina could have been the ideal person to give my brother and me a different, and more realistic, take on what was happening across the Atlantic. She might have brought us down to earth a bit and allowed us to see our hippie-style, peace-and-love, free-your-mind pipe dreams in a clearer context. One of Catrina's reasons for leaving the States was her unhappiness at the political situation in the late '60s, so she'd have been ideally placed to impart some sense of proportion and offer some first-hand experience.

I was very much committed to writing poetry all through my late teens and early twenties. By 1969, I had even acquired an older mentor from amongst the organisers of the alternative readings at the Traverse Theatre in Edinburgh. This was one of the 'Edinburgh scene' poets who ran these more left-field events to which the even more fashionable 'Liverpool Scene' poets were regular contributors, alongside a selection of singer-songwriters, jazz musicians and what we would now call performance poets. I felt I had really made it when my mentor asked me to take part in a couple of Traverse readings. And I was absolutely 'made up' when an actress from one of the Fringe shows actually complimented me on one of my long rambling recitations. I began to feel I was a part of 'the scene' myself, calling round at my mentor's back-street bohemian flat to have intense, late-night discussions about poetry and art, form and techniques. With several collections to his name, he was even advising me about where I might get published myself.

So, might the fact that my sister had been working in publishing in Boston have intrigued, even impressed me? Might interest from her, as well as from that left-field mentor, have encouraged me to keep on with my writing, to stick with the art form I was so quick to abandon only a few years later? Might it even have encouraged me to take a more considered approach to my work, to honing, editing, refining – elements the 'let-it-all-hang-out school' I subscribed to then derided.

But, I'll never know. By the time I *did* get to meet her, I had made the decision I now regret, but which I then regarded as a mature adult choice. I should 'put aside childish things', drop the poetry in favour of my teaching career. I only returned seriously to writing in my forties.

Had Catrina been introduced to her brothers on her first arrival in Scotland, I'm inclined to think I would have seen her as a slightly risqué, alternative person. I would have been gratified to have as a sister with a high 'cool' factor. She would have gained the two of us a bit of kudos in the eyes of our America-fascinated, hippie-obsessed friends.

But neither my brother nor I were ever in any danger of going seriously off the rails in the classic sense. To my parents though, and to people of their generation, I fear it may have appeared that we were. As I've already suggested, the over-extended generation gap between my parents and myself made for even less mutual understanding than the more common twenty year or so interval. Bea and Gilbert must have wondered what had happened to the family-orientated, responsible children they had brought us up to be? Why had we suddenly – in their eyes – become some species of amateur bohemian?

Strange, cacophonous music was echoing from our rooms day and night. Weird posters and abstract art prints adorned our walls. Our attempts at long hair and bizarre get-ups were embarrassing them in public. Lots of scruffy, dishevelled friends were calling round at all hours. Strange, exotic aromas wafting under bedroom doors were causing them alarm. And, what's more, I was developing interests that were unusual – that word again – interests of a nature that must have been as unanticipated as they were unwelcome. For me what mattered now were beat poetry, progressive politics, free-form jazz. Having rejected my parents' conventional church going by declaring a new-found agnosticism, I had become a member of CND, volunteered for weekend work with the homeless charity Shelter and started attending the occasional political meeting. I hung out in 'alternative' bookshops and 'underground' arts centres or got thrown out of pubs for being under-age. I spent whole nights away from home listening to 'sounds' in friends' attics and communal student flats.

By the summer of '68 I was 'on the road', hitching around Europe

Shouting the Odds

with a similarly 'switched-on' friend. By autumn '69 I was off to university and yet more 'switched-on' – or rather 'turned-on' – encounters.

1969 OK

It's another year for me and you/Another year with nothing to do
The Stooges, '1969'

Hell no, we won't go! was what they cried,
and burned their passports, ripped draft papers
into shreds. But us? We turned the TV off

and rolled another spliff, content
with marching in the street in solidarity
with what? Those teenage guys draft dodging

met on roadsides of the hitching trails,
all Afros, peace signs, Afghan coats
and dope? Their siblings, skewered and gutted

by the copter routes that turned them on
to jungle fear? Spaced out like us, though
only to supress the stuff we couldn't comprehend.

As if America could never lose. As if
empire by the backdoor had not a jot in common
with the one inherited we'd stood attention to

at cenotaphs, in school assemblies,
only children then. We skinned up, sang along
with Country Joe, mouthed Mitchell's 'Tell Me Lies',

believing this was revolution, waiting for us
as we ripped another Rizla pack to make a roach,
and rifled England's Glory for a match.

'What is it all about?' my parents must have thought. 'Where on earth are our boys headed?'

How we must have baffled them – or liked to think we did.

Years later, Catrina told me how Gilbert had discussed with her his worries about the road down which my brother and I seemed to be headed. So perhaps he had been harbouring the very hopes I have pondered here – that her introduction to the family could act as a sort of steadying influence on boys he considered wayward. A calming presence, she would have been an older, but still youthful, sibling we could both have looked up to, taken our cues from – someone to ground us. Someone to divert us from what I suspect our father mistakenly, but sincerely, believed to be a slippery slope – the one that would lead, with awful inevitability, to the rapidly approaching bad end.

He need not have worried though. Many of the friends I had then I still have today. Many of these friends must have appeared to their parents to have been heading down that same slippery slope. And yet I can think of none in my circle of close friends who did reach that projected bad end, none who even approached it. Twenty years back, at one such friend's fortieth birthday party, this was dramatically pointed up in light-hearted fashion. When a busload of his pals drew up at the pub where the party was to be held, we were all in fits as one of the friends leapt off the bus and sorted us all into groups.

'Lawyers to the left! Doctors to the right! Teachers at the back! Social workers at the front!' she intoned.

On she went to sort through another four or five professions, all of whom were represented at the party. And all of whom had come from the very same background of rebellious youth that had given my father such concerns. More recently, at our ruby wedding party, we amused ourselves by totting up – amongst the now rather ageing crowd who had escaped that same 'slippery slope' – the numbers of head teachers, professors, doctors, principal teachers and company directors, with even a solitary university vice-principal thrown in for good measure.

But what specific hopes my father might have had is impossible to say – other than uniting all of his children, of course. While no part of this is idle speculation, it *is* speculation nonetheless. Did he have any particular outcome in mind, other than the obvious emotional delight that he would have got from introducing his daughter to his sons? Had his wish come about, he'd have experienced a huge feeling of familial completion, a great emotional satisfaction.

I have two photographs from around this time, with only a few years between them. In one, Gilbert is leaning on a gate in the countryside with his daughter beside him; in the other his daughter is standing next to her brothers in my garden. How delighted our father would have been had we been able to unite these moments in a single photograph, all four of us together at last. Seeing all his children united, and getting on together, can really have been all he wanted. It is tragic that he was denied this.

* * *

Having got to know my sister well over the years, while I am not able say that welcoming her into the family while I was still a teenager would have made me change tack in any way, I *can* say that she'd have been a particular asset to the family. She could have brought about a real opening out of the rather hermetic state in which we all lived. She would have bridged that gap in generations that was particularly wide between my father and his sons. At the very least, she would have been a clear enhancement to a male-biased family group.

But equally, it is too easy to see why it wouldn't have worked – what the pitfalls might have been.

My mother, with her own secret to maintain, her own loss to bear, could not have coped. I feel sure of that. I've already shown that my father seems not to have known of Bea's illegitimate daughter, given up for adoption nine years before the couple married. It would have taken enormous reserves of empathy and understanding for my mother to have sat back and watched him introduce Catrina into the family – *her* family – while harbouring the hurt and regret of her own secret in silence. It is easy to see how impossibly hard that would have been for her, how unbelievably painful a situation it would have put her in. The agony of regret and resentment would have eaten her up. On top of that, the jealousy she would have felt at my father, experiencing the joy of his own reunion, could so easily have soured their relationship, possibly even more so than my mother's thwarting of his dearest wishes.

Judging by her reception of Catrina, after my father's secret *was* out, she never got over the resentment she felt at him getting back in touch with his daughter. How much deeper would that resentment have been if he'd persuaded her it was feasible to bring his three children together? It is clear that the small amount Bea ever did for Catrina, either before or after my father's death, was driven solely by her sense of duty – duty to her husband's wishes, duty to how convention dictated she respond to a relative, and duty to her sons' ultimate acceptance of their half-sister. But duty done through gritted teeth. After my brother and I were in on the secret, the onus was always on us to maintain contact and develop the relationship. Bea had done what she promised my father she would do by putting us in touch. Now all she had to do was make sure, 'for Dad's sake', as she *always* put it, that we stayed in touch.

Perhaps Bea *did* long for her own daughter to somehow reappear. Perhaps she hoped that the change in legislation on adoptive parent searches might bring this about. Maybe she would have felt less resentment towards Catrina if this *had* happened. And even if that longing wasn't rationally clear to her, since she'd have been aware of the difficulties it would have caused her socially, some sort of longing must have been there in a deeply embedded, almost visceral sense. That was surely the driver of her actions and attitudes. Given the internal conflict and deep-seated angst it would have engendered, is it surprising that she was neither warm nor welcoming towards Catrina at any time, either before or after we brothers were in contact with her?

This is pointed up by the way my mother treated Catrina on a later occasion when she was visiting Scotland. A few years after my brother and I had met up with our sister, she had asked Bea if she could stay the night with her in the family home. She was, I presume, hoping she might be able to forge something of a relationship with her father's widow – build bridges where none had existed. But she was also going to use the time to visit my brother and his wife in their small flat nearby.

Shouting the Odds

My mother's behaviour speaks volumes. Rather than offer my sister the spare bedroom – with its more commodious double bed where my wife and I slept on our visits – Catrina was put up in a single bed in my brother's old room. Bea curtly informed her that she preferred her not to use the spare room. Knowing my mother's foibles, this would have been no more that to save on the washing, single sheets taking less effort and smaller quantities of soap powder than doubles. But did she stop to think how Catrina would feel about this? Bea should have realised that this could only be taken as a snub.

My brother and his wife had been invited to come for their evening meal with Catrina. Throughout the meal, Bea repeatedly stated that, as Catrina was 'now part of the family', she was being 'treated to her tea'. This looks less like hospitality than obligation. Little or no attempt to actually welcome Catrina into the family or even to make her feel comfortable. More of a grudging acceptance of what my mother felt was her responsibility, her duty to her late husband, expressed in a clumsy and even alienating manner.

* * *

One possibility – albeit remote – that would have led to the firmest integration of Catrina into our family is worth considering. It is much less likely given the mores of the time, however. But it is the most likely way parents in similar circumstances would approach this in the present day, with its more open and flexible approach to the family as a unit. This approach does take as read my mother's ability to subsume her regrets over losing her own daughter though, and her being able to rise above any resentment. But, to look at it in the most optimistic light, it could have resulted in Bea acquiring that daughter – albeit a step-daughter – she so craved.

When we were quite wee, it could have been sympathetically explained to my brother and me that we had a half-sister living with her mother over in Texas. We could have been told the basic facts of our father's first marriage and divorce, simply and sensitively. We would then have had no reason to view this as anything other than part of our own family set-up. Even although my father had lost touch with Catrina in her infancy, this would have embedded her in his boys' minds as a reality. Although he may have hoped it would happen, he could never be sure of seeing her again. But who knows? Had indirect contact been resumed she might even have taken on, in our imaginations, the qualities of a slightly glamorous, slightly mysterious relative that we could look forward to meeting one day. A large number of our relations lived in distant parts, and were relatively unknown to us. Catrina would have slotted in easily with that aspect of our extended family, both naturally and completely.

Had that been the approach, when she did reappear in my father's life and the two met again after years of separation, we could have shared in our father's excitement. On her return visit in '68, it would merely have been a case of telling us that we were having a visit by our half-sister from the States. The whole situation would have fallen into place with ease. I truly believe so. And when Catrina came back to the UK for good, she could have visited the family with whatever regularity circumstances, and growing affection, allowed.

In an ideal world, at any rate.

It *was* the '60s, after all. And in that ideal-seeking world we, as boys, might have regarded the whole thing as special, a privilege we had received. We would have been favoured in the eyes of our friends with the kudos of a Stateside sister – our own Yank in the family. We would have had a girl for a sibling, relieving the family's male bias. And we would have had all the attendant benefits of an older sibling into the bargain.

All possibilities. But possibilities in an ideal world…

16

Too Late Now

EVER COMPETITIVE, MY mother was delighted to have reached her eighty-third birthday in 1996. But this was not just down to satisfaction at achieving such an impressive age. She had only publicly admitted her actual age when she got to eighty. As long as I can remember, she had trusted that her appearance and her level of fitness would convince everyone that she was considerably younger. She was right in that. Judging by the incredulous reaction she received on revealing her true age to her golfing friends, they had never thought her to be anywhere near eighty.

No, her delight at making eighty-three seemed to have its basis entirely in her individual competitive streak. She had now beaten her own mother. Grandma had only made it to eighty-two. What an extraordinary attitude to take to growing older. But then Bea had been a competitor all her life. (Though the older I get myself, the easier it is to see her point of view. As I work on this book, I am conscious of how close I am to my father's final birthday. I have to admit that I look forward to overtaking him in the race of years.)

Since her early twenties, Bea had held down, for a woman in that era, a series of relatively prestigious jobs. She had only given up work to get married in her late thirties. But this was the way of things in the 1950s. Wives were expected to keep house and be kept in turn by their husband's earnings. To have done otherwise would have been *most* unusual for the time, at least for the middle classes. It would have been to diminish, even degrade my father as the 'head of the household' and the family's breadwinner.

Before her marriage Bea had taken part in virtually every sport available – to females, that is. Golf, swimming, tennis, badminton, skating, riding, hiking: she had succeeded at them all. That energy had to go somewhere.

Once married, she threw herself into household management and domestic organisation. Shopping, cooking, baking, cleaning, washing, ironing, sewing, knitting: she succeeded at them all. Managing a limited and constraining household budget, she was still able to make sacrifices. Somehow she managed to free up enough money to send her sons to – as she saw it – a socially enhancing and prestigious fee-paying school. Seven years into her marriage, the couple were able to afford the mortgage on a substantial stone-built, terraced house in a leafy suburban street. They were going up in the world – that was her plan. She would never have to look back.

Widowed in her sixties, she maintained her independence. She was still winning golf competitions on an extremely hilly course – against all comers of any age – well into her seventies. Disdaining trolleys, she carried her own packed golf bag over that same course until ill health drove her from the fairways.

Habitually referring to the friends with whom she played golf as 'the girls', my mother was desperately trying to hold on to her lost youth. The glamour she had kept into her forties and even her fifties was rapidly fading. Never off the golf course, her complexion was plagued by the 'high colour' induced by frequent exposure to the east coast elements, as well as by the natural ageing process. She felt the need to resort to face creams and heavy make-up to disguise what she conceived of as a deficiency. She was never able to accept that this was an inevitable result of growing older and spending hours out-of-doors in almost all weathers. Her blonde Barbara Stanwyck hairstyle was long gone, replaced by a crisp straw-coloured perm. But she wasn't to be outdone.

Throughout her marriage, my mother was always determined to be young at heart and up-to-the-minute in all things. She was a founder member of the Young Mothers group attached to her church and continued to play a part in that – at least as long as my brother and I could still be classed as children – despite the fact that she was into her fifties by then. She was a keen keep-fit enthusiast and, when we took our family summer holidays on the west coast, strode out resolutely on long walks and swam in the sea almost daily. Never liking pools, particularly heated ones, she used to enthuse about the 'glow' of a cold-water swim – a sensation I reckoned to be little more than the onset of hypothermia. Loving dancing, she did her best to keep up with the latest dance crazes as long as she was able, even winning a prize at a clubhouse social to add to those she had won on the course.

Why You Won the First Prize for The Twist

You'd barely dropped the '40s style,
that Barbara Stanwyck look you loved,
when in the '60s raged in all the brashness of their youth.

Bemused, you soon caught on, got with it,
went for trouser suits and flares, from bangs to perms,
peroxide in your urge to fight it,

age – the only snag. But *you* knew
that the beat goes on. Next summer at the golf club hop,
that Chubby Checker hit, and you were *it*.

They couldn't keep you in your seat
as one more dance craze proved you'd kept your youth.
Twisting with the best of them, you took the prize.

What was it? Did you ever say?
Truth is, it was the way you wore your years;
your grip strong on each iron, every wood; on being you:

that someone always called a girl – who lived it too.

Still harking back to the terminology of previous eras, she was as determined to be 'with it' as she had previously been to be 'in vogue' or just 'the tops'.

The trouble was, her idea of this was as out-dated as her vocabulary. Like her growing pile of still-to-be-read newspapers, her fashions always seemed to be a good while out of date. Happiest latterly in sports gear, at least since turning seventy, she would step out in violently coloured jumpers, tweed-effect crimplene slacks and golf caps of every variety, wearing these on almost every outing as well as on the course. But her style gelled with those of her friends 'the girls' – and she still felt one of the crowd right up until ill health took hold of her.

These friends, though, were little more than acquaintances. They were partners with whom to play a round of golf or to have a coffee with up at the clubhouse. That was all. Bea had never been regularly sociable in the way of inviting friends round to the house, and since my father's death, fewer and fewer visitors were there to engage her. I still wonder if that confining of her social life to outwith the family home was another symptom of her fear that the various secrets of the past might come out. She had long ago lost any regular contact with her best friend, my 'Aunty' Joan and, barring Christmas cards, was not in touch with more than a handful of correspondents. She had continued to keep up with relatives but, with most of her generation passed away, Bea was increasingly lonely.

She was also out of sorts with the modern world. This she saw rapidly running away from her. I had tried to keep her 'up to speed' with changes, but I fear this was a fruitless task. At one point I bought her a radio/cassette player to listen to tapes of her favourites from the past – but it was only the radio part she used. The recordings I made for her – Fred Astaire, Jack Hylton, Al Bowlly and the like – were all unplayed, as I discovered after she died. She had never so much as broached the cassette deck. Perhaps it was the preponderance of the Sony Walkman that put her off. She railed about people's inability to be separated from their music and couldn't understand why the streets were full of listeners on the hoof, all ear-pieced up. More likely, she was just unfamiliar with the technology and a bit baffled by it (a trait I myself am increasingly prey to). She would never countenance getting a mobile phone – not even for emergencies – and I did repeatedly try to persuade her that this would be a sensible precaution. It took her ages to accept that a remote control for her telly was a good idea. Only as she got more infirm towards the end of her life, did she grasp the benefits. Previously, she'd seen a remote as promoting idleness. She was right in that, of course.

Despite being taught to drive by Gilbert in the late '50s, and using the car independently for ten years or so when we were boys, she abandoned driving as soon as my brother and I had passed our tests. It was the move from column shift gear changes to stick shifts that threw her, I think. She never got used to those. When our father died, it would have made all the difference to her if she'd been an independent driver, but she was adamant she couldn't go back to it.

'It's too late now,' was all she ever said.

My mother did manage a few independent holidays after my father's death. Pairing up with a cousin, she was able to join other relations for a fortnight on the Hebridean island of Iona for a number of years. Ultimately she found this frustrating. The cousin in question, though younger than Bea, was nowhere near as fit. On walks, Bea would be constantly frustrated at not being able to keep to the long-striding pace to which she was accustomed. But she felt she couldn't leave this cousin behind and forge off on her own. Even if she'd wanted to do so. She was of the generation where women never did things singly. We had also tried to persuade her to holiday on her own. None of the cruises or tours specifically aimed at older singles ever seemed to appeal to her. Even the small-scale cruise we suggested, round the Highland west coast she so loved, failed to catch her interest. But it wasn't the locations. It was the idea of holidaying solo that put her off.

'What on earth would I *do* on my own?' she'd always ask.

'You'd be bound to meet people,' I would reply, 'you're such a great talker. You're never stuck for something to say.'

'But people are always in couples – I'd just get in the way,' she would respond, always having an answer to every suggestion.

It was no good. I couldn't sway her.

But she still had her golf. She still had her 'girls' to socialise with, to compete with, to best if she was able. She could still cut a figure on the course – one of Edinburgh's steepest and most challenging. As long as she had that, she was relatively content.

* * *

Despite her competitive rejoicing at making eighty-four, by then Bea was far from happy. Her health had been robust throughout her life. She had suffered from only one bout of serious illness I can remember from my childhood and was always the one to minister to other sick members of the family. But things were starting to go wrong. She couldn't rely on staying fit any more.

By eighty-four, she was not in a very good state. A series of ulcers on her legs had finally prevented her from playing her beloved game – virtually her *raison d'être* – and she was becoming morose, even morbid. This was the frame of mind that prompted my poem 'Clearance'. Such a mood tended to lead Bea to talk about her own approaching death. Not my favourite subject, and one I would try to deflect her from whenever I could. But, despite my efforts at changing the subject, she would return to it almost as a default setting. During one such conversation, I tried to cheer her up by flippantly suggesting that she had nothing to worry about in the afterlife.

'St Peter's just going to fling the pearly gates open wide,' I joked, 'and welcome you with open arms.'

Her brow clouded at this remark and she looked me straight in the eyes. For a person with genuine religious convictions and an almost literal form of belief, what she said next was chilling.

'I have done some really terrible things in my life,' she told me in all seriousness, insisting that she wouldn't be welcomed into heaven at all.

How does one face such a statement? If I'd had more faith myself, perhaps I would have offered to pray for her. Instead, I only remember laughing it off. Trying to cheer her up, I resorted to further light-hearted and fatuous quips. At any rate, nothing more was said on the matter. My mother never enlightened me as to what these 'terrible things' might have been. Though, of course, I had my own suspicions.

At the time, I thought she had been referring to her resistance to my father's wish to bring his first-born daughter together with his sons. I imagined Bea was feeling guilty about her intransigence in this matter. Maybe beginning to regret how she had managed to stand in the way of Gilbert's dearest wish until it was too late for him. This was undoubtedly on her conscience. After my mother died, I discovered that, in her final years, she had written to Catrina to apologise for her actions and express her regret that Gilbert's wishes had only been honoured after his death. Clearly a guilty conscience.

But now I wonder. Was she attempting to set the scene for some sort of confession? A life-long member of the Church of Scotland, she was not of a denomination that regarded confession as central, even particularly important. To the Presbyterian, faith is largely a lonely covenant with God. While much church-going was – indeed still is – a matter of living the conventional life and of maintaining standards, my mother was more heavily committed than that. She would even, on occasion, request advice from her minister on doctrinal matters. I have never forgiven the man for his crass insensitivity in coldly informing her, when she asked about some relatives' children, that unbaptized babies were inevitably destined to be excluded from heaven. She accepted that pronouncement at face value and, repellent though the notion is, never thought to question it. All the core beliefs were givens for Bea. She took communion regularly and attended the Sunday services close to weekly. While there was undoubtedly a socialising aspect to her church attendance, she nevertheless always had a feeling she had 'let the side down' when she missed even a single week.

So, in her raising the question of those 'terrible things' she felt she had done, might my mother have been gearing up to confess the secret of her own first-born daughter? Was she attempting to enlighten me about the context in which she had found it impossible to accede to my father's wishes? To find a way for me to understand her attitude to my father's first family? It would certainly have had that effect. It was only after discovering my mother's secret that I gained any real understanding of why she had thwarted my father's longed-for union of all his children. Even if I don't approve of or agree with those reasons, I can at least now see what motivated her. The sheer psychological pressure she must have been under is obvious.

But I am still haunted by her remark. I cannot help wondering what it was she regarded as so terrible. Was this the act of giving birth illegitimately, or of having a sexual relationship – or even several – while unmarried? Both, of course, are against conventional Christian morality. There was no doubt that she was a more convinced Christian in her later years, so these youthful acts may well have been preying on her mind. Or was it the subsequent action of giving her baby up for adoption? Did she regard that as 'terrible', as a dereliction of her duty as a mother? She truly needn't have, as the baby went on to have a happy and secure childhood with her adopted family. At the time, there was a 'genuine and widespread conviction' that illegitimate children would have improved chances in life with adoptive parents. This would ensure, as Jane Robinson points out, that they were 'unencumbered by the stigma and the other unlovely disadvantages of illegitimacy.' So Bea had done what was right, in the circumstances.

But most likely she was simply weighed down by an unspecified burden of guilt attendant on the knot of secrets she had been harbouring for most of her adult life.

The episode, though, is reminiscent of the similar occasion a couple of decades previously when my father had used the loan of his cufflinks to hint at the existence of his first wife. I had failed to follow up on that one too. Perhaps Bea had hoped her bleak remark would prompt my delving further into what she was referring to. Was she seeking a way to unburden herself of the secret she, like Cousin Lil, had carried for so long? The secret so many people had died unable to relive themselves of? If that had been her intention, did my own urge to lighten the mood thoughtlessly deprive her of that opportunity? The incident remains yet another never-to-be-solved mystery.

My father's long incarceration in hospital after his heart attack had given my brother and me the time to say the things that our unemotional, almost repressed, upbringing had prevented us from saying previously. But we had no such opportunity with my mother, something

I'll always regret. Might her hints at serious wrongdoing have been an attempt to spark a response from her son? Was she looking for an expression of love and sympathy, such as I'd given to Gilbert during the last few weeks of his life? I only wish I had been more open to that sympathy and taken her remark more seriously. As with so much else, I'll never know what lay behind it, never know what my mother was reaching for.

Bea died in the early spring of 1998, shortly after her eighty-fifth birthday. Collapsing of a sudden in her sheltered flat, she had summoned an ambulance via the emergency bell. She was rushed into hospital with a ruptured aneurysm. Informed immediately, my brother and I were soon at her bedside. Her descent was rapid. She was in severe pain and was heavily sedated, so it is unlikely that whatever halting words we found at the time would have registered. But again – we'll never know. We *can* hope though.

★ ★ ★

All families have secrets, of one sort or another. That is clear. The revelations after my parents' deaths, and others' accounts of similar experiences, have underlined that. But such secrets need not solely be things hidden from family members, as in my case. They can be that most pernicious sort – the violent husband, the drunken mother, the demented child – where a whole family conspires to keep silence, using guilt as the driving force and emotional blackmail as constraint. Or they can be the sort whose presence is acknowledged, but can never be spoken of – the relative in an asylum, the unmarried parent, the unmentionable terminal disease. But, whatever their nature, the secrets are almost always there, almost always somewhere.

Why should I have expected my own family to be any different? In 1976, the first revelation felt unique. In 1998, after the second, the symmetry seemed to provide a further unique element. The dual discoveries of two half-sisters may well be uncommon, as may their sudden revelations at precisely the same interval after each parent's death. But such secrets, it is clear, are very far from unique. For so long I thought the revelations had stolen the truth of my childhood. I now know they have not. It is still there, just the same. Trying to dismiss these discoveries from my mind was no use. It was actually my attempt to do so that was stealing my childhood. Now that I have told *their* story – the story of these revelations – it has become something separate. Something distinct from that other story – the one of my own family's past as I lived it, experienced it at first hand. That is unchanged. It still remains, still endures.

The abiding image of my boyhood family – of us united and on the move in my father's company car, his rather classy Ford Consul or its later replacement, the Cortina – *has* been somewhat tarnished. But it has neither been destroyed nor fundamentally undermined. The family we were back then, we always will be. Self-contained and comfortable; Gilbert driving while Bea is admiring the view; the 'grown-ups' in the front seats, the boys in the back; the car windows up to preserve my mother's hair-do; the transistor radio playing on the parcel shelf; and us all bowling along on holiday or off to the seaside. The scene I portray in my poem 'Wild Thing'.

We were our own 'human limited company'– to echo Lorna Sage's description of her family in the same period. And, as Sage goes on to say, 'the car…played a part in making us one'. Together we were 'travelling along life's highway, socially mobile, [our] own private enterprise', the Johnstone family firm bound together by mutual support, by mutual investment. In my childhood, it had all seemed so immutable. But really, all I need to recognise – and to accept – is that my own family's private enterprise had that bit more of the private in it than I could have imagined at the time.

* * *

It may appear that I am bitter over the two revelations that so altered my view of my family. I have been so at times, I have to admit, but ultimately I am not. Although the emotions, doubts and resentments I went through on discovering the hidden secrets of my parents' pasts were very real, and still have a certain hold on my imagination, in the end I am glad – grateful, even – for their disclosure. Much loss has been attendant on them but from loss, strangely, often comes gain. And while the anticipated outcomes of each half-sister's contact with her birth parent's family failed to materialise, there has been much gain made from these occurrences – in my case, substantial gain.

For one, there is the connection with my Cousin Lil. She is someone whom I would probably never have met again, let alone got to know, had these family mysteries never been revealed. Our exchange of letters eventually resolved as many of the questions my mother's secret had thrown up as was possible. But the correspondence continued for the rest of her life and resulted in my wife and I making a number of visits to Lil in London in the early part of this century. By the time I got to know her she was in her nineties and living in sheltered housing in South Kensington. The contrast between her circumstances and my mother's was stark. While Bea had in her final year moved to a bright, airy flat with two bedrooms, lounge, kitchen and bathroom, Lil was confined in a single room, little more than a bed-sit, with a small en-suite bathroom and a cupboard containing a kettle and a two-ring Baby Belling cooker. Taking up at least two thirds of the space in this room was her piano – a Bechstein boudoir grand – which she had been bought by her father after she won a prestigious piano competition in her youth. Although by the time we got back in touch with her she was no longer able to play, she felt she could never part with it. Recently rehoused from the flat she had lived in for many years, due to developers refurbishing the building, she had given up the chance of a move to a more commodious, but smaller-roomed flat in order to find space for her beloved piano.

'It has been my life,' she told us, 'and it'll stay with me until the end.' The claustrophobic bed-sit was the only option.

Perched in cages on top of the piano, its polished surface protected by a plastic sheet, were her two companions, a pair of budgies. While they offered Lil her only constant companionship, their droppings, which she relied on her carer to clean up, did lend the room a rather stale air. Housebound since the death of her last close friend a year before our first visit, she relied on these carers for shopping, meals and much else. Most of her time was spent watching the goings-on in the busy side street in which she lived, but she was still mentally agile and read a great deal each day. I was honoured to be able to present her with a copy of my first collection which she was sufficiently taken with to write a response to in some detail, telling me about her own early excursions into writing sonnets.

One of the topics we discussed both in person and by post was my mother's family photographs which I had inherited. On first entering Lil's room I had immediately noticed a hand coloured, 19th century print hanging on her wall. This was, Lil told me, a studio portrait of her grandmother, my great-grandfather's first wife. The picture had caught my eye as I had its companion pieces in my own collection – similarly hand coloured portraits of my great-grandfather in his younger days and his mother, my great-great-grandmother, whose birth takes us back as far as 1815. Since Lil's death, all three portraits have once again been reunited.

That photograph prompted me to ask for Lil's help in identifying a number of individuals who appeared in the old family snaps I had received on my mother's death. Despite much discussion, we never got very far with the identifications. Lil wrote:

> I'm afraid you have me floored this time! I'm sorry but I can't put names to faces I don't know. It's difficult to recognise all the uncles from before I was even born! I suppose I know so little of the Edinburgh relatives because Mother died when I was thirteen and, after that, our regular visits up from Newcastle dwindled. Before then we used to drive up in Dad's car – a grey, open-topped Morris. We were all frozen going over Soutra. If you reached 40mph you were travelling!

Hours were spent looking over these images, which prompted Lil also to tell me about her father's involvement in the Amateur Cinematographers' Association in Newcastle. Having already admired his skill as a still photographer, this other angle on his art didn't surprise me. Although Lil was unable to give me dates, her father's era meant he had been involved in the very early days of film making. Unfortunately, all his film work was lost in air raids during the War, but Lil gave me a bit of background to his – and, she explained – her work in this field.

When we were all members of the Association, Dad's film of a story I wrote for them called 'Beyond the Horizon' was shown at the Annual Public Screening. It was filmed at the tiny fishing village of Cullercoats. It was a beautiful film showing the beauty of the sea in all its moods. The fisher folk were fascinated and lent us the genuine costumes which they wore. The girl who played Kirsty, the fisher girl, was ideal for the part. We had a lot of fun but when war came it was disbanded and, after that, many films were missing which was sad, so much had gone into their making.

Despite not visiting Edinburgh regularly after her thirteenth birthday, Lil was also able to pass on several stories of my mother's family decades back. All of these were new to me. From one story it would seem that my mother's insistence on 'proper English' while I was growing up had not been a concern a couple of generations before. Lil continues:

I would be seven when we first went to our grandmother's big New Year celebrations in the house in Viewforth. I remember her gatherings so vividly. There were no radios for Big Ben to announce midnight then. So, on one occasion, Grandma looked out of the window and remarked, 'It canna be twelve yet – the folk are still walkin' aboot.' Then my uncle's rejoinder, 'Whit dae ye expect them tae be daein'? – lyin' doon?'

Lil lived to a very great age, dying just short of her 102nd birthday in 2011. Although her mind was reasonably sharp until the end, the infrequency of our visits meant that she was increasingly unable to place us. Inevitably age had taken its toll on her memories and my wife and I had slipped back into the blur of the recent past. But I would never forget the dozen or so years we had been in touch, nor all the stories she had been able to tell me about the more distant past.

Similarly, without the revelations I might never have known more than the parents of my own childhood – the apparently conventional, somewhat staid couple of my early years. With the discovery of their secrets, two whole new people have become embedded in my consciousness. A couple who had vivid and eventful lives before meeting, and whose own meeting was by no means straightforward. Of course, rationally, the knowledge that my parents' earlier lives *must* have differed from what I was aware of as a child is self-evident. But the radical difference in the circumstances that have been uncovered is that I would never have known the details of this had the secrets stayed hidden. That is a gain of real value to me. Similarly, the discovery that Gilbert and Bea were two people who had spent their own early years confronting and working through similar feelings and experiences is a gain. Even though it is almost certain that one of them wasn't aware of the losses and anguish the other experienced through illegitimacy and forced adoption, I have been able to bring these stories together and, in a strange way, reconcile them.

In effect I have, through an extraordinary congruity of circumstances, been able to construct my own versions of my parents' memories. Memories that, I like to think, they would have divulged at least some of, had our family been living in the more open climate of recent decades. The upshot is, I have got to know them all the better. I have lived with them both more intensely and more intimately during the writing of this memoir than I have at any time since their deaths – and arguably at any time since my childhood. Uncovering the facts and imagining the detail of their pasts has connected me to them adult to adult in a way both unexpected and unanticipated. They are here with me now as I write the final chapters of this book, as I draw this story to a close.

Stories and more stories. Histories and more histories. These seem to be characteristic of my mother's family. 'History is a string full of knots,' says Jeanette Winterson, 'all you can do is admire it, and maybe knot it up a bit more.' While plenty of knotting has gone on in this story, it is the untying – the following of Ariadne's thread – that I have been exercised by. But I can see now that new knots of a less tangled nature have been made, and they are welcome. Ultimately my family's secrets served to make links and connections, to trace back some of the threads that had previously been so muddled and entwined. I am only too aware that none of this would have happened without the initial revelations, without the path they put me on.

★ ★ ★

I have many things to be grateful to my parents for, not least their example of a long and successful marriage. It is significant that both my brother and I, although married young, have gone on to enjoy lengthy and sustained marriages. We have both been happy and settled with our chosen partners. The upsets and uncoverings of the past have not altered that.

Rather than bitterness, my abiding feeling is one of regret. I bear no grudges against either parent. This memoir is an attempt, in some way, to make up for the fact that I was never able to tell them that. I think no less of either of them for the things in their lives they got caught up in. It was the attitudes of their time, not any inherent malice or mischief, that made them act the way they did. It is these very attitudes, coupled with their cultural background, that prevented, or dissuaded, them from being open with their sons.

The poet and writer Tom Pow, in his book of travels *In Another World*, reports one of the people he meets as speaking very wisely on this. 'You can't compare different times… You can't judge by hearsay, only by your own experience,' he writes. What the speaker Pow quotes is certain of is that experience teaches us all not to pass judgment. 'After all, you can't choose when to live,' he concludes.

How much closer to our parents would we brothers have been, particularly as adults, if we'd been able to show that we valued them no less for these things that were later revealed? How much happiness could we have given to my father, whom we had sorely tried through our fractiousness as teenagers, if we'd been able to share his joy at reconnecting with his daughter? How much relief, both spiritual and emotional, could we have given my mother if we'd been able to welcome her daughter into the family circle? Or at least to reassure

Mum that she was not judged for the acts of her past?

My ultimate sadness is that, effectively, I never knew either parent as a fully rounded whole. Large parts of their lives – parts that made them who they were in later years – were hidden from me. Much has now been revealed, or imagined, but it is still not the same as sharing it at source. While I was growing up, in that superior way of the self-assured – but self-obsessed – adolescent, I would routinely ascribe their actions to motives that bear not the slightest connection to the reality of their situation.

I am saddened that it is all too late. Neither of my parents will ever know that I would have had no less regard for them because of all the things I have discovered since their deaths. I would have understood them more – but I would have loved them no less, for any of it.

17

To Whom it
May Concern

A NNIVERSARIES COME ALONG with the inevitability of tides. Cente-
naries too, but with less frequency. So the date of a parent's 100th
birthday – whether that parent is living or not – is necessarily a notable
one. In June 2007 such a date came round.

On what would have been our father's 100th birthday, my sister
Catrina, my brother and I travelled to Penrith, the town of his birth, to
mark the day. Meeting Catrina at the station was oddly reminiscent of
our first meeting back in 1977. Only this time it was my sister waiting
on the platform, while I was the one looking out for her from the train.

Thirty years had gone by since that tentative first encounter. Now
this celebration was something we could do as a family, its members
genuinely united. We have met up many times over those thirty
years – in London, in Edinburgh, in Fife, in the Lake District – but all
three of us siblings have been together only rarely. As the centenary
approached though, we had agreed that this was something we'd like to
do together – something we'd like to do 'for Dad's sake'. Armed with
the evidence turned up in Catrina's archival research, we bore with us
various birth certificates, testimonials and school leaving certificates. So

furnished, we three mature offspring of the one and same man set off to explore the locations of his early life.

A long unanswered question had been cleared up in the interim. Although I was aware he had been brought up in England, I had never been sure of where precisely our father had been born. This had not particularly worried me, but I was inquisitive nonetheless. He had never specifically said that his birth took place north of the border. But as someone who was definite about being Scottish, this seemed to make sense. I had always wondered though – was this inference for the benefit of us boys, secure in our national identity as we were; or for my mother, always proud of her Aberdonian roots?

An older cousin had cleared up the mystery, if mystery it was, some time ago. Seemingly, in his younger days, my father had been wont to jest about this with his brother, our Uncle Joe. This uncle had been born in Scotland before the family moved to Penrith. But not so Gilbert.

'While I had the good fortune to be conceived in Scotland,' Gilbert used to joke, 'I had the misfortune to be born south of the border.' That same old joshing attitude to England so typical of Scots.

This was not a remark my brother and I had ever heard from him. But perhaps it was one that would have emerged before too long – especially if I had been able to build on the few adult conversations I'd had with my father in the months before he died. Like myself, where he had been conceived seems to have mattered to Dad.

Relying on my recollection of the geography of the town, I steered our party to a narrow street of small, cramped houses beyond the main railway lines. Catrina too had become familiar with Penrith in those intervening thirty years and spotted the name plate at the end of one of the rows of near-identical dwellings. The street was not the most commodious in town. It was easy to see how in the past this would have been, if not a slum, at least a down-at-heel, marginal district. With its red sandstone façades close-packed together on either side of the narrow thoroughfare, it had a dim and oppressive feel.

Before the move to Penrith, Gilbert's father – our grandfather – had been the manager of a grocery business in the Dumfriesshire town of

Annan. On encountering some difficulty of either a professional or family nature – we still do not know which to this day – the family had moved south to start out again. From Gilbert's quip about his conception, this must have been within months of his birth. The imminence of that may well have prompted the desire for a fresh start on the part of his parents.

Having noted the address from Gilbert's birth certificate, we found the actual house easily, along at one end of the street. Two up, two down, with a scullery out the back, this was the very terraced house where our father been born in the first decade of the twentieth century. On the market at the time, it was empty and unfurnished. Gazing at the front door and narrow façade and peering through windows at the cramped rooms, we wondered if, given the nature of their new home, they had come down in the world. The Annan house they had left to move south was a traditional Scottish one-storey cottage, twice as long as it was broad. While modest, it had seemed to be more spacious and was in a bright, open district close to the river.

When the next move came we can't be sure, but it spoke of increased prosperity. Rather than the tiny, cramped house in a desolate street beyond the tracks, Gilbert's second address was on a main road leading into the town centre. Now busy with a constant flow of traffic, it would be a tiresome spot to live in today. But in the 1910s, while the street would have been just as busy, the nature of the traffic would have made it quieter and the house was certainly well placed and prominent. Facing it across the road was a primary school. This was the very Boys' Council School at which Gilbert had been a pupil up to 1920, the year in which he moved on to take his place at the grammar school.

This house backed onto a leafy and spacious Victorian garden square. It was there we were headed next. This was where the family had moved to for a third time. We didn't know precisely when, but their trajectory was evidently upwards. The square was immediately recognisable as the one my brother and I had visited with Dad on our way home from a childhood holiday in the '60s. The handsome, end terrace house they'd occupied still dominated its south-east corner. Also built in Penrith's ubiquitous red sandstone, its three storeys were entered up a flight of steps to a front door with a pair of high sash windows to its right. These commanded a view up one side of the square and across to the tree-lined garden that took up the central space.

It is just up the street from this house that a photograph was taken of my father astride a striking-looking motorbike of the period. Given his lack of the right kit, we cannot be sure if the bike was his own. However, since the photo seems to be a professional enlargement, rather than a snap shot or contact print, it might be the specially posed portrait of a young man with his first independent means of transport. And the shot *is* carefully taken to frame the family home in the background, just over Gilbert's shoulder.

The bike, research has revealed, is a New Imperial with a side-valve engine in the region of 250 to 300cc, powerful enough for the young man my father clearly is. It dates from the middle of the '20s but Gilbert's get-up places the picture in the early '30s. Was this a second-hand motorbike bought with savings from his first post-apprenticeship job – or perhaps with a 'sub' from his parents? A 'flat-tanker', the bike was nearly obsolete. There had been big improvements in design in the late '20s. This meant that 'flat tankers', even though they might have been only a year or two old, were suddenly a decade out of date. Does this mean the bike could have been bought by Gilbert at a more accessible knock-down price? Certainly, in the early '30s, a New Imperial would have been a typical bike for a student or an apprentice.

Was this the very means by which Gilbert was able to take up his first away-from-home job as a salesman, travelling around the local farms? We just don't know. Either way, the photo shows him as a noticeably younger man looking relaxed and confident in the sunny surroundings of the square, a few doors up from his family house. And remarkably – for none of us ever knew him thus – he is clean-shaven and has a full head of hair.

It is difficult to make a good guess at his age, styles for youths and adults being so similar in that period. Where today, on a quick glance, we might suppose this to be someone middle aged, a closer examination would place him in his early twenties, conceivably even a bit younger. Dressed in a smart blazer and grey flannels, his shoes are well polished and there looks to be a watch on his left wrist. A modern touch that, given pocket watches were still the norm. His full head of hair – how long did that last, we wondered – is slicked back with Brylcreem, and his face is smooth and lacking in the moustache that so distinguished him in later life. A young shaver, in every sense.

This must be the young man who, since leaving school several years before this photograph would have been taken, had asked his old head-master for a testimonial and received a measured but positive account. The youth who had been successfully apprenticed to a chemist in the town; the young man who was setting out on a career as a salesman, moving on to a new job. We still have that testimonial letter, which turned up amongst Gilbert's papers after his death, so he must have been proud of the confidence it displays in his abilities.

> To whom it may concern. I have known A.T. Gilbert Johnstone, Penrith, since childhood. He was a pupil at the Penrith Queen Elizabeth Grammar School during the time I was Head Master and I have had many opportunities since then of watching his career & estimating his business abilities. He seems to me to be well equipped for the profession of traveller and I am told he has done very well in his present post. He has good intelligence, a pleasing personality and presence, a sympathetic consideration of other people's wants & can talk well on ordinary affairs. Now that he wishes to go further from home I should like to extend to him my good wishes & recommendation.

As a time-served pharmacist and newly appointed commercial traveller, Gilbert would shortly move out of the family home to take 'digs' in a nearby village. Before long, he would be the young man who wooed Catrina's mother when they met some years later at a dance at Morecambe Bay; the young man who was married from the house we visited next.

★ ★ ★

The three of us siblings moved on to a small village south of Penrith. Passing suburbs and industrial estates that have all grown up since our father's youth, we headed down the old high road. The area is now bisected by the M6, but ours was a pleasant drive out through the rural landscape on the old A road, now a much quieter artery. As the main north-south route in the '30s the road must have been much busier, even in Gilbert's time. The village is basically one long street stretching uphill and round a slight bend. And there we found the house, on the west side of the thoroughfare, its name, which we'd noted from Gilbert's marriage certificate, carved on a plaque set into the wall.

Lining up outside, we had our photographs taken as a threesome, all of us, I'm sure, thinking that this would be the closest we'd ever get to uniting our father with his children. What does one do when looking at a house like this? Try to imagine the long-deceased occupant going in and out of the door, wonder which was his room all that time ago, which view he had from his window? We were all rather lost in such thoughts until we noticed the adjoining barn, and fell to deliberating whether that was where he had kept his motorbike. Very likely, unless he had graduated to a car by the time he moved to the village.

Walking down a lane to the back of the house, we peered over the wall to have a look at the garden. For me, here was further proof of my father's love of the countryside – a definite trait we shared. The outlook from the back garden out over the Lakeland Fells is one I would have happily claimed for myself any day. Lost in my own musings, I stood and gazed at it for a good while.

I had always believed that my own particular love of the country – and my abiding desire to live in a rural setting, as I have done since the early 1970s – was something I had largely come up with myself. Doubtless, I thought, it had been influenced by frequent trips to the countryside as a child, and regular visits to my great-uncle's farm. But standing at the foot of my father's former garden and gazing at that view, I had a sudden realisation that there was more to it.

Long before he became my dad, Gilbert, like me, had lived in the country – here in this village when he first left home and later, when he was married, in the far west of Cumbria. His first adult job had been in the country, travelling round the Lake District farms. All through my childhood he had been as keen as anyone to get out of the city and into the hills, to walk the fields on my uncle's farm or take a drive through rolling landscapes of the Borders or the Highlands.

Was this the origin of my own predilection for rural living? An overlooked and, until now, unacknowledged legacy from Dad.

A MILE IN YOUR SHOES

They're going nowhere anymore,
this pair of crepe-soled brogues
that took you to the countryside
and hills, that saw you to the day
when you retired from the clutch

and hit the brake. So now I try
to walk a mile in your shoes, but
they don't fit, won't even settle
round my feet as they did yours,
a size or more beyond my own,

which cannot get them off, loose
laces that have bound them fast
to what was left to you beyond
the job. The days off, weekends,
the holidays and family jaunts,

the casual days that these soles,
wearing thin, have weathered,
but, un-welted and impossible
to stitch are, the cobbler tells me,
too far gone to ever put to rights.

Thanks to Catrina's research, my brother and I have filled in so many gaps in what we knew of our father's life. We had only the vaguest notions of his family's origins in Annan. For years this had forced us to thole depressingly repetitive jocular remarks from friends of our parents who seemed unable to stop chortling about us Johnstones being descended from border sheep rustlers – a joshing we felt as city boys we didn't warrant, despite the jokes being grounded in historical fact. We had known of the family's move to Penrith, but were not aware of the two earlier houses there, nor of Gilbert's later house in the village. Had Dad not driven the family south to visit our aunt, it's likely that he would never have taken the time to drive to Penrith to show his sons his final family home. And, aware of what it might have given away of his first marriage, there would have been little or no prospect of him ever taking us to see his house in the outlying village. So, while that brief childhood look at his Penrith home had stuck in my memory, I had had no notion that my father had lived in the countryside directly after leaving his family in his youth. Nor that my own preference for country living might well be due to his influence, might even be some sort of inheritance. This fact was a particular pleasure to turn up – another late confirmation of something we had in common.

* * *

I had been in my very early teens that sole time we had visited Penrith as a family. Being so young, I was not particularly curious about other aspects of my father's early life. But I never forgot that visit. We had stopped off on the way home from staying with our aunt in Gloucestershire. Dad had steered us through a maze of streets to the square where the family house stood. We saw where he had lived in his youth – he was manifestly keen to let us see his family home – but that was all. From what I know now, I realise my mother must have been all of a jitter as to what might accidentally have come out. There would have been no question of visiting the house from where our father had married his first wife. It is conceivable that Gilbert sprang the Penrith visit on Bea without first discussing the idea. I can't see her being at all keen on it. And I don't have any memory of her engaging with him in his enthusiasm to connect his boys with even this one small piece of his younger days. I don't even think we got out of the car. My memory is of a quick drive round the square and then we were back on the road north again.

My father was a grammar school boy and had done well enough for himself, given his background. I can dimly remember him wearing a blazer with an old college badge on the breast pocket but not, as far as I can recall, an old school tie – its lack thereof being something of an impediment to his success later on in class-bound Edinburgh, a fact I'm sure my mother was highly conscious of. Scotland's capital has always boasted an abundance of fee-paying public schools, each with its own fixed place in a rigid hierarchy. With that in mind, my mother was always very keen to stress that my father had attended a 'proper' school – Queen Elizabeth *Grammar* School, as she always referred to it in full – a 'proper' education being the making of a man, in her view.

On our own centenary trip to Penrith in 2007, we were keen to visit that same school. The staff couldn't have been more helpful. We found my father's name in various registers and other attendance records. But no school photographs to bulk him out as a boy. Taking the time to rake in old store cupboards for ledgers and file boxes that hadn't been touched for an age, the teachers helped us to build up a picture of this particular 1920s schoolboy.

There he was, duly noted: a good pupil; excellent attendances; no black marks that anyone could find. And his brother too, our Uncle Joe, similarly positively recorded. There they both were, marked on the rolls, names with ticks and crosses beside them, their attendance logged, their progress marked. It is still a regret that the staff couldn't locate any class photos including our future father. But despite that, thirty years from his death, Gilbert was putting on flesh new to all of us who had never seen a single image of him as a boy.

Leaving the grammar school in 1924, he'd gone from there to be apprenticed to a local chemist. From his attainments in that first job he went on to deal in agricultural pharmaceuticals, travelling round the farms and smallholdings of Cumberland and Westmorland. More evidence of his love of the country. I still have an odd selection of sepia photographs found amongst his belongings that I saved from the bin. No-one could see any value in them, but they struck a chord with me. They are of prize bulls, fat rams and farmers on horseback that must date from this time. It's easy to imagine the bluff country tenants proudly presenting the young salesman with mementoes of their latest champion beasts as he headed off to the next farm on his New Imperial motorbike.

★ ★ ★

Another centenary has crept up on us since then. This, though, was one we were unable to mark with a reunion of brothers and half-sister. By the time March 2013 came round, and we reached the date that would have been my mother's 100th birthday, I had lost all contact with Maria. Her final letter had arrived over ten years previously. Our correspondence, she explained, had been too much for her and she preferred to let it lapse. So my brother and I alone travelled to Aberdeen on a cold spring day that year. We were there to trace Bea's early life in the city where her family had lived until the mid-1920s.

As we had done with Gilbert, we visited the houses where her family had stayed – the terraced house in which she had been born and the impressive granite villa her family had moved to in her infancy. All of the same musings we had indulged in at Penrith took place once again. Our thoughts were of the century-old inhabitants of the houses – where their bedrooms were, which windows they had gazed out of, which rooms they had used for what – how they had lived in their homes. Photos were taken in front of each dwelling and the quirks of the places were noted and discussed. Again we went round to the rear of each house to see what we could see of the gardens and drying greens and what would have been the servants' entrances. We wandered down those Aberdeen back lanes that Bea had often reminisced about, where she had played chasing games with her friends and climbed trees with her brother, from where she had strolled out to the then-nearby countryside.

This being Bea's family, of course, we had period photographs aplenty. One series of these was particularly characterful. Taken by Cousin Lil's father, my grandfather's cousin, who was such an accomplished amateur, it showed in sequence a back garden race between the children. My youngest uncle seemed to be a babe in arms – at least there *was* a baby in the pictures – but the other three children, Bea, her elder brother and her sister were lined up in the first shot ready to race down the lawn. Well wrapped up against the east coast chill, the trio are accompanied by their favourite toys – a puppy dog on wheels, a stuffed duck at the end of a ribbon and what looks like a furry toy panda. The rest of the sequence shows my grand-mother giving starter's orders, the children toddling down the grass and my infant uncle, serious in flat cap and buttoned-up overcoat, winning the race. An unidentified woman, presumably the live-in maid, cradles the youngest uncle in her arms. Peering over the back gate, we were able to identify the boundary wall and the outhouse that appear in the snaps of that long gone infant race and imagine the whole scene taking place.

This was the house from which, a year or two after these photo-graphs had been taken, Bea – or Beattie as she was then known by her family – had first attended school. Born the year before the start of a war – the Great War in this instance – she had her first experience of education in the final months of that conflict. Amongst the many stories she told over the years was a tale that captured what must have been one of her earliest memories – her own infant encounter with Armistice Day in 1918.

Too young to know what was going on, she must have been puzzled when the teacher in her infant class announced that victory was won and that peace had been declared. But doubtless, the immediate award of a buckshee half-holiday would have convinced her that this was a special day, as would the rejoicings of the older more aware pupils and the crowds in the streets.

'I rushed home at lunchtime all excited,' she had told me, 'and dashed into the house, probably making a great deal of noise.'

The family maid had come out of the kitchen to see what was going on but, before she could quieten the five-year-old Beattie down, her father's study door swung open and he emerged, glaring at her, his work disturbed by her chattering.

'What *are* you doing home so soon? Why are you not still in school?' he had demanded, whereupon the poor child had burst into tears.

'He'd have been bound to have heard about the armistice, which took place at 11 o'clock,' Mum told me, 'but he'd have had no way of knowing that my school had given us all a half-holiday. He must have thought I was playing truant or had been sent home for some misdemeanour.'

An easy conclusion to jump to in the circumstances.

'So that's why I'll always remember the end of the first war,' she added.

Taking our leave at the front of that same house, I took a final glance at the door through which my mother had run near to a century before, excited to have an unexpected half-day off school, on an Armistice Day whose import she could never have imagined. Proclaimed as the 'war to end all wars', it had, in fact, set up the conditions for an even greater conflict whose actuality would impinge on Bea's life in ways she could also never have imagined.

★ ★ ★

For the thirty years and more since my father's death, I have lived in the country – first in villages, then in various isolated cottages. Embarking on this rural life when I got married seemed entirely natural. For as long as I can remember, I had wanted to live in the countryside. While at university, visiting various student friends' isolated Fife cottages had only served to reinforce this. In addition, my wife had been brought up in a remote part of the Scottish Borders, and hadn't taken well to her brief sojourn in the city as a student. I have had enormous pleasure from country life ever since. But, although I was always conscious of my mother's enthusiasm for beautiful scenery and dramatic views, I had never previously considered the part my father had played in setting my preference for a rural life.

All of our family holidays were, as convention demanded, taken at the seaside. But from the later '50s on, they were also taken in genuinely rural surroundings. The seaside towns of North Berwick and Elie on the Firth of Forth, and a brief foray to Alnmouth in Northumberland, were abandoned for more rural spots. My mother loved landscape, particularly the grandeur of the Highlands, but she never really considered the countryside as a place of work. She would complain bitterly if anything of a workaday nature got in the way of her beloved views. Oil rig yards were a particular bugbear of hers as were new roads cut through the moorland and woods.

'How could they bear to do that to beautiful Loch Kishorn?' she asked on one later trip, ignoring the obviously increased employment the fabrication yard had brought to the area. In her view, landscape came first.

'Why on earth did they spoil the old passing place road,' she complained as we drove along a new section of carriageway heading for Mallaig. She seemed oblivious to the locals' need to get around at greater speed and not be held up by gawping tourists. For Bea, the picturesque trumped everything.

On holiday she would even object to the noise farmers made early in the morning, complaining that it spoiled her 'beauty sleep', although this was in a more jocular tone. Thinking back, however, my father seemed much more attuned to work on the land and to the country as a working environment. Although these distinctions were never really apparent to me as a child, Gilbert's much more 'hands on' approach is evident to me now.

The first of our countryside holidays in 1959 took us to stay on a dairy farm on the Mull of Kintyre. Dad was in his element. And so were we two boys: roaming about the farmyard, playing on the hay bales in the barn, 'helping' the farmer bring in the cows, 'helping' his wife collect the eggs. Even the sight of a chicken being chased round the farmyard and rigorously strangled to be cooked for our tea failed to put us off this country life.

The beach was still part of it, but more often we'd set up for the day by a moorland burn and splash about in the pools. With Dad wellied up, and we two in our plastic sandals, we'd wade through the shallows fishing for minnows like three lads together. From then on the countryside became an annual feature of our holidays. Cornwall, Wester

Ross, Arran – in all but the latter we stayed on working farms, and in all we stayed in the country.

Throughout my childhood, the one set of relatives we did visit regularly as a family was my mother's aunt and uncle. They lived on the edge of the small village of Carlops, a dozen or so miles south of the city. Our great-uncle was a farmer running a small mixed unit on the edge of the Pentland Hills. He was probably not unlike the characters my father would have been doing business with back in the '30s. Although he retired before I got into double figures, he was still working the land when I was a young boy. Because of this, despite being city-raised, I have early memories of riding on top of a loaded hay cart, running with a pack of deer hounds in the hills and taking a turn on the back of the farm carthorse or on my uncle's hunter.

What all that gave me was an abiding affection for the countryside. But, while I still share my mother's love of landscape, I feel I am sufficiently aware that there is more to rural life than scenery.

I now realise my draw to the country was more down to my father's desire to get out onto the land and round the farm – hence the regularity of our visits – and to my old aunt and uncle for giving me the freedom of the fields and encouraging me to 'muck in'. For that I am especially grateful.

18

Anything like a Story

ONE SUMMER, AT the start of the second decade of the new century, I was back in Cumbria visiting my sister. She had a new base to which she made regular visits north, reconnecting with her past. I would join her there and together we would walk the landscapes of her childhood.

Some years before this, at the cusp of the millennium, Catrina had got married. A surprise to me since I had thought of her as a lifelong singleton, but it was a good move. The man she married is both understanding and open-hearted. Untroubled by the confusion of her family background, he is welcoming to my brother and myself. By a strange coincidence – synchronicity, almost – her husband is deeply attached to the north west of England and to the beautiful, old schoolhouse he owns in a farming village deep in the Westmorland Fells. It is thus that Catrina has acquired a base in the area, one that is not too far from our father's birthplace of Penrith and close enough to the village of her childhood in the western Lakes to enable frequent trips over there. In fact, her husband's connection with that part of the country has become an important link for my sister and me. Although not quite the Lake District, it is close to it. This special place, familiar and cherished, has given her a sense of homecoming, of completion even. Despite having lived in central London since returning to Britain, she never lost her love of the Lake District. She has always looked back on her early childhood there with fondness. It was her own rural idyll.

On this visit, as with others, my wife and I would spend the weekend socialising with my sister and my new brother-in-law. Each time we stayed, we would go walking in the hills, set off to explore the country houses in the area and make frequent visits to the village pubs. Each evening we would indulge in good craic around the table and by the fireside. Over the years we have spent days wandering the lanes, tramping the hill paths and following the becks up into the high pastures. On these walks I have got to know my sister better than ever before. We have had long conversations, as rambling as our routes, and talked out many of the family questions that have been a significant, if ultimately surmountable, barrier between us.

It was on one particular visit that I first showed my sister the manuscript of this memoir, so much of which concerns her. Sitting by the windows of the old schoolhouse, overlooking the beck that rushes by, we went through the text together, ironing out any misnomers or inconsistencies in our recollections. One of my sister's previous jobs being in publishing and editing, her help in honing the text was invaluable. But it was working through the twists and turns in the labyrinth of stories in this narrative that was a real boon. Like our many long walks, that too brought us closer together, gave us more insight into each other's feelings. We understand each other better now, we both agree. And we have each created our own picture of our father – and in particular, of his early life – in our own imaginations.

In writing of one's personal past the chief necessity is to remember. Despite widely held preconceptions, it is *not* to replay. Studies of memory tell us that our recollections in no way consist of the popularly supposed series of images ready for a press of the 'play' button – far from it. Current knowledge indicates that each instance of remembering is a new construction, a coming together of disparate elements from the recesses of the brain. It is an actual 're-member-ing' of each individual recollection – a reattaching of arms and legs, ears and eyes to create a fully embodied memory that can shift for itself. While that is not the etymological origin of the word, it is both a useful and – in itself – striking image with which to visualise its true meaning, its actual utility.

But writing this memoir has involved much more than recollection. I have worked through many other examples of the genre and read a wide variety of books dealing with the background to the concerns I am writing about. One of those to influence me most profoundly was Charles Fernyhough's study of memory *Pieces of Light*. In that book he quotes Salman Rushdie as stating that 'memory has its own special kind of truth' and goes on to suggest himself that, as 'natural storytellers', all of us 'engage in acts of fiction-making' each time we relate a bit of our own personal history. As our understanding and our emotional responses develop with age or with changing circumstances – as mine have in this narrative – so we perpetually edit and remould that supposedly immalleable history. We might well be making 'fictions, but they are *our* fictions and we should treasure them', Fernyhough says. 'Stories are special. Sometimes they can even be true'.

★ ★ ★

On an earlier visit to the Cumbrian schoolhouse, not long after my sister had been married, I was still harbouring one crucial part of the story told in this memoir of which Catrina was not at all aware. This was one crucial element of the 're-member-ing' that I believed was necessary for us both to assemble together. I was conscious that this was the final step I had to take with my sister in remoulding this story. That doing so was the one last exit from the maze of secrets I had long navigated.

A drive over to visit her childhood home has been something we have done together on a number of occasions. It is a place I love to go to as it further emphasises my father's love of country life and further brings his early years alive for me. This is a feeling always heightened by the presence of my sister. The village, in a remote vale over towards the western coast of Cumbria, is the sort of place I could happily live in myself. Still quiet and unhurried in the twenty-first century, it must have been an idyll indeed to a child in the early '40s. Together, my sister and I have walked all round the village, seen her many childhood haunts, visited the few local sights and soaked up the tranquillity of this forgotten corner of the Lake District. These visits have given me a real feeling for the rural upbringing my sister experienced as a very young child. Previously, she had been very much a city person in my eyes. Now that we have taken the time to make these trips and literally 'see where she is coming from', so much more has fallen into place.

On that one particular trip to the village, Catrina took me to see the house where she had stayed when she first returned to the area in the 1960s. This was the home of the couple, now long dead, whom she had thought of as her 'adopted grandparents'. She had often spoken of this couple and how they had cared for her and cherished her. But never before had she pointed out to me the house they had lived in. Knowing how very fond I was of my grandmother – the only grandparent I ever knew – I can almost share with my sister the fondness she had for these people, feel involved in her recollections of the one couple whose love for her made them nearest to being her grandparents.

Catrina has many such memories. She has often told me how her early childhood was enriched by the elderly residents of the village. This struck a chord right away. As a young boy I too was drawn to the company of the old folks in our neighbourhood. Walking down the village street, Catrina described the often indulgent attention she received from what would have been, due to the wartime call-up, a preponderance of the older generation.

'They taught me games and told me stories,' she said. 'They taught me all the names of the wildflowers.'

And they had shown her the special places where they grew in profusion on the hillsides and in the verges, where they still grow to this day.

One elderly friend was a cobbler who worked in the loft of a nearby barn, reached by the rickety ladder Catrina would clamber up to visit him. She remembered the little wooden clogs with their blue leather uppers that he had made for her and presented to her one birthday. Another such friend was the postmistress. The village post office had been almost next door to the cottage she had shared with her mother. There she had been given a privileged task. This was the job of dropping a blob of hot sealing wax onto the knots in the string that bound the parcels, helping her friend the postmistress to ready them for dispatch.

Her other friends were the village children, of her own age and older. In those days of little mechanisation on farms, there were plenty. Together they roamed the fells in freedom and played about the village streets. The children flourished, in spite of it being wartime. All were taught together in the village school, and all knew each other. Despite the remoteness of the area, they were well tutored and mixed well. Reaching school age in 1945, Catrina spent just a single year in the school as the War drew to a close.

'That gave me a head start,' she told me. But at the time she wasn't to know how.

'When I got to Canada I was able to skip first grade,' she explained. 'But that first year of school was a happy start to my life, which I never forgot.'

★ ★ ★

There were four of us visiting the village that day in the early 2000s – my sister and I, her husband, my wife. But, if I was to be true to my feelings at the time, there was a fifth presence – that of my mother.

Bea, who had set up so many barriers to Catrina's hopes and desires, but who had been a loving mother to me after her own fashion, still had a hold on us all. That final element in her story had to be told. I could no longer harbour it as a secret, nor did I want to. Nor did I want to lose the image of Bea that I had held in my mind almost since my childhood – and which, since her recent death, I had held on to all the more firmly. The glamour and vivacity I seem to have been able to recognise behind the façade of a highly conventional housewife was the image that was increasingly uppermost in my thoughts. The secrets she had kept all her life and that, but for unforeseen circumstances, would have gone with her to her grave had almost become part of that glamour – the sharp edge to the mirror, the dark side of the glass.

Double Exposure

CASE

A gilded-steel cigarette case, bright years later,
like the burnished square on the lid where
someone could have etched your name.

Snap it open and the spring is still keen, fresh
as a clicked finger. The bands of elastic though,
sagging with age, are each overburdened by use.

Even now the faint whiff of tobacco lingers
held in this space as empty as lack of employ,
as lack of consumer. Your fingers flickered here.

Enough room for a pack of Kensitas (coupons
religiously saved) to tuck below a band. The case
slipped into a clutch bag and you're ready for a do.

Later depleted, it would return. Some offered
round the company. A few elegantly inhaled
where all of you were sitting, at a table, by a bar.

It's the end of another night out, you're gone
but the print of your grip in lipstick's red
clings to the tip of a filter, just stubbed out.

That grip was still there, still holding on to an aspect of my connection
to my sister. What *I* was now aware of had gone a long way towards
explaining my mother's actions. Even if it hadn't excused them, at least
it had clarified their background, their origin.

It was crucial that Catrina be aware of this aspect of Bea's situation – one
that had surely coloured her thinking as regards Catrina herself – the last gasp
of my mother's hold on our story. Such knowledge would, I hoped, place

Bea's actions in context and allow Catrina, if not to accept them, at least to understand their motivation. Without that I knew, that as my mother's son, I would always have an obstacle to overcome in receiving my sister *as* my sister. That there would always be some sense of duty behind our connection, some tension in our relationship. For the welcoming sibling rapport I aspired to, this last secret had to be out in the open.

We were standing on the bank of the beck that ran by the village, opposite the cottage of Catrina's long dead 'borrowed' grandparents. We all took a while to gaze back at the house of this couple who had meant so much to her as a girl. We listened as she talked about what she remembered of its former occupants.

'They were empire builders of the old sort,' Catrina explained, 'spending forty years in northern Nigeria. They had only retired to the village in 1939, just before I was born.'

Throughout Catrina's time on the other side of the Atlantic, this couple's Christmas letters had kept her in touch with life in the village. The simple cottage they had lived in had such basic plumbing that it was considerably less convenient than what they had been used to in colonial Africa. But both of them, she told us, had lived well into their nineties, long enough to welcome her back to the village in 1966. And, two years later, when she was at last reunited with her father, Gilbert and Catrina had driven together to the village where they had lived as father and daughter. There they had called unannounced on her 'adopted grandparents'. The couple had always regretted the break-up of Gilbert's first marriage. They were exultant to see that at last father and daughter were together again. As Catrina says:

When I first returned to the village in my middle twenties, they welcomed me and made me feel like their own grandchild, and when Daddy and I turned up on their doorstep at the end of our emotional reunion a couple of years later they took me in and put me back together again. They had been very fond of him and were thrilled to see us together.

'Their story is over now,' my sister said. 'They were two of the dearest friends of my childhood. But they live on in all I remember of that time.'

Slowly we moved off. A walk in the fields beyond the village would fix all of this in our minds, we thought.

At the same time, I was wondering, 'Is this the time I've been waiting for? Is this the time for that final piece in the story of my own family and its knot of secrets?'

I had waited years for that; allowing the facts to bed down in my mind; waiting for the most sympathetic moment. I needed to let my sister in on what I felt lay behind all the bitterness and hostility with which she had been treated by my mother. I needed to guide her round the last corner in the maze, past the final secret in a long litany of deceptions and half-truths.

We had just been contemplating the house of those who had meant so much to Catrina in her childhood – as my mother meant so much to me in mine. My incomprehension at the way Mum had behaved had never diminished that. Walking that day by the beck, I felt at last that the moment was right.

Tentatively, I launched into a story of my own. It contained a revelation Catrina had had no hint of whatsoever. It was one that I had felt for some time she ought to hear about – one I hoped might explain some of the things both of us had been mulling over, often uncomfortably, since we first met. One that I had been swithering about revealing for years.

'This isn't some earth-shattering secret I've been holding close to my chest for fear of its impact,' I explained.

Catrina looked not so much concerned, as wary.

'It's information I only discovered in the last few years – only since Mum died,' I added. 'I've just been waiting for a good opportunity to pass it on.'

Slowly I began to explain to Catrina about my mother's illegitimate daughter – the baby born just one year after she was born herself. About the pressure my mother had been under to give the baby up for adoption; the anguish that would have caused her. About the secret my mother had kept all her life; about how she had intended it would die with her. And about my shock at the way it was revealed to me.

Of course, my mother's daughter Maria is neither connected with

Catrina nor related to her in any way. But her existence, and the way that was hidden from me until after Bea's death, has significant bearing on the nature of Catrina's own reception by my mother back in the 1960s. It is that secret more than any other that I believe was responsible for my mother's antipathy to my sister and her determination to keep her out of the family if at all possible. But it was Bea's love for Gilbert and her promise to honour his dying wishes that had brought us together in the end.

There was a lot to take in. Having finished the story and its many ramifications, I fell quiet. We were both silent for a while. My hope was that this part of my mother's history would give Catrina some understanding of Bea's actions in the past. While I was aware that it wouldn't make it any easier for my sister to bear the consequences of these actions, I hoped it might make it easier for her to view them in context. While I could never expect her to forgive my mother's behaviour, and would not blame her were she unable to do so, my wish was that she might now be better able to understand what had brought it about.

It did seem to me that Catrina, having heard this final part of the story, could see better the terrible double bind my mother had been in, as I can see it better myself. Perhaps she could now appreciate why Bea reacted so negatively to Gilbert's quest to bring his children together. Catrina told me as much, for which I am grateful. Later her husband took me aside to thank me for explaining all of this to my sister. He was sure it had made a difference.

We had both ascribed the actions of my mother, when Catrina came back into Gilbert's life, to a combination of vanity and convention. We could both now see these actions in the light of Bea's own dilemma. It felt as if a huge burden had been lifted – from me, at any rate – and I hoped from Catrina too.

I had always been torn between love for and loyalty to my mother – despite my inability to understand her motivation – and affection for my sister as my father's eldest child coupled with sympathy with what she had been put through. I had suffered from that internal conflict for years. Sometimes I would veer towards my mother and see very little

249

of my sister; at other times I'd tend in the opposite direction and stand against Mum and her rejection of Catrina. That, at least, was behind me now – and I hoped any similar feelings were behind my sister now too. As she wrote to me later:

> I am still contemplating what you told me about your mother's daughter from before she married. A second bolt from the blue! (I being the first.) This has got me thinking about coincidences and memory and misapprehensions – how our histories are so intertwined.

It seemed that a step had been taken, a corner turned. The true way out of the labyrinth had been found.

★ ★ ★

I have already suggested that I'm not inclined to the common notion that 'blood is thicker than water'. I just can't believe that simply being related to an individual results in an axiomatic bond with that person.

When Catrina first became known to us I was only in my twenties. My reaction was not one of unbounded joy at the discovery of an unknown sibling. Once I'd got over being shocked and baffled, my reaction was one of curiosity. A sense of being intrigued by new possibilities. But I'd always known that these possibilities were only that – possibilities. They would need to be built upon, enhanced and extended if anything was to come of them.

You can never choose your siblings. 'Many children would change their situation, if they could,' Dinah Birch writes in the LRB. But, despite that, the bond can be the most sustained of any association, 'the most enduring of all social relations,' she continues. Even if you lose touch, or actively break off contact, you can never forget a brother or a sister. 'Not only do they share [your] genes', they are embedded in your psyche. Whatever quality of relationship you have, a sibling will always embody your history. However much that relationship may change, elide, become damaged, that person can never cease being your brother or sister. And if you have grown up together, shared a home and the same family life, that is enough to build an almost instinctive bond that only the direst of circumstances can break. 'Loving, tiresome, indifferent or disapproving, they represent our past,' Birch concludes.

Sad though the circumstance is, by virtue of not sharing the upbringing my brother and I experienced, Catrina could not step into that secure bond which we, as brothers, share. But, come what may, she is my sister and we have forged the nearest we are able to approximate to that relationship.

Having met in the '70s, Catrina and I have known each other for well over a quarter of a century now. Despite an initial hesitancy on my part, we have got on very well for a long while. We see as much of each other as living at opposite ends of this island permits. We visit each other most years; exchange emails, if irregularly; have the occasional phone call; and still share a great many interests. By an extraordinary bit of coincidence – as if there weren't already enough coincidences in this story – it has even turned out that we share friends with people each of us had known independently of the other for ages. In addition to that, Catrina has very good friends who are active in the poetry world, of which I've long been a member, and her husband has some connections there as well. So, happenstance has played some part in our maturing relationship too.

Over the years it has been good to see Catrina at family gatherings. What a contrast with our brother's wedding in 1976. No longer is there any panic at the attendance of a mysterious unknown guest. No longer is propriety threatened by such a presence. While it has been a pleasure to welcome Catrina for herself, it has also been a tribute to our father, his presence embodied in her bringing me closer to Dad in spirit. Through Catrina I have learned so much more about my father, so much more to make him a fuller, more rounded character in my imagination.

Through such gatherings, Catrina has been able to meet many of the friends to whom I have told the story of the two strangely coincidental revelations that emerged from both my parents' histories. For a story it is – it was – but, when I was caught up in the middle of it, it felt more like the 'wreckage of shattered glass' that Margaret Atwood ascribes to that situation. In her novel *Alias Grace* she characterises this as 'a confusion' – 'a dark roaring' like being trapped inside 'a boat swept over the rapids and all aboard powerless to stop it.' As Atwood goes on to say, it is only later that it will become 'anything like a story', when you are telling it to yourself or to others. Telling it to friends as I have often done since the appearance of my sister back in the '70s. Telling it again on the discovery of my second half-sister at the end of the century. Telling its intricacies and ramifications to friends who have heard the stories in this memoir many times over, and who have wondered at them.

As I still wonder at them myself. The sadness, the regret – the perplexity even – will never quite desert me. No-one has put this residual feeling better than the Irish poet Tony Curtis when he writes: 'I have spent / most of my life baffled. / No sooner does the light / dawn than it's dark again.' And no-one has captured the catharsis of turning all that bafflement into this narrative better than Hilary Mantel, in *Giving Up the Ghost*. Describing a feeling very familiar to me, Mantel says 'as I write, pieces of the past fall into place. Sense emerges where there is no sense. And I begin to construct myself, complete with the missing bits.' It is those missing bits for which I am grateful and on which it has been possible to build.

As I think my relationship with my sister Catrina has grown, so that with my brother too has strengthened. We have been through not only the deaths of our parents together – an experience most siblings will share – but through the double exposure of two unanticipated revelations together as well. Together we have reconstructed our reality. Our sense of identity, the story we tell ourselves that makes us who we are, has expanded to take in other shared experiences that have defined us anew. But all remains firmly grounded on the base of a common upbringing, a common stepping off point, a common brotherly love.

I am wholly convinced that love grows from commitment, can *only* grow from commitment. It cannot suddenly spring fully-formed from the occurrence of a moment. It cannot snap into place as a result of a sudden revelation, some startling and unanticipated disclosure. It requires time – time to grow, to mature and strengthen. And it is that time that I am lucky to have had with my sister, time for us to put out roots that link us, to nurture those roots into love.

One image stays with me. An image that seems to sum up the whole tangled knot that has been gradually loosened and untied. It is an image that harks back to those weeks in the '90s when I was working with my mother to clear the old family home. One of the many apparently useless items we uncovered was an old cigarette tin. It was stuffed full with what I now see was a powerful metaphor. Why had it been kept? I'll never know. Inside the tin was a slowly rusting jumble of old keys, chains and padlocks. None of the keys fitted any of the doors in the house; none of them fitted any of the padlocks. At the time, having taken a fancy to the tin – a classic 'Greys' Silk Cut Virginia cigarette tin of the '20s – I shoved it into a box, contents and all. It was only reaching the end of the trail, which had begun with that late-night phone message, that I came to see its symbolic meaning. I still have the padlocks, still unopened, as a reminder of that tangle. The keys I threw out – they didn't open anything. We did that ourselves.

The love that grew from the commitment my parents both showed to me in so many ways, and which, in my self-obsessed adolescent phase, I so undervalued, still persists and is returned even after their passing. The love between Catrina and our father, suspended for a while by years and miles, persists too. Even the love of the couple who had become almost grandparents to her, rekindled after so long, didn't fail her when the time came.

Love that grows from commitment – and is sustained by lasting commitment – cannot be diminished by any revelation, by any indiscretion, or by any miss-taken step in the past.

It is simple. I would have thought no worse of either parent if I had known, while they were alive, all that I know now. That's what love means.

Acknowledgments

THREE BOOKS HAVE been of considerable value in writing this memoir: *Pieces of Light* by Charles Fernyhough (Profile Books, 2012), *In the Family Way* by Jane Robinson (Viking, 2015) and *When Daddy Came Home* by Barry Turner & Tony Rennell (Arrow Books, 2014). Numerous other memoirs, biographies and articles – too many to itemise here – have also been of great benefit in expanding my knowledge of both the background to my narrative and others' experience of similar situations.

Several of the poems in this book have appeared in print previously. My thanks are due to Scottish Cultural Press, for poems from my collection *The Lizard Silence*, and to Arc Publications, for poems from my collections *The Book of Belongings* and *Dry Stone Work*. Thanks are also due to the publishers of *Seagate III* (Discovery Press, 2016), the Lace Poetry Competition anthology (2000) and to the editors of the journals and websites *New Writing Scotland, Magma, Chapman, Poetry Scotland, Clear Poetry* and *Keep Poems Alive* where several other poems previously appeared.

Many relatives, friends and colleagues have been of great assistance to me during all stages of this book's creation. I should like especially to thank Jennie Erdal and Greg Michaelson for their appraisal of early versions; Peter Urpeth and Jenny Brown for their professional assessment of an interim manuscript; Kirsty Gunn for her advice on placing the book; and the Ailamakis family of Crete for hospitality during various phases of writing. I am particularly grateful to my publisher, Sara Hunt of Saraband Books for her appreciation and understanding of my purposes in writing this memoir and for her sympathetic support throughout the editing process. Thanks also to Rick Parkington and Julie Poole for their research input, to Colm Lyons and Fergus Eddy for advice, to Shelley Day for a timely introduction, to my cousins Ian and David for filling in various aspects of the family background and to the staff of Queen Elizabeth Grammar School, Penrith, for their contribution to my father's history. I am considerably indebted to my brother and sister for family stories, memories and information as well as for their support, understanding and patience during the period of writing and editing.

At all stages in the creation of this book, I have been assisted hugely by my wife Jean who has acted as editor, proof reader, advisor, researcher and, not least, as muse. I owe her an immense debt of gratitude for the support she has shown me both during the planning and writing processes involved in the production of this memoir and throughout the incidents recounted in this narrative.

Sources Quoted

Non-Fiction

Charles Fernyhough *Pieces of Light* Profile Books, 2012

Jane Robinson *In the Family Way* Viking, 2015

Barry Turner & Tony Rennell *When Daddy Came Home* Arrow Books, 2014

Jenny Diski *The Sixties* Profile Books, 2009; *Skating to Antarctica* Granta, 1997

Richard Gwyn *The Vagabond's Breakfast* Alcemi, 2011

Hilary Mantel *Giving Up the Ghost* Fourth Estate, 2003

Jenni Calder *Not Nebuchadnezzar* Luath, 2004

Tom Pow *In Another World* Birlinn, 2012

John Lanchester *Family Romance* Faber & Faber, 2007

Kevin Crossley-Holland *The Hidden Roads* Quercus, 2009

Tim Jeal *Swimming with my Father* Faber & Faber, 2004

Jennie Erdal *Ghosting* Canongate, 2004

Jackie Kay *Red Dust Road* Picador, 2010

Roger Grenier *A Box of Photographs* Uni of Chicago Press, 2013

Polly Coles *The Politics of Washing* Robert Hale, 2013

Double Exposure

Lorna Sage *Bad Blood* Fourth Estate, 2001

John Peel & Sheila Ravenscroft *Margrave of the Marshes* Bantam Press, 2005

Osbert Lancaster *All Done from Memory* John Murray, 1963

Terri Apter *The Sister Knot* Norton, 2007

Poetry

Tony Curtis *The Well in the Rain* Arc, 2006

Vicki Feaver *The Book of Blood* Cape, 2006

Fiction

Richard Yates *Revolutionary Road* Little, Brown & Co, 1961

Jeanette Winterson *Oranges are Not the Only Fruit* Random House, 1985

Tatiana de Rosnay *Sarah's Key* John Murray, 2006

Margaret Atwood *Alias Grace* Bloomsbury, 1996

Journalism

Adam Mars-Jones *Mrs Winterson's Daughter* LRB, January 2012

Dinah Birch *Sisters Came Second* LRB, April, 2012

Ian Penman *Even if you have to Starve* LRB, August 2013

Jenny Diski *The Girl Least Likely To* LRB, September 2013

Tim Adams *The Man who Couldn't Make Memories* The Observer, May 2013